The Singer's Voice

The Singer's Voice

Michael S. Benninger, MD

Thomas Murry, PhD

PLURAL
PUBLISHING
INC.

SAN DIEGO
OXFORD
BRISBANE

5521 Ruffin Road
San Diego, CA 92123

e-mail: info@pluralpublishing.com
Web site: http://www.pluralpublishing.com

49 Bath Street
Abingdon, Oxfordshire OX14 1EA
United Kingdom

Typeset in 10/13 Garamond by Flanagan's Publishing Services, Inc.
Printed in Hong Kong by Paramount Printing

Library of Congress Cataloging-in-Publication Data

The singer's voice / [edited by] Michael S. Benninger and Thomas Murry.
     p. ; cm.
  Includes bibliographical references and index.
  ISBN-13: 978-1-59756-252-2 (alk. paper)
  ISBN-10: 1-59756-252-1 (alk. paper)
 1. Voice disorders–Treatment. 2. Singers–Health and hygiene. 3. Voice–Care and hygiene.
  [DNLM: 1. Voice Disorders–therapy. 2. Voice–physiology. 3. Voice Disorders–diagnosis.
 4. Voice Training. WV 500 S617 2007] I. Benninger, Michael S. II. Murry, Thomas, 1943-
  RF511.S55S56 2007
  616.85'5606–dc22

                                                                    2007050049

Contents

Preface

The Singer's Voice brings together a group of dedicated professionals from disciplines related to the care and treatment of individuals who use their voices in professional settings. Otolaryngologists, speech-language pathologists, psychologists, singing voice specialists, singing teachers, and performers have contributed their knowledge and offered insights on the various aspects of the care and management of the singing voice.

In this volume, the focus is primarily on the singer; however, other performers are included—voiceovers, dancer/singers, and instrumentalist/singers, to name a few. Each type of performer brings specific issues to the treatment team and requires special attention from various members of the team. This book identifies these individuals, presents reports on cases with special needs, and offers a myriad of solutions to preserve the voice and prevent further damage.

All of the contributors to this volume have shown a dedication to the care of the singer and performer through their studios, academic training, their research interests and experience, and their clinical and/or performance background. Most of the contributors have been on stage as a performer at some point in their lives and bring that performance history to their specialty. The contributors range from current day performers to choral conductors to past rock and roll musicians.

The book is divided into three major sections. Part I presents an overview of the world of singers, describing who they are and their various artistic styles. It also provides a short review of the vocal anatomy and physiology.

Part II is directed at how to evaluate singers and diagnose their problems. The importance of the history and interview is highlighted along with how to examine and visualize the larynx and vocal folds. Perceptual evaluations and assessments are presented from the perspectives of the medical team, singing pedagogic teacher. and the professional singer. Problems that require medical care, voice training, or adaptation to the performance world are described.

Part III describes the various ways that a singer with a problem can be treated. In this section, speech pathologists and singing voice specialists offer a broad range of treatment options for both acute and long term care of the singer. A comprehensive review of the roles of over-the-counter and prescription drugs as well as alternative medications and therapies is presented. For the rare singer who requires surgical treatment, a short review of the role of surgery is discussed.

The book ends with an appendix of general methods of preserving the voice and a comprehensive glossary of medical and singing terminology that gives readers ready access to the definitions of these often confusing terms.

In summary, *The Singer's Voice* is a comprehensive book designed for singers who want to better understand the prevention and care of the their voices, for singing teachers and educators, and for those who treat singers. The information brought to this volume by those who have dedicated their lives to singing or teaching and caring for singers is an invaluable reference for everyone who either sings or cares for singers.

Contributors

David M. Alessi, MD, FACS
Assistant Clinical Professor
University of California Los Angeles
Former Chief, Division of Otolaryngology
Cedars Sinai Medical Center
Los Angeles, California
Chapter 9

Mara Behlau, PhD
Director, Center for the Study of Voice
Professor of Voice
University of Sao Paulo
San Paulo, Brazil
Chapter 11

Michael S. Benninger, MD
Chair, Department of Otolaryngology–Head and
   Neck Surgery
Henry Ford Hospital
Detroit, Michigan
Chapters 1, 5, 15

Audrey Crummey, BS
Weill Medical College
Cornell University
New York, New York
Chapter 9

Janet Madelle Feindel, MFA, ATI
Associate Professor Voice/Dialectics and
   Alexander Technique
School of Drama
Carnegie Mellon University
Pittsburgh, Pennsylvania
Chapter 12

Jack Jiang, MD, PhD
Associate Professor
Division of Otolaryngology–Head and Neck Surgery

University of Wisconsin-Madison
Madison, Wisconsin
Chapter 3

Philip J. Lanzisera, PhD, ABPP
Senior Bioscientific Staff Psychologist
Director, Psychology Intern Program
Henry Ford Behavioral Health
Detroit, Michigan
Chapter 14

Jeannette L. LoVetri
Director, The Voice Workshop
Consultant and Faculty
Steinhardt School of Education
New York University
Adjunct Professor
Teacher's College
Columbia University
Singing Specialist for the Brooklyn Youth Chorus
   Academy
New York, New York
Chapter 13

Nicholas E. Maragos, MD
Associate Professor of Medicine
Mayo Clinic
Rochester, Minnesota
Chapter 2

Thomas Murry, PhD
Professor of Speech Pathology
College of Physicians and Surgeons
Clinical Director of the Voice and Swallowing
   Center
Columbia University
New York, New York
Chapters 1, 5, 11

Sharon L. Radionoff, PhD
Director, Sound Singing Institute
Singing Voice Specialist/Voice Technologist
Team Member—Singing Voice Specialist
Texas Voice Center
Houston, Texas
Consultant Singing Voice Specialist
University of Texas Health Science Center at
    San Antonio
Department of Otolaryngology-Head and Neck
    Surgery
Chapter 4

Josef Schlömicher-Thier, MD
Consulting Physician to the Salzburg Festival
Consulting ENT Surgeon Private, Clinic Wenle
    Salzburg
Chairman, Austrian Voice Institute
Salzburg, Austria
Chapter 8

Michael D. Seidman, MD, FACS
Henry Ford Health System
Director Division of Otologic/Neurotologic
    Surgery
Medical Director Center for Integrative Medicine
Detroit, Michigan
Chairman Committee for Complementary/
    Integrative Medicine for The American
    Academy of Otolaryngology–Head and
    Neck Surgery
Chapter 10

Rahul Shrivastav, PhD
Assistant Professor
Communication Sciences and Disorders
University of Florida
Gainesville, Florida
Chapter 7

Matthias Weikert, MD
Specialist in ORL, Voice and Speech Disorders,
    and Pediatric Audiology
Consultant Surgeon, Department of Head and
    Neck Surgery
St. Hedwig Hospital of the Catholic Hospital
Regensburg, Germany
Chapter 8

Judith Wingate, PhD
Clinical Assistant Professor
Communication Sciences and Disorders
University of Florida
Gainesville, Flordia
Chapter 7

Peak Woo, MD
Professor of Otolaryngology
Eugene Grabscheid, M.D., Voice Center
Mt. Sinai Medical School
New York, New York
Chapter 6

This book is dedicated to our families;
Kathy, Ryan and Kaylin
Marie-Pierre and Nicholas

It is their love and support that has made this book possible and
our lives meaningful.

Part I

Overview

Chapter 1

INTRODUCTION

Michael S. Benninger
Thomas Murry

"Your voice is the mirror of your soul."

Our voices influence nearly every part of human interaction and culture. Until relatively recently in human history, the voice was the sole method of communication. Early human history and recording of events was exclusively through oral history. It is only in relatively recent history that communication has been both written and oral. Despite the information explosion in written, printed, and digitalized/computerized recordings, most people still use their voices as their primary means of communication. Even when people are alone, they will use their voices, to sing or to "speak to themselves."

Voice communication begins at birth. The birth cry is the first sign of life. The cry soon becomes the communication link between baby and mother. The voice of the mother soothes the crying voice. As the child develops, his or her voice plays a pivotal role in satisfying the needs of hunger, pain, and play. Some children develop pleasurable sounds while others use their voices strenuously and develop hoarseness or harshness. Still others find that humming or singing brings pleasure and reinforcement from family and friends. And, that is often how these children go on to bigger and more prominent acting and singing roles in primary school, high school, and beyond. For some adults, singing is an enjoyable hobby while for others it becomes their passion and finally their profession. Even for those who did not get the principal part in the high school musical, training and practice under watchful eyes and ears help to develop the voice for later success in a vocally demanding profession. Eventually, these individuals become the voice professionals.

Who are professional vocalists? Loosely defined, professional vocalists are individuals who rely on their voices to be the major part of their occupation. This includes teachers, salespeople, coaches, politicians, broadcasters, singers, orators, clergy, and numerous other professionals. The voice demands, the techniques and style of use, and the overall quantity of use may vary considerably among these groups. Similarly, the quality demands and the ability to maintain their professional value may differ. Newscasters must talk rapidly with clear articulation, teachers must talk for long periods of the day, and sports coaches must talk loudly. Ultimately, however, the need to maintain a strong, effective, and clear voice affects each of these professionals and contributes in some way to their success. Without their voices, these individuals can no longer perform the duties required.

One unique group of professional voice users is professional singers. Of all the voice professionals, singers are perhaps the most affected by problems with their voices, even subtle ones. There is a general expectation that a singer will always perform at his or her best, with a strong, pure, and clear voice with a broad range and unique character. Minor changes in quality are immediately scrutinized, far more so than minor hoarseness in other voice professionals. Because of these voice expectations, singers tend to also spend the most time of any voice professionals developing their voices through practice and training. They demand a higher quality for their own voices than even their audiences do. They are driven to perfection and will work diligently to crystallize their quality and refine their vocal style whether it is opera, gospel, or cabaret. This perfectionistic drive and focus on hard work and repetition is not only what leads to excellence but may increase the risk of injury. Any injury to the singer's voice has dramatic implications not only on their voices but also on their psyche and sense of self-worth.

> "First, I lost my voice, then I lost my figure and then I lost Onassis!"
> Maria Callas

What happens when a singer is injured and cannot perform at a level that either they or their audiences expect? That depends on many factors including the professional level of the singer, the magnitude of the injury, the importance of the performance, the experience of the singer, the type of music to be sung, and the expectations from the audience for the performance. It is a simplification to suggest that the expectations of the performance of an elite opera singer are greater than that of a rock singer. There are too many variables to think like this. The demands of the performance vary for each individual and for each performance. Even for the experienced, elite opera singer, there may be an important difference between a Metropolitan Opera premiere and a light-hearted recital at a hometown outdoor venue. The audition for entrance into a school of music is usually more critical to a developing young singer than the third performance of the weekend in the school play.

For some singers and for some performances, "the show must go on." But there is a danger in thinking like that. Singers usually injure their voices when they are sick, fatigued, or under strain. When the experienced singer feels that he or she cannot perform to a known level, he or she will cancel the rehearsal or the show. Canceling at the last minute, however, becomes more difficult for the lead singer at a small college in the Midwest where there is no one else to take over the role. The need to perform must always be balanced against the probability of vocal injury. When the singer cannot use his or her full voice, the decisions must be made with the singer's long-term career in mind. For some, it is simply of matter of rest and hydration; for others, their show cannot go on unless they seek treatment from knowledgeable individuals who understand the ramifications of voice care and vocal injury.

> *Madonna Cancels NJ Show*
> A sore throat forced Madonna to cancel the final NY area date of her Drowned World tour last night at the Meadowlands Arena.
> *New York Times*, August 2001

To treat singers, one has to be aware not only of the important principles of anatomy, physiology, and pathology of the voice, but also the critical interfaces between the voice, the sound produced, and the unique aspects of each individual singer. A comprehensive understanding of the differences in individual voice production, between musical styles and the more complex relationships the singer has with teachers, audiences, agents, and promoters, is necessary to comprehensively address the singer's voice needs. Each singer is different and each needs to be considered individually. Although there are a number of variables in the assessment and treatment process, the best rule to approach an injured singer is that there are no rules. Knowledge, education, compassion, and a thoughtful, deliberate approach bolstered by appropriate tools and equipment for evaluation and treatment are needed each time a singer comes to the clinic or studio with a voice problem.

One fortunate aspect of the treatment of singers is that the characteristics of hard work and drive that can lead to injury are usually also applied to assessment, treatment, and rehabilitation. Singers sing because they love it. They rehabilitate their injured voices to resume their profession. They respect a knowledgeable voice clinician and will often follow the advice and recommendations without hesitation. In a large sense singers are vocal athletes. Their bodies are the source of their vocation and like other athletes they base their careers on a somewhat fragile machine that is prone to injury.

And, like athletes, they will do what is necessary to return to performing. In doing so, they rely on the specialized voice practitioners, primarily otolaryngologists and speech-language pathologists who specialize in voice disorders, and colleagues in the music community to help them return to their careers at the same level as before their injury.

Actors and actresses also require exacting standards for their speaking voice. Projection, articulation, and endurance in the speaking voice range require training and practice. Injuries may occur in actors' voices that restrict use and therefore income. Medical care and rehabilitation of the injured actor's voice also falls to the otolaryngologist, speech-language pathologist, vocal pedagogist, and singing teacher.

The current approach to caring for the performer's voice is to use an interdisciplinary team of clinicians. The performer's voice care team is usually under the direction of an otolaryngologist or laryngologist. Laryngologists are otolaryngologists who specialize in diseases and disorders of the larynx. However, the performer's internist should always be kept apprised of changes in the performer's health status and of the prescribed medications.

Speech-language pathologists are an integral part of the performers' voice care team. Speech pathology encompasses many subspecialties of communication disorders. Relatively few have special training or intimate knowledge of the anatomy and physiology of the vocal mechanism or even an interest in the performing population. Most speech pathologists who routinely treat performers are closely aligned with an otolaryngologist and work together with the injured performer to achieve rapid and safe recovery of vocal injuries.

Phoniatrists, singing voice specialists, and vocal coaches are also involved in the care of the performer. Phoniatrists are specialists in European countries who are trained as physicians but not as surgeons. They may prescribe medicines and offer behavioral treatments. Singing voice specialists are usually singers who go on to study the medically related aspects of voice use.

They are usually affiliated with voice care teams and offer special singing-related information to the singer and the members of the voice care team.

There is a wealth of information available to the singer with a voice problem since the advent of modern voice care. Singers should be educated by their voice care team and team members owe it to the singers to share the most up-to-date practice methods that are available. It is important for the voice care team to communicate with the performer's other health care specialists, voice teachers, and others in the performing industry so that conservative and appropriate care is given when there is a voice injury.

This book is written to present the most current and comprehensive approach to the care of the singer's voice. The important anatomic, physiologic, and pedagogic principles of voice production for the singer will serve as the foundation for the care of the singer. The authors represent a wide array of people who have dedicated their careers to the prevention of voice injury, the diagnosis, treatment, and rehabilitation of the injured singer, and the education of others who continue to advance the science and art of voice care through education, research, and clinical practice. The diversity of the authors supports the important principles of the multidisciplinary approach to the care of the vocalist, particularly the singer.

This book serves as a concise reference for the otolaryngologist or speech-language (voice) pathologist who wishes to focus their practice on the evaluation and care of vocalists, particularly the professional singer. It also provides a strong foundation in the understanding of the singer's voice for singers, teachers of singing, pedagogues, and those who contract and produce vocal performances, and others who have already developed a foundation in voice and wish to become more familiar with the intricate principles of the performing voice. Ultimately, we hope that this book will continue to strengthen the fundamental foundations of voice care and will expand the multidisciplinary interests in the care and preventive treatment of the singer's voice.

Chapter 2

ANATOMY OF THE VOCAL MECHANISM: STRUCTURE OF THE VOICE

Nicolas E. Maragos

The mechanism that produces voice is, on the surface, a rather mundane structure that mostly is taken for granted. We know intuitively that everyone's voice is a little bit different, but even though we use the sound of someone's voice to figure out very quickly who is on the telephone, and whether or not they are sick or tired or worried or in a hurry, we still do not think much about it. For the singer, however, and for others who tend to stretch the vocal mechanism "to the limit," the voice and its health take on added importance. To understand the conditions that may do harm to the voice we must, therefore, understand what it is that produces the best sound over the course of a lifetime. Thus, the study of the anatomy of the vocal mechanism is paramount to understanding the basics of vocal health, hygiene, and preservation of our gift of voice.

VOCAL MECHANISM AS A WHOLE

Although the larynx ("voice box") generates the vocal sound, it is neither the beginning nor the end of the vocal mechanism. Before delving into the finer details of the larynx itself, we should spend some time understanding the anatomy of the remainder of the vocal

mechanism. Voice is produced when the lining tissue of the vocal folds, the mucosa, is put into oscillation and changes a steady stream of air into a rhythmically interrupted airstream.[1] The air, of course, has to come from the lungs, and the power pushing the air out of the lungs comes from the contraction of the abdominal and chest muscles, and the relaxation and recoil of the diaphragm. Normal exhalation takes place with a larger flow of air at the beginning of exhalation and a quickly decreasing flow thereafter. This pattern is fine for quiet breathing, but for a smooth, steady, and prolonged vocal output the airstream needs to be modified for a steadier flow. Thus, anything that hampers the normal action of the diaphragm, chest, or abdominal muscles may have a great impact on the voice.

The action of diaphragmatic contraction is mediated through the phrenic nerves on both sides. The phrenic nerves are a mix of motor nerves from the third through fifth cervical roots (C3–C5) in the neck and come directly out of the spinal cord through spaces between the vertebral bodies (spinal column).[2] Branches from roots C3 to C5 combine into a single nerve high in the neck on each side, travel downward in the neck to the posterior mediastinum between the lungs, and finally lie next to the heart before reaching the top surface of the diaphragm. Because the diaphragm is dome-shaped curving upward, contraction of the diaphragm through phrenic nerve stimulation leads to an increase in size of the chest cavity and inhalation.[3] Thus, if one or both phrenic nerves are injured or weakened the person is not able to breathe in to stay alive. The most recent well-known individual suffering from this was actor Christopher Reeve whose spinal cord was injured above C3, that is, above the formation of the phrenic nerves. He spent his last years on a portable respirator because of his total loss of diaphragmatic function.

The intercostal muscles of the chest and the abdominal muscles also receive their motor nerve supply through the spinal nerve roots exiting the spinal column farther down. The intercostals span the distance between adjacent ribs and pull the ribs together when they contract. The abdominal muscles surround the abdominal contents and squeeze everything inward during contraction. The balance of tension between the abdominals and intercostals on one hand (pushing air out) and the diaphragm on the other (pulling air in) is what voice professionals and, especially, singers spend years mastering. A deficit in this part of the vocal mechanism will, therefore, lead to a decrease in peak performance and a less than optimal vocal output.

VOCAL MECHANISM AT THE CENTER

"The living voice is that which sways the soul" (Pliny the Younger—*Letters*. Book ii. Letter iii. 9). Educators, writers, and philosophers from ancient civilizations understood well the meaning and essence of voice. From Pliny the Younger's quote from the first century AD to Longfellow's more recent quote that "the larynx is the voice of the soul," people knew there was something special about good vocal production. At the center of euphonia ("good sound") is the larynx, and it follows that a normal or near-normal laryngeal organ must be available for the voice user to produce the sounds that "sway the soul" of the listener.

The larynx is a composite structure situated in the midneck, or rather suspended in the neck from the skull above. Muscles connected to the larynx from both above and below act upon it to change its position in the neck and help it carry out its three vital functions: airway closure during swallowing, airway opening during breathing, and airway modulation

during voicing. These outside (extrinsic) muscles are often those which the voice teacher, either consciously or unconsciously, tries to manipulate to improve the student's voice. Those muscles that raise the larynx in the neck are called elevators, and those that lower the larynx are named depressors. The hyoid bone at the top of the larynx is the primary point of attachment of these elevators and depressors. The names of these suprahyoid (above) and infrahyoid (below) muscles are not important to the student, but speech pathologists, voice therapists, and voice teachers need to be reminded of their existence and the great value (or harm) that may come to the student if these muscles are injured, too tense, or malfunctioning in any way.

VOCAL MECHANISM: EXTERNAL SUPPORT

The larynx by definition includes those bony, cartilaginous, and internal soft tissue structures spanning from the top of the hyoid bone to the bottom of the cricoid cartilage (Figure 2–1). The rigid external skeleton from superior to inferior includes the hyoid bone, thyroid cartilage, and cricoid cartilage. These structures form a semirigid tube that normally can be bent forward and shortened in a superior/inferior direction, but cannot be bent from side to side. This tube is also rigid when rotated making it possible to operate on the posterolateral larynx with this maneuver in the awake patient. All the internal cartilaginous and soft tissue structures are attached to the thyroid and cricoid cartilages or are supported by them through a system of muscles, ligaments, and membranous sheets of thicker fibrous tissue.

The thyroid cartilage is the largest cartilage of the larynx and is formed by two relatively flat and broad plates of cartilage fused anteriorly at the midline of the neck. It connects posteriorly to the hyoid bone above and the cricoid cartilage below through two pairs of horn-shaped projections, the superior and inferior cornua, respectively. The superior cornu attaches to the hyoid bone above through a ligament on each side, the lateral thyrohyoid ligament, as part of the suspensory system of the larynx mentioned earlier. The inferior cornu forms a joint with the cricoid cartilage on either side, the cricothyroid joint, which allows the forward flexing of the thyroid cartilage on the cricoid cartilage but not sideways flexing. The anterior angle of the two lamina of the thyroid cartilage are different in men (90°) than in women (120°), hence, the greater protrusion of the man's thyroid cartilage, which prompts the term, "Adam's apple." The cricothyroid joints, as we will learn in a later chapter, are important for the normal action of the cricothyroid muscles during vocal pitch modulation.

Two of the most important structures of the larynx are the paired cricoarytenoid joints (Figure 2–2). As their name implies, these joints connect the cricoid cartilage to the arytenoid cartilages. Located posteriorly and just below the level of the vocal folds, these joints support arytenoid movement including a gliding motion for adduction and abduction of the vocal folds,

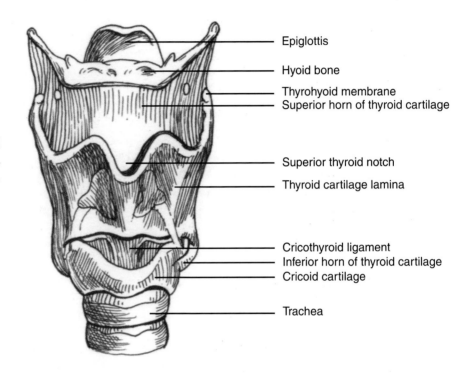

Figure 2–1. External structure of the larynx, anterior view.

- Epiglottis
- Hyoid bone
- Thyrohyoid membrane
- Superior horn of thyroid cartilage
- Superior thyroid notch
- Thyroid cartilage lamina
- Cricothyroid ligament
- Inferior horn of thyroid cartilage
- Cricoid cartilage
- Trachea

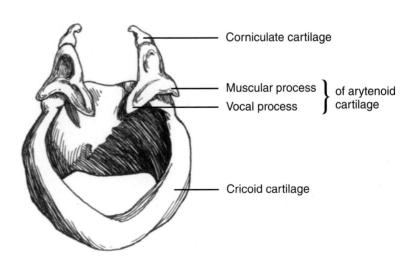

Figure 2–2. Cricoarytenoid joints, anterosuperior view.

- Corniculate cartilage
- Muscular process } of arytenoid
- Vocal process } cartilage
- Cricoid cartilage

tilting forward and backward to put the vocal processes in better vertical alignment during phonation, and a rotation around a vertical axis. The cricoarytenoid joint capsule and, in particular, the posterior cricoarytenoid ligament hold the arytenoid in place on top of the cricoid.[4] Without this support the arytenoid would fall into the larynx from its rather precarious perch atop the cricoid. Abnormalities of these joints (scarring, arthritis, etc) will impact laryngeal function by affecting vocal fold movement and position. Better treatment of these problems is one of the future directions in laryngeal surgery.

VOCAL MECHANISM: INTERNAL SUPPORT

The study of medicine and human anatomy may be daunting and, at times, confusing, but the language of medicine is actually very simple once one understands a few rules of the system.[5] So it is with the anatomy

of the larynx and all the structures therein. For example, we can now use all the information given above regarding the laryngeal external support system to understand and remember the intricate and fascinating internal structures of the larynx. Thus, the muscle of the vocal fold itself, beginning at the thyroid cartilage anteriorly and ending at the arytenoid cartilage posteriorly, is named the *thyroarytenoid* muscle, not the "arytenothyroid" muscle, because its origin is at the thyroid cartilage.

The arytenoid cartilages are the heart of the larynx. The attachments to these cartilages include the muscles, ligaments, and fibrous tissue important in voice production. The arytenoid cartilages are mostly pyramidal in shape with three processes or points of attachment to other structures. These are the vocal process anteriorly, the muscular process laterally, and the superior process.[6] The vocal process protrudes from the anterior portion of the arytenoid body and attaches to the medial thyroarytenoid muscle and ligament (vocalis muscle and vocal ligament, Figure 2–3). Attached to the muscular processes are the lateral and posterior

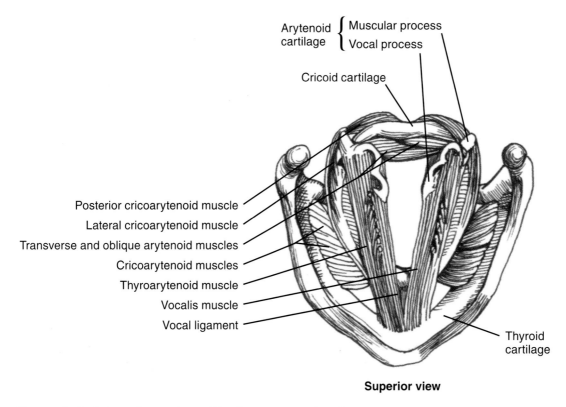

Superior view

Figure 2–3. Internal muscles of the larynx, superior view.

cricoarytenoid muscles, and spanning the distance between the arytenoid cartilages posteriorly is the interarytenoid muscle. These latter muscles position the arytenoid cartilages in the airstream to facilitate breathing, swallowing, and voicing.

As mentioned above, the vocal folds are suspended between the thyroid cartilage anteriorly and the arytenoid cartilages posteriorly at the vocal processes of the arytenoids.[7] The thyroarytenoid muscle makes up most of the body of the vocal fold. As most muscles contract when stimulated by their motor nerve supply, the action of the thyroarytenoid is to pull the arytenoid toward the thyroid cartilage to both shorten the length of the vocal fold and bulk it up isometrically. The lateral cricoarytenoid muscle arises from the anterior and lateral cricoid cartilage and inserts onto the laterally placed muscular process of the arytenoid, whereas the posterior cricoarytenoid muscle arises from the posterior surface of the cricoid cartilage and also inserts onto the muscular process (Figure 2–4). Contraction of these muscles moves the arytenoid into its various positions so that the larynx may complete its normal functions. Finally, contraction of the interarytenoid muscle will pull the arytenoids closer to each other and fill the interarytenoid space with folds of overlying soft tissue and mucosa, thus effectively obliterating any opening between these cartilages.

All the above-mentioned muscles obtain their motor nerve supply from the recurrent laryngeal nerve.[6] The last muscle affecting the voice, the cricothyroid muscle, acts indirectly on the vocal fold. It is situated on both sides in the anterolateral space between the cricoid and thyroid cartilages. Its motor nerve supply is through the external branch of the superior laryngeal nerve. Cricothyroid muscle contraction changes the tension of the vocal fold by increasing the distance between the vocal process of the arytenoid and the anterior attachment of the vocal ligament and thyroarytenoid muscle to the thyroid cartilage. This is accomplished through the cricothyroid joint mentioned earlier, a joint that allows pivoting and anterior flexion of the thyroid cartilage upon the cricoid. Alterations in

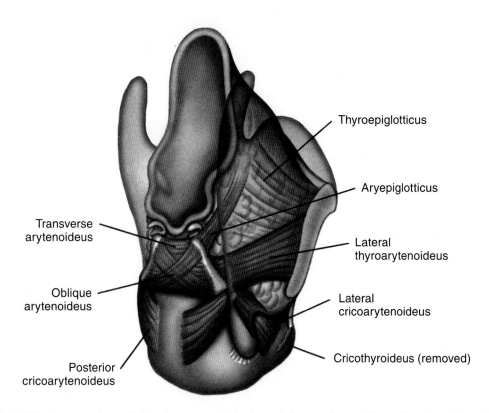

Figure 2-4. Intrinsic muscles of the larynx, posterior oblique view. (From Tucker HM. *The Larynx.* New York, NY: Thieme Medical Publishers, Inc; 1987:14 with permission).

cricothyroid muscle strength or imbalance of strength between the right and left sides is probably the most overlooked deficit of the vocal mechanism but one that is extremely important to singers and other voice users alike.

Some laryngeal structures are not directly responsible for vocal production. However, they do impact the resonating quality of the voice, especially if they "get in the way" of the outflow from the larynx. These are the epiglottic cartilage and the false cords. The epiglottis sits anteriorly and above the vocal folds and is attached by its petiole to the inside of the thyroid cartilage, and the false cords reside above and lateral to the vocal folds. The primary purpose of these supraglottic (above the vocal folds) structures is to help protect the airway during swallowing. However, they may partially or totally obstruct the vocal output in those patients with, for example, muscle tension dysphonia or spasmodic dysphonia. Without an easy passage through the larynx the voice will be impaired.

The medial thyroarytenoid muscle and the vocal ligament make up the body of the vocal fold over which the flexible mucosa of the vocal fold moves. Ultrastructural studies have shown a division of the submucosal fibrous tissue in this area, also called the lamina propria, into three distinct parts: superficial, middle, and deep layers (Figure 2-5). The superficial layer of the lamina propria is the most important of these layers for its sparse and pliable collagen binds this tissue loosely and allows the shearing force from the airstream out of the lungs to rhythmically open and close the airspace between the vocal folds during

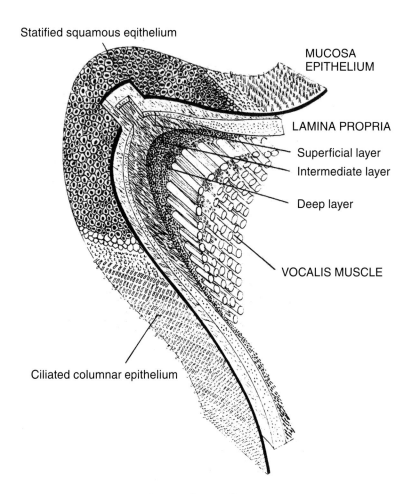

Figure 2-5. Ultrastructure of the vocal fold. (From Hirano M. Phonosurgery—Basic and Clinical Investigations. *Otologia (Fukuoka)*.1975;241 with permission).

normal phonation. Sound production without this movement leads to a dysphonic voice. The importance of the middle and deep layers of the lamina propria are its increased ability to produce thicker fibrous tissue (scarring) after injury, thus having a negative impact on the voice.

VOCAL MECHANISM: VASCULAR AND PHYSIOLOGIC SUPPORT

The arterial blood supply to the larynx comes mostly from the inferior thyroid artery through its inferior laryngeal branch.[6] After entering the larynx posterolaterally with the anterior branch of the recurrent laryngeal nerve just above the cricothyroid joint on both sides, this artery joins branches from both the cricothyroid artery anteriorly and the superior laryngeal artery superiorly to form a rich anastamosis inside the thyroid cartilage.[8] As these vessels further divide into smaller and smaller vessels, they finally reach the submucosal tissue and, in the vocal fold, they run parallel to the edge.

The capillary supply to the vocal folds and surrounding structures brings nutrients in and takes metabolic waste products away, but it also removes the heat generated in the mucosa from the energy expended during phonation (mechanical movement, muscle contraction). Increased capillary flow, however, is not the most efficient way to protect the vocal folds from harm. Mucous glands occupy the superior mucosa of the anterior vocal fold in the ventricle, and the mucus secreted here is used for cleaning, lubricating, and protecting the vocal folds. Thus, the anatomy of an area of the body and its physiologic function once again go hand in hand.

VOCAL MECHANISM: NEUROLOGIC SUPPORT

The peripheral motor nerve supply to the larynx is well known and has been mentioned already. The internal laryngeal muscles are supplied by the vagus nerve which gives off two branches to the larynx before it continues downward to supply the rest of the

gastrointestinal or GI tract.[9-11] These are the superior and inferior (recurrent) laryngeal nerves. The superior laryngeal nerve (SLN) further divides into an internal sensory branch and an external motor branch. The internal branch enters the larynx between the hyoid bone and thyroid cartilage and pierces the thyrohyoid membrane one centimeter in front of the superior cornu of the thyroid cartilage (Figure 2-6). It carries information from touch-sensitive receptors, heat-sensitive (thermal) receptors, and mucosal receptors sensitive to chemical changes back to the brainstem. In addition it picks up information from the internal muscles and joints of the larynx as well. Meanwhile the external branch of the SLN is dedicated to supplying motor innervation to the cricothyroid muscle but also picking up sensory information from the anterior subglottic mucosa.[12]

The inferior or recurrent laryngeal nerve (RLN) takes its name from its course through the neck and into the upper chest, and its subsequent looping

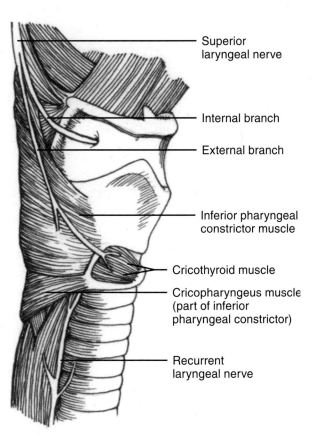

Figure 2-6. Innervation of the larynx, right lateral view.

Labels on figure:
- Superior laryngeal nerve
- Internal branch
- External branch
- Inferior pharyngeal constrictor muscle
- Cricothyroid muscle
- Cricopharyngeus muscle (part of inferior pharyngeal constrictor)
- Recurrent laryngeal nerve

around the aortic arch on the left and the subclavian artery on the right. It then "recurs" in the lower neck running in the groove between the trachea and the esophagus and traveling upward to finally reach the posterolateral larynx.[13] As the RLN reaches its target muscles it sends motor fibers in succession to the posterior cricoarytenoid muscle, the interarytenoid muscle, the lateral cricoarytenoid muscle, and the thyroarytenoid muscle. It also has sensory branches connecting to the subglottic mucosal sensory receptors and the internal laryngeal muscles. If the patient has a congenital anomaly of the right subclavian artery a "nonrecurrent" RLN will be present.[14] However, the RLN *always* enters the larynx just above the cricothyroid joint to gain access to the internal muscles it must innervate.

SUMMARY

The vocal mechanism is an intricate system of balances between the abdomen, chest, neck, and head. It is no wonder that physicians and philosophers throughout recorded time have marveled at the human ability to communicate vocally with other people. The voice is part of our individual identity, and to protect that part of our identity we must, therefore, understand how the voice works and how to maintain it throughout our lives. Learning vocal anatomy is the fundamental step in preserving our gift of voice, and one well worth taking.

REFERENCES

1. Tucker, HM. *The Larynx*. New York, NY: Thieme Medical Publishers, Inc; 1987:136-137.

2. Anson BJ, ed. *Morris' Human Anatomy*. 12th ed. New York, NY: McGraw-Hill Book Co; 1966:1059.

3. Anson BJ, ed. *Morris' Human Anatomy*. 12th ed. New York, NY:McGraw-Hill Book Co; 1966:30.

4. Sellars I, Sellars S. Cricoarytenoid joint structure and function. *J Laryngol Otol*. 1983;97:1027-1034.

5. International Anatomical Nomenclature Committee. *Nomina Anatomica*. 6th ed. Edinburgh, New York: Churchill Livingstone; 1989.

6. Anson BJ, ed. *Morris' Human Anatomy*. 12th ed. New York, NY: McGraw-Hill Book Co; 1966: 1409-1427.

7. Hirano M. Phonosurgery—basic and clinical investigations. *Otologia (Fukuoka)*. 1975;21:239-298.

8. Mihashi SK, Okada M, Kurita S, et al. Vascular network of the vocal cord. In: Stevens KN, Hirano M, eds. *Vocal Fold Physiology*. Tokyo:University of Tokyo Press; 1981:45-58.

9. Strong MS, Vaughan, CW. The morphology of the phonatory organs and their neural control. In: Stevens KN, Hirano M, eds. *Vocal Fold Physiology*. Tokyo:University of Tokyo Press; 1981:13-20.

10. Tyler HR. Neurology of the larynx. *Otolaryngol Clin North Am*. 1984;17:75-79.

11. Kambic V, Zargi M, Radsel Z. Topographic anatomy of the external branch of the superior laryngeal nerve: its importance in head and neck surgery. *J Laryngol Otol*. 1984;98:1121-1124.

12. Wallach JH, Rybicki KJ, Kaufman MP. Anatomical localization of the cells of origin of efferent fibers in the superior laryngeal and recurrent laryngeal nerves of dogs. *Brain Res*. 1983;261:307-311.

13. Caiot P, Bousquet V, Cabanie P, et al. The nerve loops crossing below the subclavian artery and their anatomical variations. *Anat Clin*. 1984;6: 209-213.

14. Saunders G, Uyeda RY, Karlan MS. Nonrecurrent inferior laryngeal nerves and their association with a recurrent branch. *Am J Surg*. 1983;146: 501-503.

Chapter 3

PHYSIOLOGY OF VOICE PRODUCTION: HOW DOES THE VOICE WORK?

Jack Jiang

The production of voice requires the interaction of many physiologic processes whether one sings an aria or simply has a conversation. Most commonly the word, "phonation," conjures images of vibrating vocal folds. The vocal folds serve as an energy transducer; they are responsible for converting aerodynamic power into acoustic power. There are many other contributors to speech, however. The aerodynamic power necessary for voice production is generated subglottally by the chest, thorax, and abdomen. Then, above the vocal folds, resonators modulate the sound into a human voice. This chapter looks more in depth at how these physiologic processes interact to create the voice and how singers can control and master their voices.

THEORIES OF PHONATION

Theories and models of vocal fold vibration have undergone considerable development over the past 150 years. As early as 1741, the vocal folds were demonstrated to be the source of sound production.[1] A model from the 1950s termed the neurochronaxic theory described each vibration as being controlled by individual nerve pulses.[2] The neurochronaxic theory has now been rejected in favor of more empirically validated models, namely the myoelastic-aerodynamic theory and the body-cover theory.

Myoelastic-Aerodynamic Theory

Published in the late 1950s,[1] the myoelastic-aerodynamic theory is now one of the most widely accepted theories for how vocal fold vibration is initiated and maintained. This theory is most appropriately studied by breaking it into its two components.

Myoelastic refers to the gross neuromuscular control of vocal fold tension and elasticity during phonation. Regulation of elasticity in turn influences the vibration characteristics of the vocal folds. Muscular control over how close the vocal folds are held is also important. During normal exhalation, the vocal folds are about 60% apart, or abducted.[3] During phonation, the muscles are contracted to adduct (bring together) the vocal folds into the stream of airflow. By controlling the configuration of the glottal aperture (opening between the vocal folds), the body can influence pressure differences above and below the glottis. This helps drive the aerodynamic features of vocal fold vibration.

The aerodynamic component of this theory emphasizes the role of fluid dynamics during phonation, specifically the continuity law and Bernoulli's principle. The continuity law assumes an incompressible flow confined in a duct. At all points in the duct, flow must be equal; this is the proverbial "what goes in must come out." Airflow is equal to the cross-sectional area multiplied by the particle velocity. Therefore, if the duct narrows, the velocity must increase proportionally to maintain constant flow (Figure 3–1). In algebraic form:

$$v_1A_1 = v_2A_2 = \text{constant},$$

where v is the particle velocity and A is the cross-sectional area at a given point.[4]

This leads to Bernoulli's principle, which deals with the conservation of energy of a flow confined in a pipe. At any point in the flow, the total energy of the fluid is composed of two components: the kinetic energy due to the particle flow and the potential energy due to the pressure on the walls of the pipe. Total energy in the fluid must be conserved. Thus, when the particle velocity increases at a constriction and the kinetic energy of the fluid increases, the potential energy of the fluid must decrease. This is observed by a reduction in pressure on the walls of the pipe. This is especially relevant during the opening and closing of the glottis during phonation; as air passes through the narrowed glottis, it increases in velocity and decreases the pressure exerted on the glottal walls.[4]

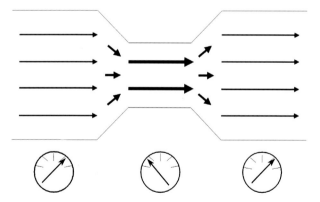

Figure 3–1. Bernoulli effect. As an incompressible flow enters a constriction, flow must remain constant. This is accomplished by increasing velocity, as represented by arrow width, proportionally to the reduction in area. The gauges beneath the diagram indicate relative pressure at each point in the tube.

At a simplistic level, Bernoulli's forces are credited for maintaining vocal fold oscillation. As air passes through the narrowed glottis, the particle velocity increases (continuity law) and the pressure subsequently drops (Bernoulli's law). This reduced pressure draws together and collapses the vocal folds. When subglottal pressure builds up, it reportedly blows the vocal folds apart and allows the cycle to repeat. This repetitive process goes on hundreds of times each second of phonation.

This explanation is inadequate, however. Bernoulli forces are present in the glottis without preference to whether it is opening or closing. Although these forces are effective for drawing the vocal folds together, they ultimately will lead to vocal fold damping. In other words, the Bernoulli forces are such that, instead of maintaining vibration, they will eventually lead the vocal folds to rest.

The additional input necessary to maintain vibration comes from the supraglottal air column. The air column has a degree of inertance, or resistance to change. When air passes through the glottis, it collides with the stagnant air particles already in the supraglottal air space. This creates an area of high pressure (a compression) that aids in driving the vocal folds together. Similarly, when the vocal folds collide with each other, they cut off airflow, but the air above the glottis continues moving forward. This creates an area of low pressure (a rarefaction) that aids vocal fold reopening.[4]

These forces can all be incorporated into an explanation of how vocal fold vibration takes place (Figure 3–2). To initiate phonation, the vocal folds are adducted so there is only a narrow channel between them. As expiratory pressure builds up from the lungs at the glottis, the air pressure pushes against the elasticity of the vocal folds. Eventually, the pressure reaches the minimum pressure needed to begin vibration, the air pushes the vocal fold tissue aside, and air flows through the vocal folds. The difference between the subglottal and supraglottal pressures combined with the deflection of the vocal fold mass creates a positive pressure which draws air up through the trachea. As described by Bernoulli's law, the airflow increases in velocity as it flows through the narrowed glottis.

As air escapes through the glottis from the subglottal reservoir, the subglottal pressure decreases, thus decreasing the force holding the vocal folds apart.

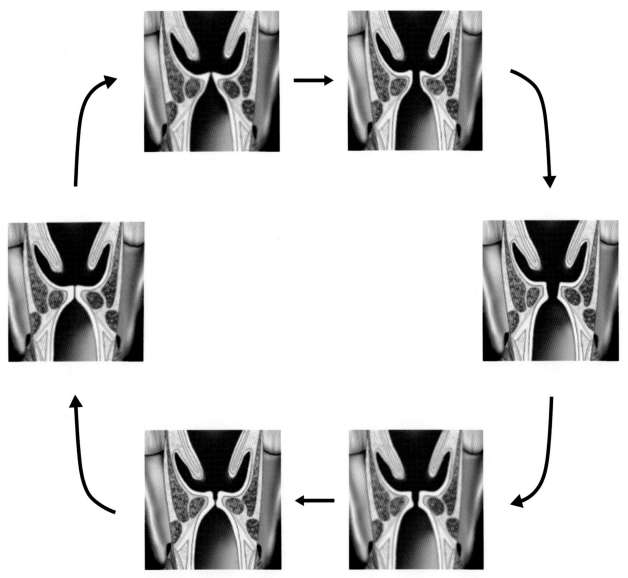

Figure 3–2. Vocal fold movement during one complete cycle. Beginning at the left, the vocal folds are adducted, followed by opening of the lower margins, opening of the upper margins, closure of the lower margins, and finally closure of the upper margins. (Adapted from *Vocal Parts*, 2001[24])

The Bernoulli effect generates a negative force, which pulls the vocal folds medially together again. Also, closure is aided by the passive recoiling (elasticity) of the vocal folds as they return to the position they were held in before being deformed by the transglottal pressure.[5]

When the vocal folds are drawn medially together, they once again obstruct the airflow, and the cycle repeats itself in what is termed the glottal cycle. The key point of the myoelastic-aerodynamic theory is that each glottal cycle is repeated without the need for repetitive muscular contraction after the vocal folds are initially brought together. Vibration is maintained through aerodynamic principles.

The number of times the vocal folds open and close each second is referred to as the frequency. The average frequency is 110 Hz in males and 200 Hz in females, but the human voice has a tremendous range and depends on many complex interactions.[5] The Bernoulli theory suggests that the effective mass and tension of the vocal folds, which are under neuro-muscular control, are the most important factors for controlling frequency.

Body-Cover Theory

The body-cover theory asserts that the five layers of the vocal folds can be classified into two groups to help account for vocal fold motion (Figure 3–3). The cover consists of the epithelium and the superficial and intermediate layers of the lamina propria. The cover is noted for being pliable and elastic but not muscular, and therefore not contractile. The deep layer of the lamina propria and the thyroarytenoid muscle fibers comprise the body. Active contractile properties of the body allow for adjustments of stiffness and concentration of mass.[6]

The morphologic structure of the vocal folds is important for controlling the tension of the vocal folds. The effective tension relies on the coupling of the vocal fold cover to the adjustable body. When the thyroarytenoid contracts, the body stiffens.[7] This contraction causes the distance between the arytenoids and the thyroid to shorten, so the cover becomes lax and pliable. The influence of the thyroarytenoid contraction on the fundamental frequency depends on the depth of vocal fold movement. If vibration is occurring primarily at the cover level, contraction of the thyro-arytenoid will make it more lax and thus lower the fundamental frequency. If vibration is deeper, however, and involves the body of the vocal folds, the increased tension for contraction of the thyroarytenoid will lead to an increase in fundamental frequency.[8]

The body-cover theory is used to account for the very large number of modes of vibration possible in the human vocal folds. Due to the loose coupling between the cover and the body, the cover can move independently of the body in an extremely variable ripple of tissue deformation.[6] This nonuniform tissue movement is characterized by normal modes of vibration, which detail the vibration patterns of the vocal folds. For instance, the lower margins of the vocal folds typically lead the upper margins in opening and closing of the vocal folds. This creates an alternation between convergent (closed at the top) and divergent (open at the top) shapes in the vocal folds whose asymmetry helps to sustain the oscillations.[4]

The more flexible the vocal folds are, the more potential there is for self-oscillation, and consequently, the more difficult it is to describe their movement. Current study of the vocal folds lacks consensus on the contribution of nonlinear dynamics to the vibration; multiple variables likely interact as either linear interactions of nonlinear systems or nonlinear interactions of linear systems.[5] Chaos theory (fractal analysis) has been employed to try to explain the complexity and redundancy of vibratory patterns.[9]

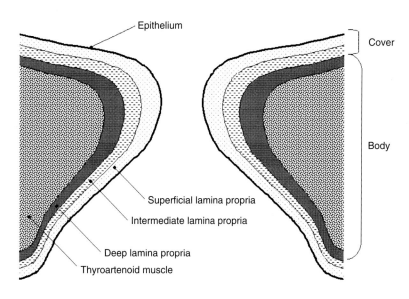

Figure 3–3. Layers of the vocal folds. The epithelium and superficial and intermediate layers of the lamina propria comprise the cover while the deep layer of the lamina propria and the thyroarytenoid muscle comprise the vocal fold body.

Mucosal Wave Movement

In addition to theories detailing how vibration is maintained, there is a clear model detailing how the vocal fold mucosa opens and closes in a wavelike pattern.[10] It is a common misconception that the sound produced by the vocal folds is a direct result of their vibration, much like a vibrating guitar string. On the contrary, the sound produced by the vocal folds is the result of small bursts of air that escape while the vocal folds vibrate. The vibration consists of an alternating sequence of medial (closing) and lateral (opening) movements. The asymmetry of these movements, which begin at the lower margins and travel to the upper margins of the vocal folds, helps to maintain oscillation. This movement is termed the mucosal wave because of its similarity to how waves travel in a fluid media.[5]

Canine larynges have been studied with videostroboscopy and other methods to show how different variables affect the mucosal waveform. Mucosal wave velocity has been shown to increase with vocal fold lengthening,[11,12] greater airflow,[11] greater subglottal pressure,[13] and laryngeal muscle contraction associated with higher fundamental frequency.[13]

PHONATORY INPUTS

The vocal folds are often thought of as the source of voice. Although they are essential in the conversion of aerodynamic power to acoustic power, the vocal folds do not act alone. Voice production requires contributions from subglottal pressure, the vocal folds, and supraglottal resonators.

Subglottal Pressure

Vocal fold vibration is powered by subglottal aerodynamic inputs. When intrathoracic pressure exceeds atmospheric pressure, there is a positive subglottal pressure. This subglottal pressure is primarily controlled by the lower respiratory airway, particularly the elastic properties of the chest walls and the active muscular contraction of the chest, diaphragm, and abdominal muscles. However, changes in the larynx

and upper airway can also influence subglottal pressure. These changes are dynamic and influence the phonation threshold pressure and glottal resistance. To respond to these changes, there must be complex and rapid feedback systems. Although not fully understood, feedback systems may include a combination of pressure sensors, proprioreceptive sensors, muscle tension/stretch sensors, and auditory sensors.[5] This feedback helps the body to regulate the amount of subglottal pressure required to start phonation.

The phonation threshold pressure, the minimum subglottal pressure required to initiate and sustain vocal fold vibration, is very important in the study of phonation. A low phonation threshold pressure means that relatively little respiratory effort is required to drive vocal fold vibration. The phonation threshold pressure decreases when there is a decreased prephonatory glottal width (the vocal folds are closer together), the viscosity of the vocal folds is decreased,[14] the thickness of the vocal folds is increased, or when the pitch is lowered. Phonation threshold pressure is elevated in dehydrated vocal folds,[15] patients with vocal fold polyps,[16] and patients with Parkinson's disease.[17]

This necessary subglottal pressure cannot be generated without glottal resistance, which is the ratio of transglottal pressure to transglottal airflow. This ratio was originally constructed in an effort to define something invariant about the glottal region of the airway. However, it has been difficult to tabulate due to the large number of geometric factors that affect the ratio, including glottal width and shape.[4]

A more useful number to characterize flow through a constricted area, such as the glottis, is a measure called the Reynolds number. This number is defined as:

$$Re = (vd)/\mu,$$

where Re is Reynolds number, v is air particle velocity, d is the effective diameter of the constriction, and μ is the kinematic viscosity. When Reynold's number exceeds a certain critical value, the fluid exiting the constriction will exhibit turbulent flow, like raging whitewater. Below the critical value, fluid exiting the constriction will exhibit laminar or steady flow (Figure 3–4). Usually the flow resistance increases with turbulent flow because of the increased energy dissipation. This can be useful for phonating certain

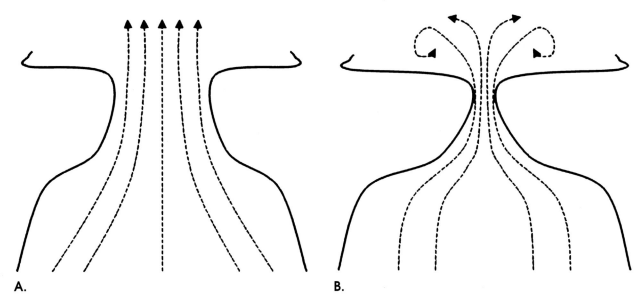

A.   **B.**

Figure 3–4. Reynolds number. **A.** If the speed of air is slow enough and the glottis wide enough, air exiting the glottis will exhibit laminar flow in parallel sheets. **B.** If these factors combine to give a Reynold's number above the threshold, turbulent flow will result.

sounds, like [h], but is not desirable for other sounds such as vowels.[4] It should be noted that most singers attempt to maintain laminar flow throughout phrases in the music.

Biomechanical Properties of Vocal Folds

Vibration of the vocal folds is a complex process whose characteristics are modulated by the biomechanical properties of the vocal folds. Specifically, the mass, stiffness, and viscosity of the vocal folds are important to regulating their vibration.

The fundamental frequency of vibration is inversely related to mass, as defined as the amount of vocal fold material that is effectively vibrating. While the actual mass of the vocal folds is fairly constant except in cases of edema or growths, the mass per unit length is easily modifiable. Longitudinal stretching of the vocal folds, as caused by contraction of the cricothyroid muscle, thins out the mass, modifies the cross-sectional shape of the vocal folds, and increases fundamental frequency. Contraction of other muscular fibers, namely, the thyroarytenoid, brings the arytenoid and thyroid closer together, thus increasing the

concentration of mass and decreasing fundamental frequency (Figure 3–5).

The second key biomechanical property of the vocal folds is stiffness, or the effective restoring force per unit of displacement. Stiffness is directly proportional to vocal fold tension and largely regulated by vocal fold length.[4] Contraction of the cricothyroid muscles increases the physical length of the tissues and thus increases the stretch tension. This is a passive state of tension because it occurs as a result of the tissue being spread over a greater area, much like a rubber band's tension increases as it is stretched. Contraction of the thyroarytenoid muscle fibers results in an active tensing of the vocal fold body. Although thyroarytenoid contraction increases the stiffness and tension in the muscular body, it reduces tension in the cover.[4] Optimum phonation requires a balance between the tension of the muscular body and the cover; the more closely the tensions of the body and cover are matched, the more efficient the conversion of aerodynamic to acoustic energy. This balance is not determined by the absolute level of contraction of each muscle but rather the differential control between them.[4]

Finally, viscosity is an important biomechanical property of the vocal folds. Viscosity is a measure of how resistant the vocal fold tissues are to change.[4]

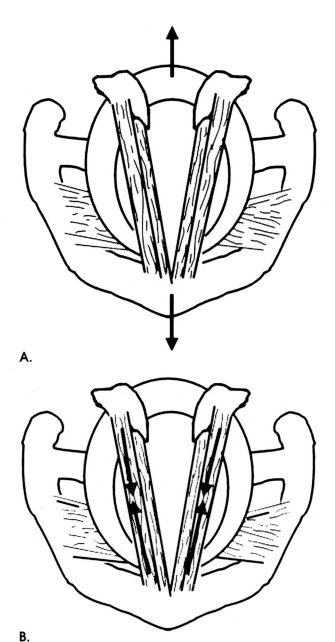

A.

B.

Figure 3–5. Muscular tuning of fundamental frequency. **A.** Contraction of the cricothyroid will elongate the vocal folds putting a passive stretch tension on the vocal fold cover. **B.** Contraction of the thyroarytenoid muscle results in an active tensing of the vocal folds.

Higher viscosity, such as results from dehydration of the vocal folds, translates to greater internal friction, greater energy loss in the form of heat, and a higher phonation threshold pressure. Viscosity is not independent of mass

and tension; longitudinal tension increases viscosity, whereas the greater vocal fold thickness that results from contraction of mass reduces viscosity.

Supraglottal Resonance

The sound exiting the glottis consists of the fundamental frequency plus many harmonics, or overtones. The supraglottal vocal tract helps to shape those sounds from raw noise into a human voice. The filtering effects of the supraglottal vocal tract modulate the acoustic output of the glottis and regulate the acoustic power. The higher frequencies are more susceptible to energy loss because of the damping characteristics of the source spectrum of glottal vibration.[5]

When the waveforms reflect off other structures, resonance occurs. To appreciate resonance, we turn to the analogy of a bottle with a narrow neck. When one blows across the top of the neck, the air in the bottle resonates at a certain frequency. The resonant frequency is a characteristic of the bottle, not of the air being blown across it. Pouring liquid into or out of the bottle will change its resonant frequency by changing the air column's size and shape.

Similarly, air will resonate at a certain frequency in the supraglottal vocal tract. Each resonance in the vocal tract is called a formant. Changing the size and shape of the airway by moving the tongue, jaw, lips, and any other structures in the upper airway will change the resonant frequency. Lengthening the airways causes a decrease in formant frequencies, the energy regions of vowels. The resonance in the supraglottal air tract is responsible for the perceived differences in vowels. Each vowel is defined by the lowest two formants, which are a characteristic of the supraglottal vocal tract.[4]

PHONATORY CONTROL MECHANISMS

Pitch

As described by the myoelastic-aerodynamic theory, two main factors interact to control pitch: tension and mass. The tension involves both the passive tension on the vocal fold cover and the active stiffness of the vocal fold body. Lengthening the vocal folds increases stretch tension on the vocal fold cover. Increasing the length also decreases the mass per unit length, which leads to an increase in frequency. The average person can control these changes to have an overall pitch range of about two octaves.

Raising the pitch primarily relies on contraction of the cricothyroid muscle. Contraction of the crico- thyroid causes the vocal folds to lengthen and the medial edge to thin. Because the cricoarytenoid mus- cle limits the movement of the arytenoid cartilages, contraction of the cricothyroid also causes an increase in vocal tension. All of these factors can be fine-tuned to elevate the pitch. Breath pressure has also been shown to covary with pitch. This has been demon- strated in both excised larynges and computer models, but it is a complex relationship that is not yet com- pletely understood.[18] Current evidence shows that while pitch and pressure are related, they do not have a causal link.

There are two mechanisms for lowering the pitch. From a higher pitch to a lower pitch, one simply relaxes the muscles in the larynx. The natural elasticity of the vocal folds returns them to the tension required to produce their normal pitch. Further lowering of the pitch requires contraction of the thyroarytenoid mus- cle. This draws the arytenoid and the thyroid cartilages together, thus increasing the concentration of mass and decreasing tension on the cover.[7] This rounds the medial edge of the vocal folds and allows for greater amplitude of vibration. Contraction of the thyro- arytenoid can be used to lower the pitch below the normal pitch At high frequencies because there is little movement of the deep tissues, contraction of the thy- roarytenoid is used to fine-tune the pitch.

Loudness

Loudness of voice is a measure of how we perceive pressure or power differences. The largest determinate of loudness is the intensity of sound, which is the phys- ical measure of power or pressure ratios. Increased intensity requires the vocal folds to open and close with more vigor. Control of this is possible at the subglottal, glottal, and supraglottal levels. This control relies on the same basic mechanism that controls

frequency, so it is difficult to vary them separately. There are two contributors to subglottal regulation of vocal intensity: subglottal pressure and tracheal airflow.[19] At the level of glottal regulation, intensity is linked to the level of medial compression.[20] When the vocal folds are more tightly compressed, more force is required to blow them apart. They then are drawn together more forcefully and close more rapidly. Tightly compressed vocal folds stay closed longer and thus increase the intensity with which each burst of air escapes the vocal folds. This level of regulation is especially impor- tant at low pitches.[21]

Supraglottal factors can also affect vocal intensity. The size, shape, and placement of resonators are impor- tant. Trained speakers learn how to effectively control frequency and intensity independently. Trained singers can also increase vocal intensity with less respiratory and vocal effort by changing the shape and stiffness of the vocal tract to tune formants. It is well known that there is a major hump in the voice spectrum around 3000 Hz known as the "singers' formant" that allows the singer's voice to soar over the accompaniment.[4]

Voice Quality

One of the main ways to evaluate vocal quality is through vocal registers, which are perceptually distin- guishable modes of phonation. The ideal phonation register is modal, or chest. This register is present in the middle frequency range. Because it is the most effi- cient mode of phonation, it is the mode used most commonly in daily conversation. Speech-language pathologists focus on teaching their clients to use this mode of phonation.

Below modal phonation is the pulse or glottal fry register. This low frequency of phonation (30–90 Hz) is distinguished by its crackly, "Strohbass" (straw bass) sound. It is important to note that it is not simply a lower frequency of phonation; it is a different mode of phonation that contains a secondary syncopated beat. During this syncopated vibration, two opening cycles occur in close succession followed by a prolonged closed phase that may last for up to 90% of the cycle. It requires only low subglottal pressure to maintain because the vibrating margin is flaccid and thick. The lack of tension allows air to slowly bubble through the vocal folds instead of pushing them into rapid vibration. To eliminate the crackly quality of this voice, one must increase the tension of the vocalis muscle.[22]

On the opposite end of the vocal spectrum is the high frequency (300–600 Hz and above) loft or falsetto register. The falsetto register is defined by a very short, or completely absent, closed phase with the vocal folds making contact only briefly. During this type of phonation, the vocal folds are thin and reedlike. The cricothyroid and thyroarytenoid muscles both exhibit heightened activity.[23] When the vocal folds reach the maximum possible contraction, they must use a different mode of increasing pitch. The posterior portion of the vocal folds is damped, and there is a reduced degree of movement.[22]

Two common variations on these modes of vibration are breathy and pressed voice. Breathy voice results when the vocal folds remain slightly abducted during vibration. This mode is inefficient because it causes air wastage and vocal fatigue, but it is not damaging to the phonatory mechanism. However, breathy phonation may be an indication of an underlying pathology, like vocal polyps, that is preventing complete closure of the vocal folds. On the other side of the spectrum, pressed phonation results from full glottal adduction. This variation on the voice is often viewed as strong and commanding but it is actually abusive to the vocal folds and can lead to damage.[5]

Nonregistered voice quality can be described based on its stability. Phonation with long-term modulation of intensity may be labeled as persistent, variable, or controlled; the terms traditionally given to these modulations in intensity are "tremulous" in pathologic voices, "nervous" in emotional voices, and "vibrato" in singing voices. Involuntary variations in stability are labeled "hoarse." Hoarseness may result from glottal incompetence in vocal fold paralysis, lesions that affect vocal fold mass, or vocal fold hyperfunction. For an objective evaluation of hoarseness, clinicians often refer to signal-to-noise ratio, or SNR.[5]

Overall voice quality, or timbre, is defined by the partial emphasis of different overtones. Essentially it is an evaluation of the qualities that make each voice unique and humanlike. Timbre is influenced by selective amplification by the walls of a series of resonators in the pharynx and mouth. Timbre is closely related to the skewing of the glottal volume velocity. This refers to the fact that the flow maximum occurs after the maximum glottal area. Skewing is linked to the iner-tance, or resistance to change in airflow, of the airway. When phonation occurs, the stagnant air in the vocal tract must be pushed out. The resistance of the stagnant air increases supraglottal pressure and thus decreases translaryngeal pressure. Elongating the vocal tract with maneuvers such as lowering the larynx or protruding the lips can increase inertance. Greater inertance means greater skewing of the flow maximum, and the more the flow maximum is skewed, the more energy is in the higher harmonic frequencies of the voice.

SUMMARY

Overall, voice production involves the interaction of many physiological systems. It begins with the aerodynamic pressure generated by the chest, thorax, and abdomen. Muscles in the larynx can be used to control the width of the glottal opening and the tension in the vocal folds, which when combined with the pressure inputs, drive the vocal folds into a series of rhythmic vibrations. The result is a wave of air pressure changes sent to the upper vocal tract where it can be modulated by resonators and filters to produce the instrument known as the human voice.

REFERENCES

1. Van den Berg J. Myoelastic-aerodynamic theory of voice production. *J Speech Hear Res*. 1958;1: 227–244.
2. Tucker HM. *The Larynx*. 2nd ed. New York, NY: Thieme Medical Publishers; 1993.
3. Stemple JC, Glaze L, Klaben BG. *Clinical Voice Pathology Theory and Management*. 3rd ed. San Diego, Calif: Singular Publishing Group; 2000.
4. Titze IR. *Principles of Voice Production*. Englewood Cliffs, NJ: Prentice Hall; 1994.
5. Jiang JJ, Lin E, Hanson DG. Vocal fold physiology. *Voice Dis Phonosurg J*. 2000;33:699–718.
6. Hirano M. Morphological structure of the vocal cord as a vibrator and its variations. *Folio Phoniatr*. 1974;26:89–94.
7. Titze IR, Luschei ES, Hirano M. Role of the thyroarytenoid muscle in regulation of fundamental frequency. *J Voice*. 1989;3:213–224.

8. Titze IR, Jiang J, Drucker DG. Preliminaries to the body-cover theory of pitch control. *J Voice.* 1988;1:314-319.

9. Baken RJ. Irregularity of vocal period and amplitude: a first approach to the fractal analysis of voice. *J Voice.* 1989;4:185-197.

10. Hertegård S, Gauffing J. Glottal area and vibratory patterns studied with simultaneous stroboscopy, flow glottography, and electroglottography. *J Speech Hear Res.* 1995;38:35-100.

11. Jiang JJ, Yumoto E, Lin SJ, Kadota Y, Kurokawa H, Hanson DG. Quantitative measurement of mucosal wave by high-speed photography in excised larynges. *Ann Otol Rhinol Laryngol.* 1998;107(2): 98-103.

12. Titze IR, Jiang JJ, Hsiao T-Y. Measurement of mucosal wave propagation and vertical phase difference in vocal fold vibration. *Ann Otol Rhinol Laryngol.* 1993;102:58-63.

13. Nasri S, Sercarz JA, Berke GS. Noninvasive measurement of traveling wave velocity in the canine larynx. *Ann Otol Rhinol Laryngol.* 1994;103:758-766.

14. Finkelhor BK, Titze IR, Durham PL. The effect of viscosity changes in the vocal folds on the range of oscillation. *J Voice.* 1988;1:320-325.

15. Verdolini K, Titze IR, Fennell A. Dependence of phonatory effort on hydration level. *J Speech Hear Res.* 1994;37:1001-1007.

16. Jiang JJ, O'Mara T, Conley D, et al. Phonation threshold pressure measurements during phonation by airflow interruption. *Laryngoscope.* 1999; 109:425-432.

17. Jiang J, Vlagos D, O'Mara TG, et al. Aerodynamic measurement of patients with Parkinson's disease. *J Voice.* 1991;13:583-591.

18. Shipp T, Doherty ET, Morrissey P. Predicting vocal frequency from selected physiologic measures. *J Acoust Soc Am.* 1979;66:678-684.

19. Holmberg EB, Hillman RE, Perkell JS. Glottal airflow and transglottal air pressure measurements for male and female speakers in soft, normal, and loud voice. *J Acoust Soc Am.* 1988;84:511-529.

20. Berke GS, Hanson DG, Gerratt BR, et al. The effect of airflow and medial adductory compression on vocal efficiency and glottal vibration. *Otolaryngol Head Neck Surg.* 1990;102:212-218.

21. Isshiki N. Regulatory mechanisms of voice intensity variation. *J Speech Hear Res.* 1964;7:17-29.

22. Seikel JA, King DW, Drumright DG. *Anatomy and Physiology for Speech, Language and Hearing.* 3rd ed. Clifton Park, NY: Thomson Delmar Learning; 2005.

23. Zemlin WR. *Speech and Hearing Science.* 4th ed. Needham Heights, Mass: Allyn and Bacon; 1998.

24. *Vocal Parts* [computer program]. Version 2.5. Lynnwood, Wash: Blue Tree Publishing Inc; 2001.

Chapter 4

ARTISTIC VOCAL STYLES AND TECHNIQUE

Sharon L. Radionoff

Voice professionals work in a wide range of disciplines and genres. The voice professional who is a singer may choose to use his or her vocal instrument as a singer/music educator, a singer/choral director, professional singer (opera; oratorio; musical theatre; clubs—pop/rock, jazz, country, mariachi, salsa), or as a professional actor/singer (theatre), to name a few. Each discipline demands peak vocal performance for longevity of career.[1]

In order to have a healthy singing voice, it is important to know how to: (1) Sing with healthy technique (ie, balancing airflow, phonation, resonance, articulation, agility), (2) sing in the correct voice category/range, (3) sing in the correct tessitura (pitch area where voice comfortably sits), (4) choose music that has a tessitura (pitch area) and range that matches one's own tessitura and range, and (5) sing the genre of music with the healthiest possible stylistic tools.[1]

In regard to vocal styles and stylistic tools, there are many vocal sounds that can be made but some sounds have the potential to be harmful. For example, "grit," "growling," and glottal onsets are stylistic effects found in rock, country, and pop music. These tools must be used with the least amount of tension needed to avert damage. Also, if used too often, a tension onset may become part of one's technique and no longer employed just as a stylistic tool.[2] These habits often creep into the speaking voice adding to the harmful effects. It is possible to create a desired vocal tool (ie, grit, growl) in more than one way. The key to longevity of career is finding and understanding the "system's balance" and alignment for singing before creating stylism. Balance must be attained before power, agility, or style. This analogy can be clearly seen in sports. For example, consider a gymnast. It makes sense that a gymnast stretches and finds his or her center of gravity first, whether it be on the balance beam or floor exercise, before doing any flips, turns, or difficult combinations. One might consider a gymnast foolhardy if he or she were to attempt difficult movements before balancing the body and mind. Singers, however, are notorious for ignoring balance and head immediately to agility, power, and style. They even attempt to "warm-up" by singing what they consider to be an easy song. There are so many variables to be aligned that it is critical for the voice professional to find his or her system's balance and alignment.

BALANCING

Sound: A Balancing Act

The act of singing can be compared to being on a teeter-totter or seesaw (Figure 4–1). The teeter-totter effect occurs as follows: a person sitting on the ground seat pushes with the legs and is propelled into the air.

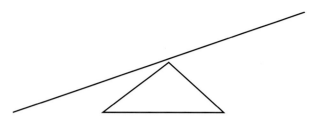

Figure 4–1. Teeter-totter.

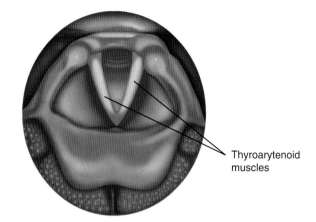

Figure 4–2. The thyroarytenoid muscle makes up the body of the true vocal folds (vocal cords). (Courtesy of Blue Tree Publishing.)

Consequently, the opposite seat, which was in the air, goes down to the ground. Keeping the teeter-totter parallel to the ground requires a "balancing act."[3]

The shifting of power action in the teeter-totter example may be used as an analogy to singing. At different times, one muscle or muscle group is more active then another and a power shift takes place. Sometimes the shift is gradual and sometimes the shift is abrupt. The complex systems for sound production that interact and must be balanced are respiration (power source), phonation (the vocal folds = raw sound source/pitch source), and resonance (the supraglottic vocal tract = the quality shaper).[3]

Questions to keep in mind regarding balancing the vocal system are: (1) where does the work occur? (2) what does the work? and (3) how much work has to happen? These questions may be examined in terms of pitch, loudness, and articulation. There are a variety of muscles that work together to create pitch as previously discussed in chapter 4. This chapter discusses the two most important muscles. In the most simplistic terms, the thyroarytenoid (TA) muscle shortens, and thickens the vocal fold.[4] Therefore, when lower pitches are produced, the TA muscle (Figure 4–2) is active. When a higher pitch is produced, the cricothyroid muscle becomes more active (Figure 4–3). The cricothyroid (CT) muscle is the principal muscle for longitudinal tension. Contraction of the CT muscle lengthens the vocal folds and thins them, which allows for a higher pitch.[5] One does not have to vocally manipulate to make pitches change because this is intrinsically how the system works![3]

In regard to loudness, when the vocal folds vibrate with greater amplitude (are wider apart), there is more airflow passing through per vibration. Also, the impact or closure force of contact of the true vocal folds is greater thereby creating a louder sound. When the vocal folds vibrate closer together, there is less airflow

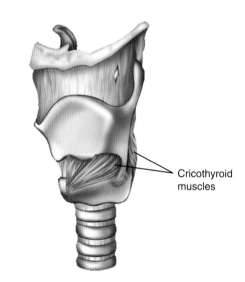

Figure 4–3. The cricothyroid muscle runs between the cricoid and thyroid cartilages. (Courtesy of Blue Tree Publishing.)

per vibration, which creates a softer sound. This is called amplitude variation and results in a change in intensity. This is perceived as a change in loudness.[4]

The questions asked above are especially pertinent to articulation. In order to have precise articulation, overwork may occur in terms of jaw clenching, chewing, tongue pressure, or excessive movement of the face and lips. For example, the consonant /n/ is created by the tongue tip moving up and touching the hard palate or, more specifically, the alveolar ridge.[6]

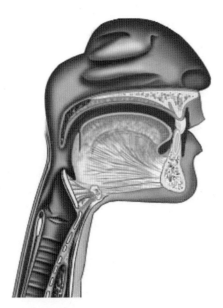

Figure 4–4. Sagittal (side) view of the resonance tract and articulators. (Courtesy of Blue Tree Publishing.)

Frequently the tongue posture for /n/ is produced with a closed or clenched jaw. This closing and/or clenching also is often true for the production of an /l/. The tongue is a powerful muscle, and a much larger structure than often perceived (Figure 4–4). Because the tongue has an attachment to the hyoid bone, tongue tension and excessive manipulation of the tongue may lead to vocal fatigue.[6]

No matter what the style of singing, balance is the key. If longevity of voice use is the desired outcome, then knowledge and excellent use of the vocal mechanism is critical. Therefore, singing and sound production are about balancing the systems necessary to achieve sound for a desired outcome in the healthiest way.[6]

BALANCING EXERCISES

Building Block Approach

Singing is like building a house. The foundation comes first, then the walls, and the roof follows before work begins on the inside. Likewise, as in building a house, there is a logical sequence when creating sound. Airflow management is the foundation (the respiratory system = power source), phonation (pitch source) is the walls, and resonance (sound shaper) is the roof. After you have layered these three systems then you can begin to work on agility, strength, and musicianship along with interpretation and style. An example of the building block approach would be the following: (1) begin with airflow on /sh/, /f/, or /s/; (2) next add phonation on a single note using /shu/, /fu/, or /su/; and (3) last add resonance by adding an /m/ to the previous phonation /shum/, /fum/, or /sum/ and repeat the pattern (shum-mum-mum). There is a direct link between the first step, airflow, to the second step, phonation. The same consonant and consonant combination for the respiratory mechanics of airflow begins both steps and then we add vocal fold vibration for the second step. Also, by adding the /m/ for resonance, the third step starts the same as the second but allows for frontal directionality for the resonance. As /m/ is the most frontal nasal consonant, it is not necessary to press or push air pressure forward. One simply closes the lips and the airflow travels forward. After the basic sound has been balanced, agility of vocal fold lengthening and shortening may be attempted. A desirable way to begin is by using small patterns so that one will not fight against oneself for control. The numbers used to define these patterns below are based on a major scale 1-2-3-4-5-6-7-8 (C-D-E-F-G-A-B-C). These patterns are 1-7-1 (C—down ½ step to B natural—back up to C), 1-2-1 (C—up a step to D—back down a step to C), and 3-2-1 (down the major scale E-D-C). Then these patterns may be added together to gradually increase the range of agility such as: 1-7-1-2-1, 1-2-1-7-1, 3-2-1-7-1, and so on.[7]

Stress Release Exercises

The voice can be misaligned for many reasons. It may simply be that one has just woken up and the brain and body are not awake enough to connect at the highest level. It may also be related to external or internal stress. A certain amount of stress is normal as one goes through the rigors of life, and stress can result from a variety of things. Just the pace of a busy day can induce the physical reaction of stress. This reaction will cause the body to tighten and the result will be less access to airflow. Less airflow means a diminished power source and the body and voice will feel pushed by the end of the day if one does not learn how to release body and mind tension. A good way to release stress and tension is to do a few repetitions of airflow management exercises—blowing air for a comfortable consistent length of time using /sh/, /wh/, /f/, or /s/ and after blowing, releasing the abdominal area, letting the body fill up with air and repeating.[8]

Vocal Tension Release Exercises

After airflow exercises, the next step would be "vocal tension release" exercises. These exercises consist of vocal slides using the phonemes /f/ and /v/ in combination (beginning with the unvoiced consonant and then moving down the slide on the voiced consonant) or /shu/. The main object of these exercises is to feel the air at the front of the mouth (f/v) with ease of sound, not listening for beautiful sound. It is important to do these exercises starting in a comfortable middle range and not in the high range. First, start on a comfortable middle range pitch and slide down to a comfortable low range pitch. It should be a moderately slow glide. Be sure that the upper teeth touch the bottom lip appropriately when using the f/v combination. Airflow should be felt behind the top teeth. The teeth should touch the bottom lip at the vermilion border. If one feels the airflow coming out between the teeth then one does not have the teeth touching the bottom lip enough or there is a gap between the teeth. This exercise may also be done by using an undulating wavy slide (Figure 4–5). Don't try to make exact pitch definition. Again, the important issue is a lot of air at the teeth and ease of sound. Another phoneme cluster to use is /shu/. Remember that when using /shu/ the tongue tip will not be behind the bottom teeth for the consonant cluster /sh/ but will then need to come behind the bottom teeth for the /u/ vowel. If you use the f/v combination then the tongue can be behind the bottom teeth the entire time.

Voice Balancing Exercise

The last exercise presented is called a voice balancing exercise. This consists of choosing a comfortable note in the speaking range. On a single note (eg, A3, Bb3, B3, or C4 for women—C4 = middle C) use the con-

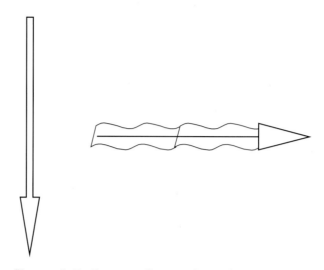

Figure 4-5. Descending and small wavy slides.

sonant vowel combination *"Bum" or **"Buhm." The object is to simply say easy repetitions of the combination of choice in slow and faster repetitions (bum-bum-bum-bum-bum). It is not necessary to push pressure forward into the /m/. Simply by choosing one of these combinations you will feel the sound move forward as /m/ is the most frontal nasalant consonant. All that one does is open and close the lips for the combination.[8]

Never forget that as a voice professional, the entire body is the instrument. What you do with your body will directly affect your voice. Also, because you only have one larynx, what you do with your voice when you are not singing will affect what you are able to do with your voice when you sing.[7]

BODY-MIND-SPIRIT CONNECTION

Another concept that warrants examination concerning vocal health is the understanding that each person is composed of body, mind, and spirit. One can put into practice all the appropriate exercises but the psyche can either hinder or help progress. When someone sings, all aspects of the persona are entwined. Our singing voice is our body, mind, and spirit. We cannot separate the influences of these elements.[9]

---

*International Phonetic Alphabet (IPA) used unless otherwise noted.
**Not IPA

Body

For healthy singing technique, the tongue and the neck are two common pitfalls to monitor. The tongue often gets us into trouble! The tongue is composed of 8 to 10 muscles that are interdigitated. In fact we can only see a small part of the tongue. We often try to control sound by controlling the position of the tongue (ie, pulling it back too far, pressing it down in the center) instead of having the most efficient "home resting place" for the tongue tip while we are producing different vowels. Of course the tongue will have to move for consonants and change shape for vowels, but we usually overwork with pressure and manipulation of the tongue rather than simply having the efficient position of the tongue for certain consonants.

Along with the tongue, the neck is often a source of control and manipulation. A stiff and stubborn neck is a sign of the inability to manage stress. Some singers often hold it stiff with extrinsic muscle tension to feel physical control for sound in the area of the larynx. This may be done in order to psychologically "feel" control.[10]

Mind

The impulse or idea for making sound begins in the cerebral cortex of the brain.[11] The brain is the control panel or central processing unit (CPU) of our body (Figure 4–6). It sends information to all the systems that have to balance in order to sing. The singing voice is trained by the concepts that we cultivate with various exercises. Please remember that practice makes permanent and not necessarily perfect! What we practice is what becomes a learned behavior. What we dwell on is what becomes part of us.

Manipulative control often happens with the tongue, jaw, neck, or torso to psychologically "feel" voice before it can leave out of the mouth. Learning efficient technique and the tools to sing facilitates healthy singing. However, as one learns efficient, healthy technique, one has to get out of the way, let go, and trust. Despite the overriding need to control, manipulate, and hold to make sound happen, one must consciously let go, trust, and believe that it will happen.[10]

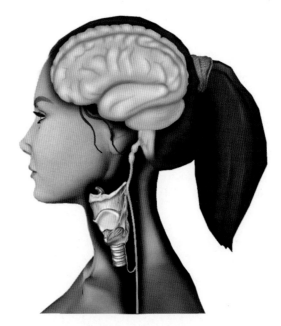

Figure 4–6. Sagittal (side) view of the brain, nerves, and laryngeal skeleton. (Courtesy of Blue Tree Publishing.)

Spirit

What drives or motivates someone to sing? Is it a burning passion within or a desire to prove something? Is it the need for self-expression or applause? Does singing bring joy? Whatever the case may be, there is an internal reason why one chooses to sing. The essence or spirit of a person is expressed through music when they sing. If the technique is not at the level of the emotion or essence, then one will try to force singing to occur. In our vocal journey we can choose to approach singing by either "make my voice be" or "allow my voice to become." As stated above, efficient technique of course aids in healthy singing. Remember, however, that singing takes faith. We have to get out of the way, let go, and trust.

STYLES

Balance and alignment of the vocal instrument, comprising the body-mind-spirit connection, is just the beginning for the performer. If one knows where his or her center of balance is, then one can experiment with how far one may go from the central balance point for coloration and effect and still have integrity of technique. It really does not matter what style of music someone sings. What truly matters is the balance point of the voice. If a singer knows his or her balance point, then he or she will be able to experiment with breath, resonance (eg, nasalance), articulation, straight tone, and delayed vibrato (along with other aspects) for coloration and effect. It is no different than a painter having a palette with many colors to choose from to create nuance in his or her painting.

Broad Categories

Style is often discussed in terms of two broad categories: Classical music and commercial music. Vocal pedagogue Carolyn Binkley in Nashville defines classical and commercial music as the following: "Classical" is a term which represents many genres including opera, oratorio, art song, symphony, chamber music, and the manner of performance associated with those genres. "Commercial" can include the styles jazz, rock, country, pop, rhythm and blues, big band and swing, alternative, contemporary Christian, gospel, rap, hip-hop, and heavy metal but to name a few. These two terms are not descriptive of two areas, rather they are commonly used terms that are widely recognizable throughout the musical world (C. Binkley, personal communication, 1999). Although the acronym CCM is currently another reference to commercial music, one must be careful as the acronym has been used specifically to refer to the genre of Contemporary Christian Music for the past 25 years. There is a magazine called *CCM* devoted specifically to this genre of music as well (L. Poquette, personal communication, November 29, 2005). Furthermore, the term commercial music is well entrenched and used by colleges and universities to define a specific degree plan such as found at Belmont University in Nashville, Tennessee and Miami University in Miami, Florida.

Western

Classical music (as we know it) may be further categorized into "Western" classical music. A note is neces-

sary here about the term Western versus non-Western categories of classical music. Music historians often use this separation. However, noted ethnomusicologist Dr. Robert Trotter who taught "Music in World Cultures," preferred a more inclusive terminology (personal communication, 1987). This is especially relevant today given the culturally expanded nature of the world.

Non-Western

Non-Western music includes Latin styles such as Salsa, Cumbia, Merengue (which has its roots in the German polka and African drum beat), and a mixed style of music called Reggaeton (rap/hip-hop/Caribbean). There are also Hispanic styles such as Tejano and Mariachi music. In addition, the musical styles of Indian and Middle Eastern cultures vary significantly from what the Western ear is used to hearing. This list of non-Western music is by no means exhaustive. It is only meant to show that a plethora of diversity exists.

Choral

Another broad category subset is the choral tradition that exists in a variety of settings. Choral music exists in the school, community, and religious settings. In the school setting, ensembles may range from small chamber ensembles (12–20 voice, mixed chorus) to medium-size chorales (40+ voices, mixed chorus) to a larger oratorio chorus (150+ members, usually mixed). The larger choral works may include such diversity as "The Dream of Gerontius" by Edward Elgar to the well-known work the "Messiah" by Handel. In these large ensembles it can be difficult to hear oneself sing: Consequently, it is easy to "push" voice production to create more volume in order to hear oneself. Also, in the school setting there are show choirs with choreography and a live band as well as jazz ensembles with accompaniment ranging from a combo to a full jazz ensemble. Choreography and the different types of accompaniment both pose potential problems for healthy singing. If the singer pulls in the abdominal area when dancing then the breathing will be high and shallow. When there is a live band the singer will often push to hear him- or herself. This happens with and without monitors simply because of the sheer amount of sound from the instruments and prompts the singer to compete because of the inability to hear him- or herself.

In the community setting there are chorales, symphony choruses (often 250+ members), as well as Barbershop, Sweet Adelines, and Madrigals groups. The sound of the Barbershop/Sweet Adeline style is often described as a "laserlike" pinpoint sound. It is easy to get caught in a trap of using excessive pressure to create a frontal, laserlike sound if one is not careful.

In the religious setting there is a wide range of styles and service music. There is music for the traditional service versus the contemporary service (found in Catholic, Protestant, and nondenominational churches). Even within the contemporary service definition there is a wide diversity of style and definition. Some consider anything other than high-church music contemporary while others consider only current music contemporary. Two churches that have brought contemporary music to the forefront are the Brooklyn Tabernacle and Houston's Lakewood Church (choir roster of approximately 650 members). Cindy Cruse Ratcliff, Lakewood's Music Director, defines their style of contemporary music as "diverse and eclectic. It ranges from Rock to Pop to Rhythm and Blues (R & B) to Gospel and even Latin" (personal communication, October 15, 2005). She notes that the music often changes style within a song. A song may start as Pop-oriented while the bridge is in a Gospel or R & B style. A good example of mixed style would be "Gloria" from Lakewood's CD *We Speak to Nations* which has a Latin salsa feel but also incorporates a traditional "Gloria" from the carol "Angels We Have Heard on High."

In the contemporary tradition, amplification is used for the singers as well as for the instrumentalists. The volume of energy created by all this amplification can trick the singer into feeling like he or she needs to sing louder in order to be heard. This happens more when there are no monitors for the singers but can happen even with monitors (ear buds as well as wedge style). Many singers who use ear buds actually prefer to use only one in order to hear room sound and feel the audience energy. Also, when singers try to create the contemporary sound they frequently do this by using tension to stop vibrato (ie, straight tone) and sound more "pop" in style. To sing without vibrato actually takes more airflow, not less. This same issue of inefficient production can be found in churches that ask sopranos to produce a young boylike sound in order to emulate the English Cathedral Choir sound.

Musical Theatre

In musical theatre, the performance practice "sound du jour" has historically gone through changes. In the book *The Complete Professional Audition* by Cohn and Perilstein, one can find songs and musicals in a variety of categories. Vocally, there is variation in singing style depending on when a musical was written. In the first chapter, Cohn[12] organizes shows into groups that encompass similar styles ranging from Country-Western influence (*Oklahoma*), Teens/Children (*Into the Woods*), Pop/Rock (*Jesus Christ Superstar*), and Outcasts/Underdogs (*Hairspray*) to name a few. In regard to different vocal sounds, there are musicals that are considered more classical in sound such as *Oklahoma* and *Phantom of the Opera*, while *Rent* and *Jesus Christ Superstar* use a contemporary pop/rock sound.

Those who perform the principal roles of a musical production are rarely asked to perform or play more than one character in an evening. However, *Jekyll and Hyde*, for example, demands two very different vocal productions from the male lead in every performance. It is very difficult to perform at the extremes of range and style every night and stay healthy. Other shows that have principals perform more than one character in an evening include: (1) *Into the Woods*, (2) *The Apple Tree*, and (3) *I Love You, You're Perfect, Now Change*. Also, in *Sunday in the Park with George* the cast plays different roles in the first and second act. Other difficulties include the use of character voices such as: (1) Little Bird (*Seussical*) and (2) Adelaide (*Guys and Dolls*). When creating a character voice, one has to be careful not to pass the point of healthy coloration and effect whether it is producing a cartoonlike voice or using nasalance. Each singer has a window of opportunity for coloration and effect and must experiment with how far he or she may go from the central balance point and still have integrity of technique. Another interesting twist is bringing Disney characters to life on the theatrical stage. It can be difficult to create an inanimate object such as a clock, teapot, or candle (*Beauty and the*

Beast) and keep integrity of body alignment (potential to adversely affect airflow).

Two terms that broadly categorize musical theatre are "legit" and "belt." Legit style includes such standards as *Oklahoma* and *Carousel*. Legit is defined by singing voice specialist Jeanette LoVetri (personal communication, November 8, 2005) as classically based vocal production generally using unmodified vowels. She further defines *belt* as chest register carried up above the traditional break, approximately E4–G4, at a loud volume (high intensity). The term belt is often treated as a dirty word. However, if done in a healthy manner, it can be a viable option. One can take pressure off the larynx by using more nasalance in this instance. Broadway belt includes shows as *Jekyll & Hyde* and *Wicked*. The advent of *Evita* however, brings about use of the mixed sound combining "belt" and head voice (P. House, personal communication, October 20, 2005).

In the August 2005 issue of *Opera News*,[13] Michael John Lachiusa (composer, lyricist, and librettist whose works include *Lady Suite*, *Hello Again*, and *The Wild Party*) discusses two other issues in regard to categorizing musicals. He defines what he calls the "faux" musical and the "jukebox" musical. He lists *The Producers* and *Hairspray* as two examples of the faux musical genre. He labels these musicals as "faux" because they are based on cult films, not original ideas. The other category of musical, referred to as "jukebox" musicals, is defined as such because they are basically a catalogue of songs by a group or solo singer. Examples of this include: *Good Vibrations* based on music by the Beach Boys and *Movin' Out* which is based on the music of Billy Joel. The musical that is given credit as being the first of this kind is *Mamma Mia*, which is based on the music of ABBA. Although these categories may have merit for organizational purposes, they do not detract from public interest in attending the performances.

There is potential for difficulty when music by well-known artists is used. It is possible that some of the listeners may be disappointed because they will compare the vocal sound of the performers in the current show to the original artists. Furthermore, a singer may be chosen to perform in these shows because he or she is able to mimic the sound of the original artist. However, if the vocal production is a manipulation for the singer, it has the potential to cause vocal problems after a period of time. If, for example, the lead singer in *Movin' Out* has to scoop his tongue in the center to press his larynx down to a lower than normal position to mimic the timbre (quality) of Billy Joel, then he has the potential of creating vocal distress in regard to his natural range and flexibility. Also, the lead singer(s) in the show may need a different key from the original. Hopefully, this will be taken into account. These same issues hold true for singers who primarily perform cover songs in clubs.

Currently, career marketability of young singers requires a broader ability than ever before in regard to genre. It is of note to mention that in 2002, an entire month's issue of *Opera News* (August)[14] was devoted to the crossover phenomenon between opera and the theatre. There has never been a time when being a crossover singer has been as important as now. Many opera and lyric opera companies include musicals in their programs. It behooves the singer to learn the elements of what makes a style a style.

SPEAKING VOICE

Theater Versus Musical Theater

In nonmusical theater, the actor may play one role throughout an evening's performance, or he or she may play several different characters. In Houston's Alley Theatre production of *The Devil's Disciple* by Bernard Shaw, one actor played both the British General Burgoyne and the commoner Uncle Titus; the comportment and voice of each were vastly different. The same actor, in the two-hander *Stone's in His Pocket* by Marie Jones, was required to use six different Irish dialects with a character age range from 6 to 78. Indeed, all the characters in this production were portrayed by only two actors. The virtuosity required to satisfy the textural and pitch demands in such instances is very taxing on the voice and can do damage without proper vocal technique (T. Waite, personal communication, September 28, 2005).

TOOLS VERSUS TECHNIQUES

The performer must remember that healthy technique must precede stylism and use of stylistic tools. It is also prudent to be reminded that there are some sounds that have the potential to be harmful. The examples outlined previously included "grit," "growling," and glottal onsets which can be found in rock, country, and pop music and must be used with the least amount of tension necessary in order to avert damage. There are also tools that are common in different styles of music. In Country music prominent stylisms also employed include yodeling, crying, and "riding" an "r." In Rock music screams are employed. In Jazz agility with scat singing and breathy voice are employed. In Alternative music, glottal tension and vocal fry are employed. In Musical Theatre we have "belt," "legit," and "pop" stylisms. Remember, if used too often, a tension onset may become part of one's technique and no longer employed just as a stylistic tool.[2]

SUMMARY

Learning to balance the voice and creating healthy phonation is an excellent foundation for a performance career. The balanced voice is like clay; you need to have it to be able to mold the sound into a shape (character/style/genre). Once you have the clay, then you will be able to shape it into a creation of your own choosing. The performers voice is the vehicle for expression. So, it is not about the person, but about being a communicator with the voice as the vessel or vehicle for communication.

Acknowledgments

Pictures for Figures 4-2, 4-3, 4-4, and 4-6 are courtesy of Blue Tree Publishing. The author thanks Inkwater Press for liberal use of content from the book *Faith and Voice* for the sections called Body, Mind, and Spirit. The author thanks *Texas Sings* for republication of material from several journal articles. The author thanks the following people for their support and editorial assistance: Leonard Radionoff, Jackie Gartner-Schmidt, Todd Waite, Cindy Cruse-Ratcliff, Lee Poquette, and Paul House.

REFERENCES

1. Garrett JD, Radionoff SL, Rodriguez M, Stasney CR. *Vocal Health*. Lynnwood, Wash: Blue Tree Publishing; 2003.
2. Radionoff SL, Binkley CK. *Commercial Singing for Classical Singers*. Professional workshop presented at The Voice Foundation's 25th Annual Symposium Care of the Professional Voice, Philadelphia, Pa; June 1996.
3. Radionoff SL. Sound: a balancing act. *Texas Sings*. 2005(Winter): 8-9.
4. Sataloff RT. *Professional Voice: The Science and Art of Clinical Care*. 2nd ed. San Diego, Calif: Singular Publishing Group; 1997:111-130.
5. Baken RJ. An overview of laryngeal function for voice production. In Sataloff RT, ed. *Vocal Health and Pedagogy*. San Diego, Calif: Singular Publishing Group; 1998:27-45.
6. Bunch M. *Dynamics of the Singing Voice*. New York, NY: Springer-Verlag Wien; 1993:113.
7. Radionoff SL. The music educator: a high-risk professional voice. In Stemple JC, ed. *Voice Therapy Clinical Studies*. 2nd ed. San Diego, Calif: Singular Publishing Group; 2000:397-409.
8. Radionoff SL. Choral directors vocal health and reviving the tired voice. *Texas Sings*. 2003(Fall): 4-5,11.
9. Radionoff SL. Sound: A balancing act—part II: body, mind, and spirit. *Texas Sings*. 2004(Winter): 13,19.
10. Radionoff SL. *Faith and Voice*. Portland, Ore: Inkwater Press; 2005:2-38.
11. Sataloff RT. The human voice. *Sci Am*. 1992(Dec): 108-115.
12. Cohn D, Perilstein, M. *The Complete Professional Audition: A Commonsense Guide to Auditioning for Musicals and Plays*. New York, NY: Back Stage Books; 2005.
13. Lachiusa J. *Opera News*. 2005(August).
14. Rauch RS (ed). *Opera News*. 2002(August).

Part II

Assessment and Diagnosis

Chapter 5

CASE HISTORY, INTERVIEW, AND VOICE HANDICAP ASSESSMENT

Michael S. Benninger
Thomas Murry

THE CHIEF COMPLAINT

The most important step in the evaluation and assessment process of any person with a voice disorder is the elucidation of the history of the current complaint or concerns. The singer comes to a voice clinic because he or she has specific concerns about the quality of his or her voice. In some cases, the singer will give a very concise description of the problem, such as, "I fatigue after the first 4 or 5 songs" or "I am no longer able to reach the upper few notes of my range since I performed three weeks ago." At other times, it may be very difficult for them to articulate their concerns and it is incumbent on the practitioner to take extra time in this important step to clarify as specifically as possible the problems the singer is experiencing. A few extra minutes during the initial interview will allow the clinician to focus the evaluation on the singer's primary concerns and create a directed approach to specific treatment. It should be remembered that, despite a primary concern, there may be other factors that must be teased out slowly.

Care should be taken to elucidate the chief complaint as this will often play a major role in the ultimate diagnosis. Common chief complaints are shown in Table 5–1. We have found that the chief complaint can

Table 5-1. Chief Complaint and Probable Diagnosis

Complaint	Probable Diagnosis
"Hoarseness"	Abnormality of the vocal fold (laryngitis, reflux, edema, masses)
Fatigue	Overuse of voice
Breathiness	Inability to approximate vocal folds (laryngitis, edema, masses)
Need for prolonged warm-up	(reflux)
Volume disturbances	Technique, intrinsic voice limitations, pathologic processes, age, neurologic disorders, hearing loss, endocrine dysfunction
Pain	URI or laryngitis, musculoskeletal strain, arthritis, reflux
Scratchy, itchy voice	Reflux, acute laryngitis, vocal abuse
Foreign body sensation, globus	Reflux, voice abuse

often serve as the primary mechanism for making the diagnosis. Table 5-2 lists some causes of overuse or improper use of the voice. The clinician should discuss each as multiple factors often occur over time to bring on the problem. Tables 5-3 and 5-4 list other considerations or conditions that may bring on the voice problem or contribute to changes in the voice of the singer.

A thorough history that focuses on the issues related to performance and postperformance voice changes along with a complete physical examination of the ears, nose, and throat will usually serve to crystallize the diagnosis. For example, a complaint of hoarseness might suggest a vocal mass, but examination is needed to confirm this diagnosis and identify the specific pathology.

The interviewer will be the most successful during the initial discussion with the singer if he or she engages the singer in aspects of lifestyle, rehearsal schedules, performances, and so forth. In this way, the singer will be more likely to discuss details about the onset of the problem. Other factors such as whether or not the singer is also a dancer, actor, or musician may also help the clinician to understand the reasons for seeking help.

As professional singers and actors are not the primary caseload of most otolaryngologists and speech-language pathologists, it is wise to have a prepared questionnaire. There are extensive ones such as that used by Sataloff[1] or shorter forms that are specifically for singers.[2] With a prepared questionnaire, the clinician is likely to identify issues that go beyond the current primary hoarseness or fatigue complaints.

The singer's initial interview may be aided by the presence of the singing voice specialist. He or she may offer the singer time to explain the details of the onset of the complaint, the feelings associated with the changes since its onset, and relay the concerns to the other clinicians. In any event, allowing extra time for the interview will put the performer at ease and demonstrate the clinician's interest in the details of the singer's problem.

Table 5-2. Common Causes of Vocal Overuse

- Time and duration of practice
- Excessive performing
- Conducting and teaching
- Environment of performances
- Singing/talking excessively
- Singing/talking over noise
- Singing/talking under tension
- Social speaking
    Voice use different in speaking than in singing
    Expert training lost or ignored
- Noise volume—children, noisy backgrounds
- Telephone—sound amplified
- Airline travel—speaking over ambient background noise, dryness

Table 5-3. Additional Sources of Dysphonia in Singers

- Inadequate preparation
    limited practice and rehearsals
    poor or inadequate training:
        in general
        singer's voice and level of training not suitable for the role
- Insufficient warm-up
- Poor environment for practice, rehearsing
- Working through injury
- Errors in technique
- Excessive muscle tension in tongue, neck, or larynx
- Excessive volume
- Poor or inadequate abdominal support

Table 5-4 Environmental Influences on Voice

- Humidity, dryness, mold
- Dust, dirt (set construction)
- Second-hand, primary smoke
- Smoke, fog machines
- Pollution
- Allergies
- Travel schedule
- Other vocal irritants

MEASURING QUALITY OF LIFE

Efforts to evaluate quality of life (QOL) in medicine have moved into voice clinical practice and research. The application of QOL to patients and the result of treatment or nontreatment are referred to as measuring outcomes. This section describes some general concepts of outcomes measures, the outcomes and quality of life research movements in medicine, and the present status of these movements as they relate to voice care, and the implications in determining treatment options for the voice patient.

ASSESSING THE SINGER'S QUALITY OF LIFE AND OUTCOMES

Health is a multidimensional concept that, according to the World Health Organization, incorporates physical, mental, and social states.[3] Handicap is defined as "... a social, economic, or environmental disadvantage resulting from an impairment or disability," and disability is defined as "... restriction or lack of ability manifested in the performance of daily tasks."[4] The degree of change in the parameters of physical, mental, or social status is considered an outcome. These outcomes, however, depend on a number of factors including the baseline level of function, other concomitant medical conditions, a person's perception of quality of life, and cultural or societal influences. In general, medical care strives to prevent and eliminate disease and thereby improve the quality of a patient's life. Traditionally, assessment of physical function was the only means of determining the impact of health or disease. This practice limits the clinician's ability to also assess the emotional or social impact of disease or its treatment. An acknowledgment of these limitations led to the development of a whole new way of looking at health and disease, and has been coined the "*outcomes*" movement.

Traditional assessment of outcomes in medicine has largely been through the perspective of the treating physician or clinician (ie, doctors, nurses, speech-language pathologists.) Therefore, an outcome was identified via changes in the physical examination, an improvement or change in symptoms and functions, or changes in laboratory tests or X-ray examinations. Classically the simplest two measurements of an outcome of treatment are the presence or absence of disease. In many ways, this distinction is very important, but it is often inadequate for assessing general life impact. For example, surgical treatment may be successful for a vocal fold polyp, yielding complete return of normal voice function. However, if the polyp and its treatment resulted in the singer missing an important performance, its effect on quality of life might be significantly different. Thus, when we consider the performer's voice, quality of life and outcome take on meanings that have fully yet to be understood.

The medical profession's early attempts to assess quality of life revolved around questionnaires that served to identify key issues that patients may have in relationship to their disease.[5] These questionnaires usually focused on questions that the physician or other person administrating the questionnaire felt were important, often not including factors that the person completing the questionnaire was most concerned about. Over time, following multiple revisions and adaptations, these questionnaires tended to address, to some degree, both these perspectives. Furthermore, questionnaires were not statistically validated, and, therefore, one could not be sure that they truly measured what was intended to be measured or that responses by individuals with the disease were different from those without the disease. It was also not clear whether or not the questionnaire maintained its validity over time so that a person who had no change in status would answer questions similarly at different times.

A realization that there are many critical issues related to the presence of a disease or the treatment of disease and efforts to measure the entire impact of health on individuals and society have driven the outcomes movement. Outcomes research attempts to observe patients in their typical clinical environment and uses patient-centered measures. In other words, they are measures of how the voice disorder affects function and quality of life.

Quality of life measurement instruments have been developed to try to measure the multidimensional nature of health with the questions and items within these tests usually clustering around broad health-related areas that can be measured in direct relationship to disease or response to treatment. Probably the most well-recognized and utilized quality of life measurement tool is the Medical Outcomes Study 36-Item

Short Form General-Health Survey, or "SF-36."[6-8] This instrument is self-administered and assesses 8 domains of health that are commonly affected by disease or its treatment: physical functioning, role functioning, social functioning, mental health, bodily pain, general health, vitality, and health transition.[6-8] Each of these subscales provides a score that is reliable and a valid measure of health for that particular dimension. The SF-36 has been used to evaluate a wide range of health issues and to compare quality of life as it relates to different disease processes.[9]

One of the disadvantages of using general health measurement tools to evaluate specific disorders is that they may not assess well the specific impact of the disease on an individual and how it may be affected by other medical conditions. This has led to an effort to develop disease-specific outcomes measurement tools.[8] The creation of these outcomes measurement tools requires a comprehensive, statistically validated assessment of reliability, predictability, reproducibility, responsiveness, and interpretability. In general, they should be easy to use (low burden) and should assist in the evaluation of the specific problem they were designed to assess.

MEASURING VOICE OUTCOMES AND QUALITY OF LIFE: STATE OF THE ART

Outcomes research is in its infancy as it relates to the care of people with voice disorders. Past attempts at trying to assess the impact of a voice problem on quality of life were limited by the types of tools that were available. Even with objective tests, there are often no generally agreed-upon gold standards of measurement. Furthermore, different objective tests have been designed for different measures of function, such as pitch, frequency range, airflow parameters, perturbation, or vocal fold vibration. Variation occurs among clinicians in the interpretation of these tests. These limitations have prevented valid comparisons between the impact of an intervention in different environments or in comparing two different interventions. Although it would be expected that improvements in objective tests would correlate with improvements in outcome, severity of disease as measured by these

tests does not necessarily measure its impact to an individual. Minimal variations in pitch for a performing vocalist would likely have a much greater impact than for a person who has minimal voice demands. A cured small laryngeal cancer may prevent a singer or other professional speaker from performing but would probably not limit the quality of life for a weekend volunteer choir singer. The impact on their quality of life would be expected to be significant and likely poorly represented by objective tests.

A recent study showed significant differences in perception of quality of life between patients with dysphonia and unaffected average people in the United States.[7] When evaluating the specific domains of the SF-36, we found significant differences in the domains of "emotion" and "physical" between individuals with dysphonia and normal speakers. These two domains deal with the ability to perform work and other daily tasks as a result of the physical or emotional impact of their disorder. As voice problems might be expected to have an impact on work and other daily activities, this finding is not unexpected. The "social functioning" score was also worse in patients with dysphonia. Because "physical functioning," "vitality," and "mental health" scores were also worse for dysphonic patients than for normals, it can be extrapolated that these disorders may affect a broader sense of well-being than would be expected from the types of problems people would generally be expected to have with a voice disorder. Objective tests of voice function or questionnaires would not be expected to measure these impacts on quality of life of dysphonia.

Traditionally, outcomes for patients with voice disorders have been measured with a clinical or biomedical frame of reference. The variables that are used to indicate a favorable or unfavorable treatment outcome do not rely on attitudinal input from the patients. In an effort to shift the focus from the clinicians' judgments to patients' self-perceptions of their voice disorders, we developed the Voice Handicap Index (VHI)[10] (Figure 5-1). The VHI consists of 30 statements that reflect the variety of experiences a patient with a voice disorder may encounter. Patients note a frequency of each experience on a 5-point, equal-appearing scale (0—never, 1—almost never, 2—sometimes, 3—almost always, 4—always), with the best score being 0 and the worst score 120.

VOICE HANDICAP INDEX (VHI)

Today's Date ☐☐ - ☐☐ - ☐☐

First Name
☐☐☐☐☐☐☐☐☐☐

Last Name
☐☐☐☐☐☐☐☐☐☐☐☐☐☐☐

MRN
☐☐☐☐☐☐☐

Birth Date
☐☐ - ☐☐ - ☐☐
Month   Day   Year

Age
☐☐   ○ Male   ○ Female

Provider
☐☐☐☐☐☐☐☐☐☐☐☐☐☐☐

Date of Operation
☐☐ - ☐☐ - ☐☐
Month   Day   Year

Type of Visit:
○ New Visit   ○ Pre-Treatment   ○ Pre-Surgical Treatment
○ Return Visit   ○ Post Medical Treatment   ○ Post Surgical Treatment

Diagnosis:
○ Functional Dysphonia
○ Spasmodic Dysphonia
○ Other Neurogenic Dysphonia
○ Bowing/Presbylarynges
○ Benign Masses (polyp/ nodule/ MRC)

○ Epidermoid Cyst/Sulcus
○ Vocal Fold Paralysis
  ○ a) unilateral
  ○ b) bilateral
  ○ c) SLN

○ Reflux Laryngitis
○ Leukoplakia
○ Benign Laryngeal Tumor
○ Malignant Laryngeal Tumor
○ Other (Describe) _____

Instructions: These are statements that many people have used to describe their voices and the effects of their voices on their lives. Check the response that indicates how frequently you have the same experience.

	Never	Almost Never	Sometimes	Almost Always	Always
F1. My voice makes it difficult for people to hear me.	O	O	O	O	O
P2. I run out of air when I talk.	O	O	O	O	O
F3. People have difficulty understanding me in a noisy room.	O	O	O	O	O
P4. The sound of my voice varies throughout the day.	O	O	O	O	O
F5. My family has difficulty hearing me when I call them throughout the house.	O	O	O	O	O
F6. I use the phone less often than I would like.	O	O	O	O	O
E7. I'm tense when talking with others because of my voice.	O	O	O	O	O
F8. I tend to avoid groups of people because of my voice.	O	O	O	O	O
E9. People seem irritated with my voice.	O	O	O	O	O
P10. People ask "What's wrong with your voice?"	O	O	O	O	O
F11. I speak with friends, neighbors, or relatives less often because of my voice.	O	O	O	O	O
F12. People ask me to repeat myself when speaking face-to-face.	O	O	O	O	O
P13. My voice sounds creaky and dry.	O	O	O	O	O
P14. I feel as though I have to strain to produce voice.	O	O	O	O	O
E15. I find other people don't understand my voice problem.	O	O	O	O	O

Figure 5–1. The Voice Handicap Index (VHI) *(continues)*

7177008628

	Never	Almost Never	Sometimes	Almost Always	Always
F16. My voice difficulties restrict my personal and social life.	O	O	O	O	O
P17. The clarity of my voice is unpredictable.	O	O	O	O	O
P18. I try to change my voice to sound different.	O	O	O	O	O
F19. I feel left out of conversations because of my voice.	O	O	O	O	O
P20. I use a great deal of effort to speak.	O	O	O	O	O
P21. My voice is worse in the evening.	O	O	O	O	O
F22. My voice problem causes me to lose income.	O	O	O	O	O
E23. My voice problem upsets me.	O	O	O	O	O
E24. I am less outgoing because of my voice problem.	O	O	O	O	O
E25. My voice makes me handicapped.	O	O	O	O	O
P26. My voice "gives out" on me in the middle of speaking.	O	O	O	O	O
E27. I feel annoyed when people ask me to repeat.	O	O	O	O	O
E28. I feel embarrassed when people ask me to repeat.	O	O	O	O	O
E29. My voice makes me feel incompentent.	O	O	O	O	O
E30. I'm ashamed of my voice problem.	O	O	O	O	O

P Scale ☐☐

F Scale ☐☐

E Scale ☐☐

Total Scale ☐☐☐

Please circle the word that matches how you feel your voice is today.

Normal   Mild   Moderate   Severe

Figure 5-1. *(continued)*

Three subscales of the VHI measure the physical, emotional, and functional impacts of the voice disorder. The VHI, therefore, is able to measure not only the physical effects of a person's voice problem but also the functional and emotional aspects. Therefore it can serve as an independent, objective measure of the impact of voice dysfunction on the quality of life.

Two examples of how the VHI is used are shown in Figures 5-2 and 5-3. In Figure 5-2, the patient, a 32-year-old teacher who also sings with a club band on

Documentation:

Teacher/Singer

Figure 5–2. Use of the VHI in treatment of a 32-year-old teacher who also sings with a band on the weekend. The data show improvement but the VHI is above normal. She opted for surgical treatment.

	VHI	F$_0$	F$_0$ Low	F$_0$ High	X flow	P.T.P.
Pretreatment	78	188	145	487	370 cc/s	5.2 cmH$_2$0
Posttreatment 6 sessions	47	201	140 Hz	600 Hz	295 cc/s	4.8 cmH$_2$0

Conclusion: Repeat examimation, consider surgery

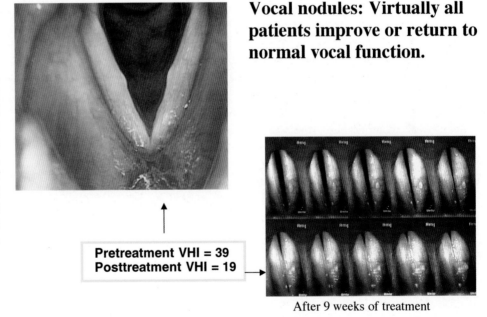

Vocal nodules: Virtually all patients improve or return to normal vocal function.

Figure 5–3. A 28-year-old actress diagnosed with vocal fold nodules. Note that her VHI reduced to a near-normal value, Her nodules appear to have resolved at her examination 9 weeks later, as seen on the right.

Pretreatment VHI = 39
Posttreatment VHI = 19

After 9 weeks of treatment

weekends, presented with a lesion on the right vocal fold. Her initial VHI was 78, indicating a severe voice handicap in her estimation. She was given 6 sessions of voice therapy and returned for re-evaluation. Her VHI decreased to 47 and her acoustic and aerodynamic measures also decreased. However, her VHI was still significantly above normal and she opted for surgical treatment.

Figure 5–3 shows a 28-year-old actress who was seen shortly after performing in an outdoor theater during the summer. She was diagnosed with vocal nodules. Following a period of voice therapy (6 sessions over 9 weeks), her voice improved, her VHI decreased, and the vocal nodules were no longer present on follow-up stroboscopic examination. Her VHI went from 39, a moderately high score, to 19, a reduction of 20 points and a range considered to be normal.[10]

Our studies also show that the impact of dysphonia on quality of life is substantial even when compared to other chronic diseases such as angina, sciatica, chronic sinusitis, or back pain, particularly in the areas of social functioning and role-playing.[10] Overall, however, other chronic diseases tend to produce worse scores than dysphonia. As the SF-36 is scaled only relating to the individual domains and not for a total score, direct overall total comparisons cannot be made. Nonetheless, by evaluating the individual domains, a comparison of their impact on quality of life can be made between such disorders.

When attempting to correlate the VHI with the SF-36, strong correlations were found between the total VHI scores and the individual subscales of the SF-36 domains of social functioning, role functioning (emotional and physical), and mental health. The greatest disability of patients with swallowing disorders is in the functional areas, as validated by this study and the relationship of the VHI to the SF-36.[9] As patients with voice disorders generally do not have significant changes in bodily pain, general health, vitality, and general physical functioning, the VHI would not be expected to be very sensitive to changes in these domains of the SF-36.

Patients with vocal fold paralysis had worse scores in many of the domains of the SF-36 than patients with dysphonia from other causes, particularly in the domains of role-playing, physical, and physical functioning.[9] This is likely due to the impact of vocal fold paralysis on lifting and straining and other daily activities. In general, paralysis patients appear to be more disabled and have poorer overall quality of life than the other categories of patients with dysphonia as measured by both the SF-36 and VHI. When evaluated with the VHI, the group with vocal fold edema, which is not uncommon in singers, had better scores for the total, functional, and physical scores than the patients with vocal fold masses (eg, nodules or polyps). Individuals with vocal fold paralysis in general had worse

scores than other individuals with voice disorders on the VHI.[9] We have found the VHI to be an excellent tool when used to measure the success of either medical or surgical treatment in vocalists.[13]

Recently, Rosen and others offered a short form of the VHI, known as the VHI-10. The VHI-10 is a valid and reliable scale of a person's handicap. The VHI-10 was validated against the original VHI. It has been shown to be reliable in a group of 100 subjects. Its value in clinical situations is that it takes very little time to complete and offers a patient's self-estimate of his or her voice handicap. It has not been applied specifically to singers; therefore, its use with singers suggests the same caveat as the original VHI, namely, that singers tend to underestimate the speaking handicap as this questionnaire does not specify the singing voice in its statements. The VHI-10 is shown in Figure 5–4.

Published reports of the use of the SF-36 in evaluating performing vocalists or singers have not been presented to date, although we and other investigators are beginning use of the VHI to assess the level of disability and response to treatment.

As the VHI was developed from a group of patients with a broad range of voice problems, it may not be sensitive to subtle changes that may affect a performer. The broad measurement of emotional and social aspects may well represent the overall general life impacts of performing voice disorders.

> Singers, actors, and voiceover performers represent unique groups and when they present with voice problems; general questions or statements about the voice may not reflect specific problems that relate clarity, loudness effort, or emotional problems that develop as a result of voice injury.

All voice problems in singers may be interpreted as serious by the singer even though quality, loudness, or endurance issues may be minimal. However, as the vocal demands increase, the singer with a minor injury may require more time off, resulting in increasing loss of income.

Evidence of the continuing need to explore singers' voice problems and singers' perception of severity

The VHI-10

1. My voice makes it difficult for people to hear me.	0 1 2 3 4
2. People have difficulty understanding me in a noisy room.	0 1 2 3 4
3. My voice difficulties restrict personal and social life.	0 1 2 3 4
4. I feel left out of conversations because of my voice.	0 1 2 3 4
5. My voice problem causes me to lose income.	0 1 2 3 4
6. I feel as though I have to strain to produce voice.	0 1 2 3 4
7. The clarity of my voice is unpredictable.	0 1 2 3 4
8. My voice problem upsets me.	0 1 2 3 4
9. My voice makes me feel handicapped.	0 1 2 3 4
10. People ask, "What's wrong with your voice?"	0 1 2 3 4

Figure 5–4. The VHI-10[13] consists of 10 statements derived from the original VHI and has been validated against the VHI.

was offered by Rosen and Murry.[12] They found that singers' scores on the VHI are significantly lower than nonsingers. Moreover, they also reported that professional singers had lower VHI scores than recreational singers or those who have income from other professions. Reasons for the low scores on the VHI for singers may relate to the lack of specific questions related to the singing voice or the fact that professional singers come in for consultation soon after they detect a change in their voice. Although the VHI provides an estimate of the patient's perception of severity, it may underestimate their concerns. Nonetheless, the VHI provides an estimate of severity that cannot be obtained by other objective measures or subjective observations.

SUMMARY

The future challenges related to outcomes research in voice, particularly for singers, will revolve on the application of these types of instruments to allow identification of factors important to the patient. The first challenge is to determine the severity of a patient's handicap or disability from a particular disorder. This will influence the aggressiveness of treatment or, in some cases, whether or not to treat. The second challenge is to utilize outcomes research to identify the best treatment. This may also be used to develop new treatments that take the singer's response to treatment into consideration. Finally, voice outcomes research should focus on how improvement of a specific disorder will affect the global quality of life for the singer and his or her family.

The future in outcomes research in voice is bright. There is much effort directed at improvement of quality of life and measurement. These efforts in combination with traditional voice evaluations, basic voice research science, and prospective, randomized clinical trials should have a dramatic impact on voice care in the future. The application of objective outcomes tools such as the VHI and the SF-36 to performing vocalists will ensure that the global impact on quality of life is measured.

REFERENCES

1. Sataloff RT. *Treatment of Voice Disorders*. San Diego, Calif: Plural Publishing Inc; 2005:365–372.

2. Greene MCL, Mathieson L. The *Voice and Its Disorders*. 5th ed. San Diego, Calif: Singular Publishing Group;1991:77–81.

3. World Health Organization. The economics of health and disease. *WHO Chronicle*. 1971;25:20–24.

4. World Health Organization. *International Classification of Impairments, Disabilities and Handicaps: A Manual of Classification Relating to the Consequences of Disease*. Geneva, Switzerland: Author; 1980.

5. Benninger MS, Gardner GM, Jacobson BH. New dimensions in measuring voice treatment outcomes. In Sataloff RT. *Professional Voice: The Science and Art of Clinical Care*. 3rd ed. San Diego, Calif: Singular Publishing Group; 2006:471–478.

6. Ware JE, Sherbourne CD. The MOS 36-Item Short Form Health Survey (SF-36). I. Conceptual framework and item selection. *Med Care*. 1972;30:473–483.

7. McHorney CA, Ware JE, Raczek AE. The MOS 36-item Short Form Health Survey (SF-36). II. Psycho-metric and clinical tests of validity in measuring physical and mental health constructs. *Med Care*. 1993;31:247–263.

8. McHorney CA, Ware JE, Lu JF, Sherbourne CD. The MOS 36-Item Short Form Health Survey (SF-36). III. Tests of data quality, scaling, assumptions and reliability across diverse patient groups. *Med Care*. 1994;32:40–66.

9. Benninger MS, Ahuja AS, Gardner G, Grywalski C. Assessing outcomes for dysphonic patients. *J Voice*. 1998;12:540–550.

10. Jacobson BH, Johnson A, Grywalski C, Silbergleit AK, Jacobson GP, Benninger MS. The Voice Handicap Index (VHI): development and validation. *J Speech Lang Pathol*. 1997;6:66–70.

11. Benninger MS, Gardner G, Grywalski C. The outcomes of botulinum toxin treatment for spasmodic dysphonia. *Arch Otolaryngol Head Neck Surg*. 2001;127;770–773.

12. Rosen, CA, Murry T. Voice Handicap Index in singers. *J Voice*. 2000;14(3):370–377.

13. Rosen CA, Lee AS, Osbourne J, Zullo T, Murry T. Development and validation of the Voice Handicap Index-10. *Laryngoscope*. 2004;114:1549–1556.

Chapter 6

LARYNGEAL EXAMINATIONS AND VISUALIZATIONS

Peak Woo

SINGERS AS PATIENTS: WHY ARE THEY DIFFERENT?

Some physicians and health professionals see singers' complaints as being dominated by psychogenic issues. It is true that singers want to see doctors earlier and more frequently than other voice professionals such as teachers and reporters. Thus, singers with their complaints often earn the undeserved reputation as psychosomatic in their complaints. Were it the only issue, most of us would be happy to send singers to psychologists and educate them on coping issues. But it is true that even well-educated, well-adjusted, and well-tempered singers experience transient voice loss and voice difficulties in a lifetime of productive singing; they may need help from a health professional when they have voice loss.[1]

Psychological issues particular to the singer's world may bring the singer to an otolaryngologist. Anthony Blunt said it best in his treatise on the singer's and actor's throat.[2]

Fame, wealth and realization of artistic ambition apart, the life of a leading international singer is not to be envied. These artists become unsettled by constant change of scene and climate, by uncomfortable traveling from airport to airport and from hotel to hotel, and also by the lack of "roots" with a home, family and close friends. Young singers, especially, suffer from insecurity and disruption of personal attachment. It is not unusual for a consultation to start on the theme of "laryngitis" and end with tears and the story of a broken engagement.

For singers who depend on their voices for a living, their voice is the instrument that expresses their individuality and their character. Singers depend on the fine-tuning of their instrument for their livelihood. This investment in time and energy may well merit the extra attention given to their instrument when it is not behaving correctly. Such concern, however, would not explain the fear, anxiety, and mental anguish that accompany some calls from singers to explain their voice difficulties. After all, trial lawyers, stockbrokers, and auctioneers all fall into similar professional voice categories. The identity of a singer is defined by his or her voice quality not by what is said or expressed in content. Thus, its potential loss is magnified to a much greater extent than for other voice professionals. For a singer, there is no greater nightmare than waking up without a voice, with the uncertainty of return of voice. This fear may seem incredible to a rational person and may indeed even seem irrational to the singer. But the relationship that a singer develops over time with his or her "voice" is unique. Often, the singer's voice has a separate identity which must be treated well, managed carefully, and coaxed into action by the singer. As if the voice "coexists" within the singer in a symbiotic fashion, it has good and bad days. The treating professional should not trivialize these feelings.

Singers are labile, sometimes emotionally fragile, and often prone to emotional extravagance. But would the public want a singer in any other way? Singers sing by tactile sensation, not by sound feedback. They sing by feeling sensations developed over many lessons and hours of practice. Sensory kinesthetic abnormalities are common when swelling, edema, dryness, phlegm, or lubrication problems of the throat become an issue. Singers feel it in the effort required for singing. They feel it in the ease in which one note melds into another. They feel abnormal when the singing gesture needed for expression is accompanied by tactile sensations at odds with those that they know are "perfect." Such need to explain the abnormal sensations are common symptoms that will bring a singer to the doctor's office before there is an audible problem in the singer's voice. This helps to explain why singers will tend to present to the doctor earlier than other voice professionals.[3]

LISTEN TO THE COMPLAINT

In the previous chapter, the common reasons for seeing an otolaryngologist (voice doctor) were presented. In addition, singers may seek an otolaryngologist simply to "bless the instrument" prior to going on with an important endeavor. The instrument, once verified to be true and healthy, can then be used with freedom and in a worry free state.[2] The singer may present with acute voice breakdown before a performance. Voice breakdown may be due to acute illness, real or imagined, or due to nonmedical causes.[1,3,4] Singers also present for a nonurgent evaluation for voice deterioration or vocal deficit due to spiraling or progressive voice loss surrounding body and life span changes.[5] Sometimes singers' failure to progress with a singing teacher or a singing technique will prompt a consultation to evaluate the vocal apparatus. Westerman Gregg has suggested that posture, respiratory support, change in hydration, phonatory hyperfunction, speaking pitch too high or low, lack of resonance, tongue tension affecting resonance and voicing are some of the factors to be explored.[6] Life span changes such as puberty, menopause, and senescence may be accompanied by voice changes that are difficult to decipher. These changes may prompt the referral for consultation.[7,8]

LISTENING TO THE VOICE

The history and the general examination have been discussed in previous chapters. Several important points should be reiterated. The history should especially inquire as to the menses in the adult female singer.[5] Prior to examination of the patient by instrumentation, it is important to note the quality of the voice. The GRBAS scale is a good scale for determining what instrument and what visualization tests to perform. The GRBAS scale rates the voice based on perceptual qualities of grade, roughness, breathiness, asthenia, and strain. Some singers will have a normal speaking voice but have specific singing difficulties. Patients with vocal strain, voice breaks, and specific voice range issues are examined by flexible laryngoscopy.[9] If the patient is complaining of a difficulty with passagio, excessive tremolo, wobble, or pain with singing, flexible laryngoscopy will be necessary. The inherent advantage of a flexible scope for evaluation of the singing apparatus without holding the tongue should be obvious.

As part of the general examination of the singer's speaking and singing voice, perceptual evaluation of their voice quality should be done beyond the GRBAS quality as discussed in chapter 7.

As part of the examination prior to instrumentation, ask the patient to sing some simple notes. The purpose of this is not to ask the singer to demonstrate his or her singing prowess but to systematically but simply test the voice. A five-tone ascending scale in the vowel "ee" or "oo" is easily modeled by the examiner and can be followed by the patient even if he or she has no prior training. The singer is then asked to progress up the scale until an audible voice break or a problem is detected. A simple tool to use is a pitch pipe, which is available at music stores for nominal cost (Figure 6–1). At the point of voice breakdown, the patient is then asked to sustain the voice at that note and the frequency is noted either by ear or by using a frequency analyzer on the stroboscope. The patient is asked to place the stethoscope of the stroboscope on the neck to pick up the fundamental frequency. Starting in the patient's most comfortable speaking voice will do. For males we start at C2, 125 Hz, for females we start at middle C, C4 or 250 Hz. The singers will then progress to approximately two octaves higher using the ascending five-tone scale. At the area of difficulty, the singer may be switched from a five-tone discrete vowel production to a voice glide. To facilitate discussion of musical notes and singing range difficulties, a musical chart of piano keys and their frequency is also useful (Figure 6–2).

In general, singers with voice problems will reveal the vocal difficulties in specific areas of their singing. These areas include:

1. High soft notes will be difficult.
2. Transition notes from chest voice to mixed or head voice will be noticeable by a break or a lack of ease during their production.
3. There will be difficulty with a fast staccato production.
4. Pitch glides may show distinct voice breaks with lack of smoothness.

Figure 6–1. Pitch pipe used for accurate modeling of singing pitch. Available in music supplies stores.

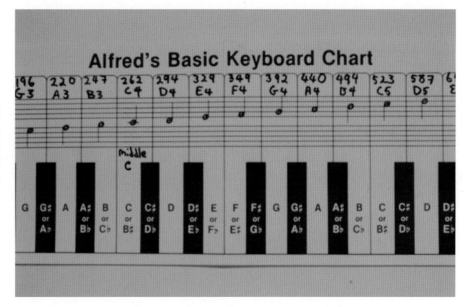

Figure 6–2. Keyboard with corresponding musical notation and frequency noted. This helps the examiner to test the frequency most troublesome to the singer.

PALPATION OF THE LARYNX AND NECK

In the examination of the neck and larynx, palpation should be done before visual inspection. Palpation of the larynx feels for evidence of appropriate laryngeal position, softness of the larynx during phonation, and confirms the presence of an easy posture without excessive tension. The common sites of excessive tension that may be elicited by palpation are:

1. Base of tongue and suprahyoid muscle tension. Figure 6-3 demonstrate the base of tongue palpation that elicits excessive tension with phonation.
2. Short thyrohyoid distance with contracted, tight thyrohyoid distance (Figure 6-4). The thyroid to hyoid distance is shortened with a barely palpable thyrohyoid membrane. This corresponds to a tight squeezed voice with a high larynx position.
3. Cricothyroid (CT) lock. Some patients have poor relaxation of the cricothyroid membrane. They have a locked distance at the CT membrane. Thus, pitch glides in the patient with fixed CT distance are associated with a higher pitch but with a strained quality. There is no closure of the cricothyroid membrane with pitch elevation and there is a lack of opening of the cricothyroid membrane with low phonation.
4. Lack of freedom of movement of the larynx with phonation.

5. Figures 6-3 through 6-7 are photographs of the different sites of palpation done as part of the examination. Palpation of the base of the lesser horn of the hyoid bone and the superior cornu of the thyroid cartilage are used to elicit extrinsic laryngeal muscle tension. The cricothyroid membrane is palpated with pitch glides to feel for adequacy of laryngeal movement.

On palpation, the larynx should be supple. With rocking, the larynx should give easily and show the normal laryngeal crepitance. Consistent finding of isolated muscle tenderness after singing is not normal. The most common findings are tenderness of the

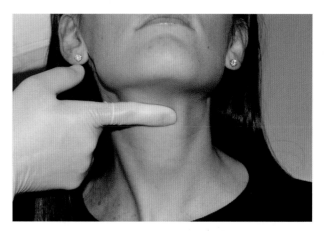

Figure 6-4. Palpation of the thyrohyoid distance and freedom during singing.

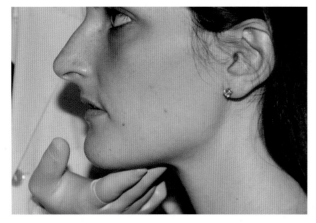

Figure 6-3. Palpation of the base of tongue for base of tongue tension.

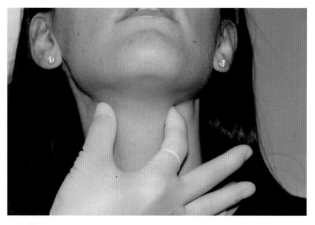

Figure 6-5. Palpation of the hyoid horn for tenderness and symmetry.

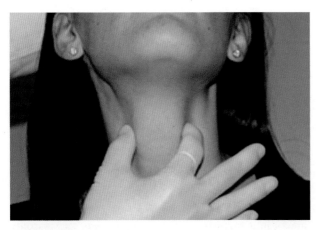

Figure 6–6. Palpation of the superior thyroid cornu for tenderness and motion.

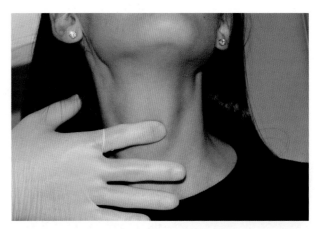

Figure 6–7. Palpation of the cricothyroid membrane during a pitch glide.

suprahyoid muscles.[10] Over-activation of the stylohyoid muscles, the sternohyoid muscles, and the laryngeal elevators will result in tenderness of the greater hyoid cornu and the superior horn of the thyroid cartilage. Laryngeal isometric tension may involve either the extrinsic laryngeal muscles or the intrinsic laryngeal muscles or both. This muscle tension results in protracted tenderness to palpation. It is usually associated with a throaty voice with other vocal faults such as low-tone focus and lack of appropriate resonance.[11]

INSTRUMENTATION OF THE SINGER'S THROAT

There are no standardized examinations that will fit all singers. Some singers need a simple rigid examination that takes as little as a few minutes; others may need extensive examinations that require both the flexible laryngoscope and the stroboscope. With the video recording systems that are available, both flexible and rigid endoscopy can be recorded and analyzed.

Specific singing problems cannot be readily diagnosed by rigid stroboscopy alone and therefore flexible endoscopy with or without stroboscopic light should always be entertained in an initial examination. Examination of the biomechanics of the singing voice is best done by fiberoptic examination.[9] Once the diagnosis is clearly related to a vocal fold edge abnormality, follow-up examinations may be shortened to include only the rigid or the flexible endoscope alone.

To efficiently conduct the examination of the singer, I prefer to start the examination in most patients with a rigid telescope. This examination is excellent for estimation of mucosal health, detection of lesions on the vibratory margins, and detection of gross movement abnormalities of the vocal folds. In the event that the vocal folds appear normal, a flexible examination of the vocal fold function is in order. Flexible laryngoscopy is the preferred imaging modality in patients with asthenic voice, vocal tremor, and vocal strain. Patients suspected of functional voice disorders and neurogenic voice disorders such as dystonia, Parkinson's disease, and dysarthria should also have a flexible laryngoscopy as the primary examination.

Fiberoptic Laryngoscopy

Fiberoptic laryngoscopy should be routinely used in singers presenting with specific problems in areas of their singing. Pitch elevation is associated with specific changes in the pharynx, base of tongue, and laryngeal position.[12] Whether these are adaptive, maladaptive, or normal depends on the clinical scenario. One may need the helpful eye of a singing teacher during such an examination. For example, if the singer is complaining of a difficulty with excessive tremolo or wobble in the vibrato, a flexible laryngoscopy of pharyngeal and laryngeal adjustments during singing will yield more valid observations than a rigid telescopic examination. Similarly, if the complaint is about difficulty during the passage or a problem in a specific note, the singing difficulty is best explored with a thin fiberscope with the singing teacher present to help with the accuracy of the sound production to be tested.

Prior to the instrumentation, the examiner may wish to ask the singer to produce the abnormal voice so that the test may focus on the problem. In patients with suspected spasmodic dysphonia or muscle tension dysphonia, the difficulties may not be during sustained vowels but may occur only with rapid onset and offset of the voice. Thus, the examiner must ask for speech and singing tokens laden with voice gestures most likely to reveal the abnormality.

The fiberoptic testing protocol is divided into three key areas. These three key areas are: (1) anatomy and mucosal health, (2) laryngeal movement evaluation with vegetative gestures, and (3) voicing gestures. Table 6–1 outlines the testing protocol.

Table 6-1. Test Protocol with Fiberoptic Laryngoscopy

A. Laryngeal anatomy and mucosal health
B. Laryngeal movement, vegetative, nonvoicing gestures
1. cough
2. eee . . . sniff
3. whistle
4. laugh
5. deep inspiration
6. rapid diadochokinesis evaluation with throat clearing
C. Voice testing
1. sustained phonation and speaking
a. pitch and loudness range testing
b. register transition
c. speaking sentences
2. singing
a. five-tone scale, steady vowel
b. glissando
c. messa de voce
d. staccato
e. singing in pianissimo
f. singing a song the patient knows

The fiberscope should be introduced with a minimum of nasal anesthesia so as not to change the sensation of the singer and cause excessive secretion. The tip of the scope should be placed at the level of the uvula and not deeper lest it cause gagging and choking. The scope should be placed into the side opposite the vocal side suspected of the lesion. Thus, a patient with a left-side vocal fold lesions or paralysis should be examined through the right nostril. This takes the advantage of the fiberscope ability to be turned to slightly look to the side, revealing more information than from the top-down view. A panoramic view of the larynx and pharynx is used to evaluate the anatomy and the function. The anatomy of the larynx and pharynx is evaluated as to symmetry and motion. Some simple questions remind the examiner to systematically inspect the structures beside the vocal folds during flexible laryngoscopy:

- Is the base of tongue forward enough to see the larynx?
- Is there lingual tonsil and pharyngeal tonsil tissue?
- Are the pharynx and larynx hydrated and without excessive mucus?
- Is there pharyngeal pooling?

After the anatomy and mucosal hygiene are evaluated, laryngeal movement is checked. The "ee-sniff" gesture is used to check for adduction and abduction. Symmetry of arytenoid cartilage motion, and symmetry of pharyngeal constriction are important to evaluate for pharyngeal or laryngeal paresis. Patients with vocal fold paresis may show excellent adduction and abduction but subtle abnormalities may be revealed with gestures that require rapid diadochokinesis of the vocal folds. Thus, whistle, laughter, and cough are used to evaluate the symmetry of motion of the vocal folds. Asymmetric vocal fold motion should raise the suspicion of vocal fold motion abnormality such as paresis or ankylosis.

Examination of the vocal folds during voice production will evaluate steady voice production in different pitch and loudness modes. The voice system is then stressed to look at voicing during rapid voice transitions such as singing in staccato voice, full voice, and with common singing maneuvers. Singers with classical voice training background will understand the request for a five-tone steady scale in ascending or descending pattern, singing through their passage, singing with a glide (glissando), and singing from soft to loud in a steady pitch (messa di voce). Sometimes asking the singer to sing in supported full voice and nonsupported voice will show differences in laryngeal and pharyngeal movement. Some singers will also readily produce the voice in their singing that is problematic. These gestures then may be recorded and analyzed.

Some common abnormal patterns readily identifiable by flexible laryngoscopy have been identified. Several authors have addressed the laryngeal gesture changes accompanied by excessive muscle tension dysphonia.[9,13] Hyperfunctional voice disorders may result in excessive base of tongue tension, excessive false vocal fold adduction, and anterior/posterior arytenoid squeeze.

Clinical diagnosis of vocal fold motion impairment suggestive of paresis may be made by flexible laryngosocpy.[14] Vocal fold paresis may be on the basis of superior laryngeal nerve injury,[15] recurrent laryngeal nerve injury, or combined nerve injury. Paresis differs from paralysis in that there is preserved adduction and abduction in paresis but not in paralysis. The degree of paresis may be variable and office fiberoptic laryngoscopy testing is the best way to elicit more subtle cases. The criterion for the clinical diagnosis of paresis is based on findings of asymmetry of vocal fold movement compared to the contralateral vocal fold. The asymmetry may be obvious in differences in degree of abduction and adduction during phonation or respiration[15] or it may only be elicited by systematic testing.[16] Patients with vocal paresis may show asymmetry in pharyngeal squeezing during phonation, or lag of the affected vocal fold during laryngeal movements that require rapid movement such as in a whistle or laughter. Superior laryngeal nerve paresis may be elicited as an axis shift of the larynx during a pitch glide and/or the presence of vocal fold bowing of the affected vocal fold.

Muscle tension dysphonia (MTD) comes in many forms.[17] Observation of the patient and laryngoscopic examination may show evidence of MTD.[18] Extrinsic laryngeal muscles such as the suprahyoid muscles and strap muscles will tend to elevate the larynx and squeeze the pharynx. Base of tongue tension will push the epiglottis posteriorly and retroflex the epiglottis, making the view of the vocal folds difficult due to epiglottis hooding. Thus, the finding of an elevated larynx during pitch glides, with retroflexion of the epiglottis would suggest the presence of excessive extralaryngeal neck muscle tension. Intrinsic muscles of the larynx may also be postured in a maladaptive way. There are typical laryngeal configurations due to intrinsic muscle tension dysphonia. Some of these are: (a) prephonatory ventricular adduction and constriction with release on phonation, (b) short thick vocal folds that fail to lengthen on pitch glide, (c) isometric tension with fixed vocal folds and a large posterior chink, and (d) false vocal fold phonation. Muscle tension dysphonia patterns have not been well studied by laryngeal EMG or laryngeal kinesthetic studies but are believed to be so on the basis of muscle imbalance during phonation. Some postulated abnormal patterns are (a) thyroarytenoid muscle hyperfunction (TA predominance pattern), (b) lack of engagement of the cricothyroid muscle (cricothyroid lock), or (c) isometric muscle tension pattern (posterior chink). Additional laryngeal research is needed to separate the different patterns.

The presence of muscle tension is indicative of adaptive or maladaptive functional compensation for the production of voice. The presence of MTD does not differentiate the problem of a primary MTD pattern from that of a compensatory MTD pattern. An example of secondary MTD is patterns of muscle hyperfunction due to reflux laryngitis.[19] Primary MTD is the presence of MTD without organic disease or injury. Thus, a singer who has spent too long during practice or lessons may show evidence of MTD after a long session. Compensation by MTD may be a consequence of adaptation after injury to the vocal folds by scar, hemorrhage, inflammation, or trauma. Therefore, a patient with an intubation injury to the larynx resulting in glottal incompetence may phonate with an MTD pattern that is adaptive to a need to generate greater subglottic pressure to drive the vocal folds in vibration. A singer with chronic reflux laryngitis may sing in a maladaptive way with MTD in response to edematous inflamed vocal folds and not as a consequence of poor singing techniques. After the examiner has identified the presence of MTD, the determination of its primary cause, be it primary or compensatory MTD, is a challenge to the diagnostician.

Chronic laryngitis (laryngeal edema) is one of the causes that promote MTD. Chronic laryngitis causes a mass effect by the edema of the vocal folds that raises phonation thresholds. In addition, chronic laryngitis affects the viscoelastic properties of the mucosal layer of the vocal folds. Inflamed vocal folds have thicker mucus making each vibratory cycle more labored. Early chronic laryngitis or laryngeal edema is one of the most difficult problems to identify. While classic posterior laryngitis resulting in gross arytenoiditis, contact granuloma, and pachyderma laryngitis is easily identified, subtle edema may show only erythema of the vocal folds with excessive mucus. Mucosal health may seem abnormal due to the thickening of the posterior pharynx and the presence of dry thick mucus throughout the upper airway. Fiberoptic laryngoscopy may give some clues as to laryngeal edema and inflammation but stroboscopy and evaluation of the vocal folds in vibration will give better details.

Rigid Videostrobolaryngoscopy (VSL)

The goal of videostrobolaryngoscopy (VSL) examination in the singer is twofold.[20] The clearest indication for VSL examination of the vocal folds is for vocal fold pathology such as cysts, polyps, nodules, and inflammation. The second and sometimes as important indication is the evaluation of laryngeal phonatory gestures that accompany the sound production.[18] VSL examination will open a new world for understanding of dysphonia. Errors and pitfalls that can be avoided by such evaluation may help to detect: (a) organic lesions previously attributed to functional etiology, (b) scarring and vocal fold injury that was not recognized, (c) unilateral polyps previously mistaken as nodules and vice versa. Clinical errors such as failure to consider multiple sources for inflammation, failure to try conservative medical or voice therapy, and recommendation for speech therapy for voice disorders when there is no evidence are far too common. Accurate stroboscopy evaluation can help to avoid such errors.

Not all patients with voice disorders should have a VSL examination. Some pediatric patients cannot be examined.[21] Good candidates for examination by VSL are based on the fact that the principle of stroboscopy is based on Talbot's law, which states that there is retention of image on the retina of 200 milliseconds after exposure. This optical illusion of apparent motion from a series of images presented with rapid

succession is the basis for motion films. Thus, by exposing rapid microsecond flashes of light on a quasiperiodic vibratory source such as oscillating vocal folds, the image may be frozen. When the flashes of light are synchronized just off the fundamental frequency of vibration, the vocal folds may be seen to oscillate at 1.5 to 3 times per second. This multiple image from VSL recordings of vocal folds oscillating in slow motion is made up of hundreds of glottal cycles and is a montage of glottal vibration. Thus, based on the principle of stroboscopy, the best patients chosen for VSL examination should be those with a vibratory source that is quasiperiodic. The professional voice user, the singer with subtle dysphonia noticeable as a qualitative abnormality in the voice, the veiled husky voice, the voice with intermittent abnormalities, are considered ideal candidates for VSL. Low gag reflex and phonation time of greater than 5 seconds are desirable but not mandatory. Ideally the VSL patient should have enough insight and cooperation to produce phonation tasks directed by the examiner at sustained pitch and loudness.

For practical VSL recording in the office, four parameters are typically recorded. These parameters and the approximate frequency ranges for singers are shown in Table 6–2.

A. Modal phonation at habitual pitch and loudness;
B. High-pitched phonation at habitual loudness;
C. Low-pitched phonation at habitual loudness; and
D. Loud phonation at modal-pitch frequency.

These are guidelines that are easily achievable by most patients. Although VSL does not evaluate the true vocal range in frequency and amplitude of vocal phonatory function, it does test the larynx and its function by using different subglottic pressures and laryngeal muscles. By adding specific tasks such as pitch glides and loudness variation, different modes of phonation such as chest, falsetto, and flute register can be examined during the examination.

A cooperative patient can have the simple protocol examination done in one to two minutes. The playback can be reviewed with the patient and interpretation and report generation based on oscillatory patterns of the vocal folds may be made from examination of the recorded examination.

Table 6–2. Four Parameters Typically Recorded During VSL and the Frequency of Phonation That They Typically Represent

Parameters	Females	Males
A. Modal phonation at habitual pitch and loudness	225 Hz 70–75 dB	125 Hz 70–75 dB
B. High-pitched phonation at habitual loudness	300 Hz 70–75 dB	200 Hz 70–75 dB
C. Low-pitched phonation at habitual loudness	190 Hz 70–75 dB	100 Hz 70–75 dB
D. Loud phonation at modal-pitch frequency	250 Hz 80–85 dB	140 Hz 80–85 dB

Interpreting the Stroboscopic Examination

As the VSL is viewed at regular speed and in slow motion, several features of vocal fold anatomy will be rated relative to normal vocal fold anatomy and physiology. After the VSL is reviewed, the clinician should be able to decide on the primary diagnosis of the phonatory disorder, make a functional assessment of vocal fold vibratory function, and based on these make therapeutic decisions as to treatment. Great variations can occur in the normal larynx. For example, the presence of a small posterior chink that permits air leakage in females is normal. Elias and Sataloff investigated strobovideolaryngoscopic findings in normal professional singers without voice complaints. "Abnormal" strobovideolaryngoscopic findings occur in this asymptomatic population of "volunteers" with great frequency. These abnormalities might have been misinterpreted as causing dysphonia.[22] Therefore, it is a good rule to review any prior videos or prints of the singer's larynx before a new diagnosis of nodule or edema or scar is made. A great deal of variation of normal occurs in the normal larynx and by inference in the normal singing larynx. A great deal of latitude must be taken prior to a clinical interpretation of a specific laryngeal gesture as abnormal.

If the examiner sees the frequency of phonation to be consistently too high or too low during the examination from that experienced without the scope in place, the examiner should have the patient practice the desired token by asking for the sound "Heeeee . . ." without the scope in place. Once the patient has a consistent ability to produce the sustained vowel, then the patient can be examined with the scope in place. It does little good to examine the vocal fold vibratory patterns in too soft, too loud, or too high a pitch.

Glottal configuration is the overall shape of vocal fold closure during sustained modal phonation. Vocal folds are judged at their most closed phase. The common patterns are: (a) complete, when the vocal folds are in complete contact from the front to the back, (b) posterior chink, when there is complete closure in the anterior aspect of the vocal folds but there is a gap between the vocal processes, (c) midfold gap, when there is good closure in the front and back but there is bowing in the midthird with incomplete closure in the midmembranous portion of the vocal folds, (d) anterior gap, when there is a gap anterior to the posterior two-thirds of the vocal folds, (d) hourglass or midfold contact, when there is contact only in the midmembranous portion of the vocal folds, (e) irregular, when there is irregular edge making contact, and (e) incomplete, when there is a lack of contact. Figure 6–8 is a montage of a singer with a small nodular swelling and a large posterior glottic chink.

Next to be rated is the phase of vibration. Normal glottal vibratory cycle at modal pitch and loudness will spend approximately 60% of the glottal cycle in the opening or closing phase and 40% in the closed phase. Edema, mass, and tension abnormalities will change this pattern to too much in either the too-open phase

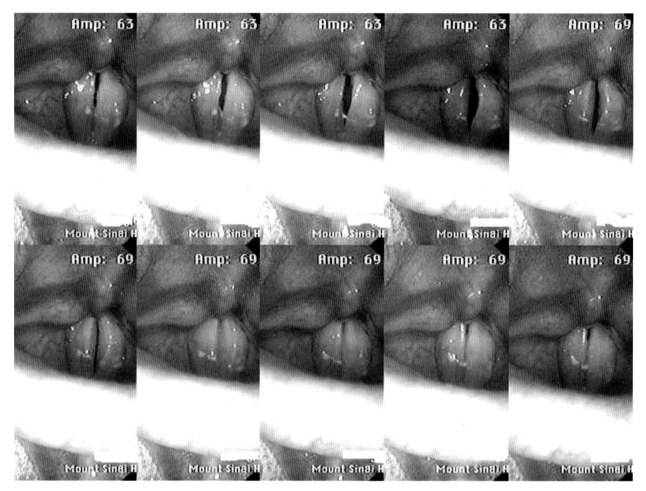

Figure 6–8. Stroboscopic video montage of a singer with nodular diathesis and excessive phlegm. Note the long opening phase and nodular swelling of the vocal margin.

pattern or too-closed phase pattern. Both soft phonation and vocal fold nodules will result in vocal folds vibrating with a long opening and closing phase. Pressed phonation or phonation in vocal fry will result in a prolonged closed phase. The rating of normal versus abnormal phase closure should have wide latitude. The ratings are simply divided into open-phase predominates, normal, or closed-phase predominates. Open-phase predominates is when greater than two thirds of the frames of the glottal cycle are in the open position. Normal is when vocal folds are in contact with about half the glottal cycle open and half closed. Closed phase predominates is when greater than two-thirds of the frames of the glottal cycle are in the closed position.

Vibratory amplitude of the individual vocal folds is rated next. The amplitude of the lateral excursion during vibration of a vocal fold during modal phonation should be about half the thickness of the visible vocal folds. Therefore, amplitude is normal if one-half to two-thirds of each vocal fold moves aside during each glottal cycle. The extent of lateral movement is rated as normal, decreased, zero, or increased. Normal vibratory amplitude is when one-half to two-thirds of the vocal fold lateralizes during each glottal cycle. Decreased amplitude is when there is reduction in the expected lateral movement (stiff vocal folds). Zero is when there is no visible movement of the vocal fold during each glottal cycle. Increased amplitude is seen when there is a large lateral excursion with each glottal cycle (ie, in patient with presbyphonia or vocal fold paralysis).

Mucosal wave is the traveling wave which crosses from below the folds to the superior surface. The mucosal wave travels on the surface of the vocal fold and is distinctly different from the vibratory amplitude. A normal mucosal wave should be visible across the superior surface and coincides with the opening of the upper lip of the vocal folds during each glottal cycle. More than the vibratory amplitude, the smoothness of the propagation of the mucosal wave is an indication of the intact nature of the superficial layer of the lamina propria. Its presence indicates the pliability of the Reinke's layer. The mucosal wave is larger when the vocal folds are shorter and are driven with large subglottic pressure. The mucosal wave is also larger in males than females. Mucosal wave is less distinct at higher pitch and soft phonation. Therefore, great care must be given to obtain consistent pitch and loudness recordings when one recording is to be compared to another. When there is scar or inflammation, the mucosal wave will usually become affected either locally at the site of scar or globally when there is diffuse inflammation or edema. The mucosal wave is rated as normal, absent, or reduced. Absent mucosal wave is a lack of visible traveling wave across a part or whole area of the vocal fold. Reduced mucosal wave is wave limited to the medial edge. Although reduced mucosal wave is usually associated with reduced amplitude, the mucosal wave abnormalities occur earlier and may be disturbed without an amplitude abnormality.

Asymmetry of vocal fold vibration is one of the easier pickups as the abnormal vocal folds will vibrate with a lack of symmetry compared to the normal side. Asymmetry of vocal vibration can be compared to the opposite side for abnormal edge, closure, vibratory amplitude, or mucosal wave.

Vocal folds should vibrate in phase relative to each other. When they fail to oscillate in phase, these phase differences contribute to dysphonia. Normal is when both vocal folds open and close together. Out-of-phase vibration is when one vocal fold is in the open phase while the other is in the closing or closed phase. Phase shifts can occur in the lateral/medial plane, resulting in a snake dance side-to-side undulation. Phase shift may occur in an anterior-to-posterior direction as the vocal folds peel open from the back to the front or the front to the back.

Because there are many possible variations in vocal fold oscillation, some seemingly abnormal vibratory patterns are actual normal variations. In the singer, it is

especially important to recognize these normal variations lest they be a cause of undue anxiety.

The posterior glottal chink is a normal variation in many males and females. The female singer and speaker have a higher incidence of a small posterior chink. The chink is small and usually posterior to the vocal process. A small gap between the vocal processes may also be present. There is, however, rarely any extension of the posterior gap anterior to the vocal process and any gap that is present into the membranous vocal folds that is more than 25% of the length of the vocal folds should be considered abnormal. Such finding is indicative of muscle tension dysphonia, early vocal nodules, or other pathologic conditions.

Vocal swelling at the site of maximum vocal fold contact is a common finding. Nodular swelling at the midmembranous vocal folds may be present in many female singers and has been observed even in male singers. It may be present without vocal complaints. The pattern of vibration is unaffected despite the presence of soft vocal fold nodules. These findings should be labeled as soft vocal fold nodules without pathologic consequence or judgment.

Phlegm and mucous coating on the vocal folds can vary greatly. It depends on the hydration status of the patient, whether the patient has undergone vocal warm-up before the examination, the time of day, and when the last performance was finished. There should be great leeway in avoiding a diagnosis of reflux due to the presence of phlegm alone.

COMMON PATHOLOGIC CONDITIONS AND THEIR MANAGEMENT IN SINGERS

We now discuss some common findings in singers and their management.

Laryngitis

The red larynx and traumatic laryngitis are one of the most common findings in singers after loud or prolonged singing. The etiology may be due to quality or quantity of singing. After prolonged loud reading of a single passage, no significant changes were noted in trained singers but there were differences in vibratory amplitude noted in untrained speakers.[23] Prolonged voice use results are difficult to quantify but clinically they have a typical history and physical finding. The voice is characterized by early vocal fatigue. The singer has to push harder to make the desired sound. Singing in high and especially soft phonation becomes difficult and may be broken by unexpected breaks. Examination can suggest the presence of vocal fold swelling by asking the singer to sing in legato voice through the passage. Another way to test the voice is to ask the singer to glide the voice from low to high voice (glissando). During the singing passage, the examiner listens for unexpected breathiness before the sound is produced or hoarse, rough quality at the soft notes that can only be compensated by a hard glottal attack (coup de glotte). Stroboscopic examination will often show symmetrically swollen vocal folds that have either a large posterior chink or an hourglass appearance. The vocal folds during phonation may not thin out as the frequency of vibration is increased, resulting in short thick vocal folds. Vibratory examination will show a prolonged open or closed phase during the glottal cycle (hypo- vs hyperfunction). The vocal folds will have reduced vibratory amplitude with a mucosal wave that is difficult to see. Sluggishness of the mucosal wave is typical. The surface of the vocal folds may have a paucity of thin mucus with pale whitish phlegm at the nodal point.[24]

Treatment for traumatic laryngitis is vocal rest and voice re-education with a view toward injury prevention. If the situation is temporary, a brief course of steroid may be useful to allow the singer to sing through the disability. Hydration and use of mucolytics will make the viscoelastic properties of the vocal folds favorable to oscillation at a lower phonation threshold and may be enough to tide the singer through the singing engagement.

Dehydration and Lubrication

Dehydration and lubrication problems are such common issues in the singer that they warrant mention as a separate problem. Sympathetic discharge before a performance, poor hydration, and self-medication with agents that are drying are some of the common reasons singers may sing with a dry throat. Singing with a dry throat may sound like acute laryngitis or edema but it has different stroboscopic findings. Dry vocal folds differ from red vocal folds in the lack of capillary dilation. The surface of the vocal folds of dehydration and laryngitis sicca will often be uneven with a "salt and pepper" appearance due to air drying. The mucus is often thick and the vocal folds will stick together during the opening phase of vocal fold vibration. The condition is readily managed by bland nebulization of saline or water. A hydroscopic agent added to the bland nebulization such as 5% glycerine will help to wet the vocal folds and allow them to vibrate with greater ease.

Chronically dry throat due to steroid inhalers, medication negative side effects, and Sjögren's syndrome may cause a low-grade mucositis, which mimics laryngitis sicca. Laryngitis sicca results in keratinization of the vocal fold margin, thickening of the vocal fold edge with stiffness, and a mass effect of the vocal folds. The interarytenoid area is often thickened, resulting in pachyderma laryngis. The condition is difficult to differentiate from reflux laryngitis except in the diffuseness of the involvement of the larynx. Treatment of chronic laryngitis sicca depends on a careful search for medical causes of dry throat and review of past and present medications.

Reflux Laryngitis

Reflux laryngitis is common and may present with hoarseness, chronic throat clearing, excessive phlegm, or pain with singing as described in chapter 8. If left untreated, reflux laryngitis may progress to loss in vocal range, permanent voice changes, and development of mucosal abnormalities. Scar and vocal fold damage due to submucosal fibrosis may promote fibrovascular lesions that go on to scar and sulcus formation. Acute and chronic reflux laryngitis may be serving as inflammatory cofactors that act in concert with vocal overuse and abuse to produce unwanted lesions of the vocal folds.

The stroboscopic appearance of reflux laryngitis is characterized by sluggish swollen vocal folds with reduced fundamental frequency. Vocal fold edge may be irregular but is uniformly edematous or erythematous. Figure 6-9 is an example of chronic laryngitis associated with vocal abuse resulting in an ulcerated vocal fold edge. Vocal folds vibrating with open phase

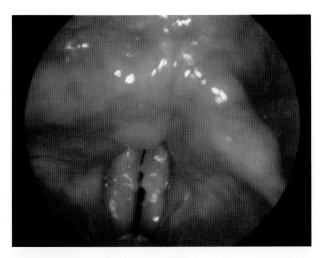

Figure 6-9. Reflux laryngitis.

predominating, and reduced mucosal wave and amplitude are other findings. There is frequently mucus collection swirling on the surface of the vocal folds. Treatment is by aggressive management of nutrition and careful mucosal hygiene. Empirical treatment by acid suppression by use of proton pump inhibition (PPI) is indicated.

Pathologic findings in singers beyond acute and chronic inflammation lie largely in the finding of benign mucosal lesions. These include varix, vocal fold nodules, pseudocysts, polyps, and cysts. Rarer problems may include sulcus vocalis, scar, and mucosal bridges. Careful differentiations between the lesions are necessary to allow the clinician to proceed with the most effective treatment. Keratosis and epithelial changes are usually of prolonged duration and are more of interest when they do not resolve as they may have implications for atypia or neoplasia.

Vocal Fold Nodules

Vocal fold nodules are the most feared lesions in singers. Nodules are difficult to diagnose accurately without stroboscopy. Nodules are symmetric swellings of the vocal fold at the margin of the membranous vocal fold experiencing maximal phonotrauma.[25] Fear of loss of the voice, income, and of permanent disability cloud the ability of the singer to judge rationally the implication of the diagnosis of nodules. This fear is not

to be trivialized. Thus, the use of the term nodules is frequently avoided.

Stroboscopic examination can differentiate between the various diagnoses that can simulate nodules. In the differential diagnosis, the following should be considered: fusiform polyps, laryngeal medina, pseudocyst, laryngeal papilloma. Some of the lesions mistaken for nodules are easily differentiated by the stroboscopy. A good VSL will readily differentiate symmetric lesions such as vocal nodules from asymmetric lesions such as laryngeal polyps. Furthermore, laryngeal nodules can be differentiated as to their stiffness. This is valuable for prognosis. Stiff vocal nodule versus soft vocal nodule can mean the difference between taking a day off versus prolonged voice rehabilitation. Cysts and pseudocysts will show abnormality on one side compared to the other. Figure 6-10 is an intraoperative photograph of a vocal fold mucous cyst. Figure 6-11 is an endoscopic photograph of a pseudocyst. Both are in singers. The pseudocyst does not have a capsule and is truly a fusiform polyp. The side with the cyst will appear to be larger and more massive. The reduction in mucosal wave will also be apparent. Vocal nodules will have a vocal fold configuration simulating an hourglass

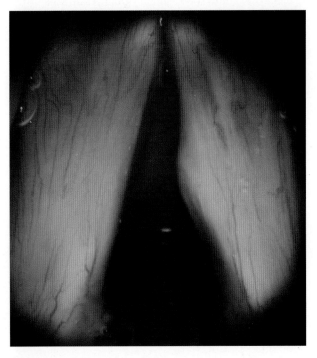

Figure 6-10. Vocal fold cyst, mucous type.

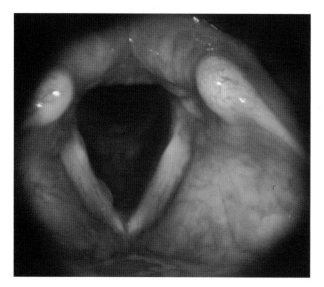

Figure 6–11. Pseudocyst or fusiform polyp on a singing teacher.

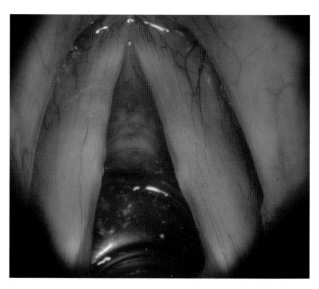

Figure 6–12. Keratosis of the vocal fold edge in a patient with mature vocal nodules.

appearance. There will be midfold contact. The contact area may be keratotic or thickened. In some patients the thick keratotic edge may not soften and surgery may be needed despite their cause from phonotrauma has been moderated. Figure 6–12 is such an example of keratosis going on to surgery due to stiffness noted on stroboscopy. The mode of vibration will show a predominantly open-phase vibration. There may be a posterior chink. In early vocal nodules, the mucosal wave will be slightly diminished but the vibratory amplitude will be good. Testing the voice at different pitch and loudness combinations will show relative stiffness as the voice is put under more strain with increasing amplitude and subglottic pressure.

The importance to diagnostically differentiate cysts, pseudocysts, and polyps from nodules is in their subsequent treatment.[26] Surgical treatment is rarely indicated in the patient with vocal nodules. Vocal nodules require vocal retraining and a consultation with a qualified speech-language pathologist (voice therapist). Pseudocyst, polyps, and vascular lesions should be treated differently. Although these asymmetric lesions are often responsive to therapy such as steroid treatment, they do not uniformly respond to voice therapy. Surgical management of these benign mucosal lesions should be considered.

Pseudocysts

Pseudocysts differ from vocal polyps in the following way: pseudocyst is an excess of mucosa due to the shearing force from a harsh phonation. Polyps, on the other hand, come from submucosal hemorrhage leaking into the submucosa or lamina propria. The site of pathology in vocal polyps and pseudocyst also differ. Vocal nodules are primarily a dysfunction of the epithelium and the basement membrane. Pseudocyst is caused by redundancy of the squamous epithelium. Laryngeal polyps are due to an increase in the protein layer in the superficial layer of the lamina propria. Mass effect on the affected vocal fold will result in the heavier vocal fold vibrating asynchronously from the thinner, more pliable vocal fold.

Pseudocysts are more common in female singers. More often, this is an affliction of females undergoing classical singing training. It appears to affect singers with a higher tessitura. The onset of this condition is usually quite distinct. Sometimes, it is preceded by laryngitis or a cold. Occasionally, it is a combination of heavy singing surrounding a brief period of illness. After the illness is gone, the loss in the voice persists and does not completely resolve. The voice quality is often described as veiled with airiness to it. If the patient has had a prior examination, the patient often has been diagnosed to have laryngitis. Only videostroboscopy will show evidence of asymmetry and redundancy of mucosal membrane.

Vascular Ectasias

Vascular ectasia and varixes can form on the vocal fold margin. Their etiology is obscure but may be related to microtrauma as they form usually at the striking zone of the vocal fold margin.[27] The vessels may be on the superior or the inferior surface of the vocal fold margin. They cause difficulties by swelling during prolonged phonotrauma and may swell excessively during menses. The presence of dilated vessels on the superior surface of the vocal fold should prompt the examiner to seek additional vessels on the undersurface of the vocal folds. The undersurface of the vocal folds can best be examined by asking the singer to sustain a loud chest voice. This will maximize the phase difference between the upper and the lower lip of the vocal folds during stroboscopic examination. This gesture will allow the examiner to visualize the undersurface of the vocal folds, an area that is otherwise difficult to evaluate except under general anesthesia. Occasionally, small vessels will show a blush or frank vocal hemorrhage. Such an early vocal hemorrhage in a singer is shown on Figure 6-13.

Vocal Polyps

A vocal polyp is the most common type of lesion seen in males. It is a result of the vocal fold injury and may be related to a mucosal vessel hemorrhage. An evidence of a vascular ectasia may precede laryngeal polyps. Laryngeal polyps cause asymmetric vibratory patterns by reduction of amplitude and mucosal wave. Sometimes vocal cord polyps have a mass effect while at other times they may have a stiffness effect on the affected vocal fold. The vocal fold may lag behind the more pliable vocal fold. The mass effect from the polyp may result in a rocking motion on VSL that has its own frequency. Pedunculated vocal fold polyps are usually treated by surgery. An example is shown in Figure 6-14.

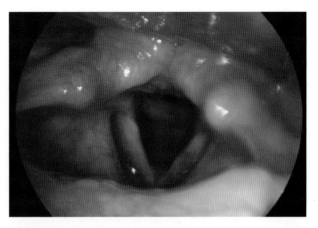

Figure 6-13. Early vocal fold hemorrhage with vascular blush on the left vocal fold.

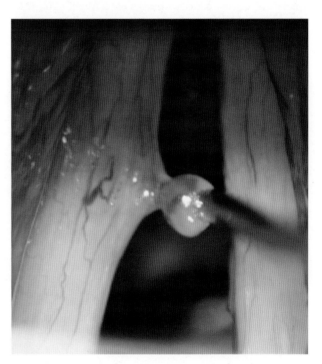

Figure 6-14. Pedunculated vocal fold polyp, intraoperative view.

Vocal Fold Cysts

Vocal fold cysts may be of keratin or mucinous type. The keratin cysts are white with usually a visible feeding vessel. The mucinous type may arise on the undersurface of the vocal fold and may mimic a nodule or a vocal polyp. The mucinous cysts are yellow to brown in color and when small can be difficult to identify by constant light endoscopy. Stroboscopy is able to identify the lesion easily as the side with the intracordal mass will oscillate with markedly reduced vibratory amplitude and mucosal wave. The vocal fold may have a visible mass within the vocal fold. Such a mass may resemble an "egg" lying within the vocal fold.

Fibrovascular deposit lesions may resemble a cyst of the vocal fold. Yet they differ from cysts in that histologically there is mass, fibrin, fibrosis, and hyaline protein but there is no cell wall to suggest a true cyst.

Sulcus Vocalis

Sulcus vocalis and mucosal bridge are difficult to identify by office endoscopy or by stroboscopy. Sometimes the sulcus is readily visible as a vocal fold duplication or striae on the edge of the vocal fold. More often, a sulcus will present with a spindle-shaped glottic closure with markedly reduced vibratory amplitude and wave on the side of the sulcus. Asymmetric loss with loss of amplitude and wave on the side of sulcus in a patient without mass or edge abnormalities should make the examiner suspicious of a sulcus condition. In these patients, recording the voice in an aspirated voice may exaggerate the sulcus and show the lesion. If the sulcus cannot be identified by office endoscopy, surgical exploration may be necessary.

Some changes seen on stroboscopy are consistently found in patients with dysphonia associated with organic tissue change. These findings are: asymmetric amplitude, decreased amplitude, short closed phase, prolonged open phase, and failure of mucosal wave propagation on the side of pathology. With successive medical, rehabilitative treatment, improved vibration will result in improved vocal fold edge, better vocal contact, greater vibratory amplitude and mucosal wave. Less important findings that correlate to an improved voice are the degree of ventricular adduction and the perceived effort necessary for sustained phonation.

SUMMARY

Singers have special needs that bring them to the physician. Although not all problems before a performance are related to vocal fold dysfunction, otolaryngologists will nevertheless be called on to perform an examination and counsel the patient. A standardized examination protocol with some rudimentary knowledge of the singing process will go a long way toward establishing communication and efficacy in the management of this group of patients.

REFERENCES

1. Sataloff RT. Professional singers: the science and art of clinical care. *Am J Otolaryngol.* 1981;2(3): 251-266.
2. Punt NA. Vocal disabilities of singers. Applied laryngology—singers and actors. *Proc R Soc Med.* 1968;61(11 part 1):1152-1155.
3. Mishra S, Rosen CA, Murry T. 24 hours prior to curtain. *J Voice.* 2000;14(1):92-98.
4. Mishra S, Rosen CA, Murry T. Acute management of the performing voice. *Otolaryngol Clin North Am.* 2000;33(5):957-966.
5. Davis CB, Davis ML. The effects of premenstrual syndrome (PMS) on the female singer. *J Voice.* 1993;7(4):337-353.
6. Westerman Gregg J. The singing/acting mature adult—singing instruction perspective. *J Voice.* 1997;11(2):165-170.
7. Boltezar IH, Burger ZR, Zargi M. Instability of voice in adolescence: pathologic condition or normal developmental variation? *J Pediatr.* 1997;30(2): 185-190.
8. Woo P, Casper J, Colton R, Brewer, DI. Dysphonia in the aging: physiology versus disease. *Laryngoscope.* 1992;102(2):139-144.
9. Koufman JA, Radomski TA, Joharji GM, Russell GB, Pillsbury DC. Laryngeal biomechanics of the singing voice. *Otolaryngol Head Neck Surg.* 1996; 115(6):527-537.
10. Morrison MD, Rammage LA. Muscle misuse voice disorders: description and classification. *Acta Otolaryngol Stockh.* 1993;113(3):428-434.
11. Morrison M. Pattern recognition in muscle misuse voice disorders: how I do it. *J Voice.* 1997;11(1): 108-114.
12. Yanagisawa E, Estill J, Mambrino L, Talkin D. Supraglottic contributions to pitch raising. Videoendoscopic study with spectroanalysis. *Ann Otol Rhinol Laryngol.* 1991;100(1):19-30.
13. Morrison MD, Nichol H, Rammage LA. Diagnostic criteria in functional dysphonia. *Laryngoscope.* 1986;96(1):1-8.

14. Ellis SF, Pollack AC, Hanson DG, Jiang JJ. Video-laryngoscopic evaluation of laryngeal intubation injury: incidence and predictive factors. *Otolaryngol Head Neck Surg*. 1996;114(6):729-731.

15. Dursun G, Sataloff RT, Spiegel JR, et al. Superior laryngeal nerve paresis and paralysis. *J Voice*. 1996;10(2):206-211.

16. Fleischer S, Schade G, Hess MM. Office-based laryngoscopic observations of recurrent laryngeal nerve paresis and paralysis. *Ann Otol Rhinol Laryngol*. 2005;114(6):488-493.

17. Belafsky PC, Postma GN, Reulbach TR, Holland BW, Koufman JA. Muscle tension dysphonia as a sign of underlying glottal insufficiency. *Otolaryngol Head Neck Surg*. 2002;127(5):448-451.

18. Behrman A. Common practices of voice therapists in the evaluation of patients. *J Voice*. 2005;19(3):454-469.

19. Koufman JA, Amin MR, Panetti M. Prevalence of reflux in 113 consecutive patients with laryngeal and voice disorders. *Otolaryngol Head Neck Surg*. 2000;123(4):385-388.

20. Alberti PW. The diagnostic role of laryngeal stroboscopy. *Otolaryngol Clin North Am,* 1978;11(2):347-354.

21. Hartnick CJ, Zeitels SM. Pediatric video laryngo-stroboscopy. *Int J Pediatr Otorhinolaryngol*. 2005;69(2):215-219.

22. Elias ME, Sataloff RT, Rosen DC, Heuer RJ, Spiegel JR. Normal strobovideolaryngoscopy: variability in healthy singers. *J Voice*. 1997;11(1):104-107.

23. Gelfer MP, Andrews ML, Schmidt CP. Documenting laryngeal change following prolonged loud reading. A videostroboscopic study. *J Voice*. 1996;10(4):368-377.

24. Mann EA, McClean MD, Gurevich-Uvena J, et al. The effects of excessive vocalization on acoustic and videostroboscopic measures of vocal fold condition. *J Voice*. 1999;13(2):294-302.

25. Lancer JM, Fisch U. Vocal cord nodules: a review. *Clin Otolaryngol*. 1988;13(1):43-51.

26. Milutinovic Z., Bojic P. Functional trauma of the vocal folds: classification and management strategies. *Folia Phoniatr Logop*. 1996;48(2):78-85.

27. Hochman I, Zeitels SM, Heaton JT. Ectasias and varices of the vocal fold: clearing the striking zone. *Ann Otol Rhinol Laryngol*.1999;108(1):10-16.

Chapter 7

PERCEPTUAL ATTRIBUTES AND ASSESSMENT OF THE SINGER'S VOICE

Rahul Shrivastav
Judith Wingate

*V*ocal performance is unique in that the performer *is* the instrument. Further, each singer's instrument is distinct from all others due to differences such as body size and vocal tract configuration. The singer's voice is a product of his or her individual experiences, emotions, training, and perceptions. The singer learns, in large part, by means of the teacher's perceptions and his or her own perception of the teacher's instructions and feedback. Therefore, understanding of the singing voice, perception of the singing voice and its role in both performance and clinical assessment is important in the care of the singer's voice.

The development of singing pedagogy in the Western European tradition had its origins in the seventeenth century Italian "bel canto" method. The method was largely dependent on perceptual assessment, relying on the "ear" of the teacher and the ability of the student to understand and respond to the teacher's instructions. The method was enhanced by the use of imagery by the teacher to elicit vocal changes from the student. In order to replicate the desired sound consistently, the student had to rely on memory as well as kinesthetic and auditory feedback when a "target" voice was achieved. This feedback based on perception continued throughout the performer's training. The significance of perceptual feedback and memory on the singing performance cannot be underestimated and its relevance in singing has been summarized well by Vennard[1(p80)]:

> Learning to sing is a slow and patient undertaking, in which a good ear is the prerequisite, the imagery is an aid supplied by the teacher, and the experience is gradually accumulated until it is so powerful that merely calling up the memory will reproduce it.

In spite of technological advances in speech and voice science and instrumentation, much singing instruction continues to follow the methods used by the early teachers of bel canto singing. Teachers typically teach in the same manner as that used by their own teacher. These traditions are passed on orally over the years in a master-to-apprentice fashion. As many of the structures involved in singing cannot be visualized without invasive means, the tradition has largely persisted, requiring singing teachers to rely heavily on perceptual methods.

Perceptual assessment continues to play a key role in the clinical assessment of singing voice as well. Each of us assesses the voices around us without conscious awareness of how we perform this task. Listeners have a referent for normal voice quality and are easily aware of a voice when it deviates from this referent. However, perceptual assessment of voice may be further refined by following a systematic approach based upon our knowledge of the auditory perceptual process. Such a method can help identify the consistencies and inconsistencies in perceptual judgments and assists in comparing these observations to the information gathered in the instrumental assessment of voice. Additionally, a thorough knowledge of how vocal fold physiology, voice acoustics, and perception relate to each other can benefit clinicians in understanding the voice problems faced by a singer in its entirety and in developing an appropriate rehabilitation program. Perceptual assessment also serves as an important measure of treatment outcome as it gives the clinician a picture of the patients' functional capabilities. Because many problems for the singer will be those of function, observation in a variety of contexts is important[2] and should include assessment of the speaking voice concurrent with the singing assessment.

This chapter is divided into two sections. The first section provides an overview of the research related to the auditory perceptual process, with an emphasis on the singing voice. This is followed by more specific guidelines that may be useful in the perceptual assessment of the singing voice.

THE AUDITORY PERCEPTUAL PROCESS

Understanding the relationship between a physical stimulus and its perception has been the focus of much research over the last century and has resulted in a distinct branch of cognitive psychology called *psychophysics*. The origin of psychophysical research dates back to the work of Weber and Fechner in the mid-19th century. Psychophysical experiments typically deal with two distinct but related questions: (1) what is our "sensory capability?" and (2) what is our "response proclivity?"[3] Sensory capability refers to the resolving power of a sensory system. For example, we may be interested in knowing the lowest sound pressure level that can be detected by the human ear. In contrast, response proclivity refers to the tendency of an observer to respond in a specific manner. For

example, when a listener is asked to assign a score to reflect the loudness of a signal, he may choose a specific ratio based on factors such as his pervious experiences, training, characteristics of the sensory system, and so forth.

Psychophysical experiments use a variety of methods to investigate perceptual phenomena. The experimental paradigms include tasks such as determination of thresholds (the smallest perceivable magnitude), difference limens (the smallest perceivable difference), identification (assigning stimuli to unique categories), judgments of equality (the magnitude at which two stimuli appear equal in some aspect), ranking (ordering a set of stimuli based on specific perceptual attribute), and others. The findings from such experiments have helped us understand how the characteristics of a physical stimulus are related to its perceptual attributes.

In the context of voice assessment our primary interest is in the vocal acoustic signal produced by the singer. There are three major components related to the perception of an acoustic signal. These include its pitch, loudness, and quality (or timbre).

Pitch

Pitch is one of the most fundamental perceptual attributes of sound. It is defined as "that attribute of auditory sensation in terms of which sounds may be ordered on a musical scale."[4] When listeners are asked to judge pitch, they can represent sounds on a single scale varying from low to high. In this aspect, pitch is often regarded as a one-dimensional perceptual attribute. Considerable research has been done to understand the processes underlying the perception of pitch and how it is influenced by changes in the physical properties of the acoustic signal.

The pitch of pure tones is related primarily to its frequency (F). Similarly, the pitch of complex periodic signals, such as those observed in speech and music, is related primarily to its fundamental frequency (F_0). As the F or the F_0 of a signal increases, it is perceived to have a higher pitch. However, this relationship is not linear. In other words, if the frequency of a tone were to change by a certain proportion, the corresponding change in pitch is not of the same proportion. For example, doubling the frequency of a tone may not result in a doubling of pitch. Although pitch is a perceptual correlate of frequency, the two terms cannot always be used synonymously.

Certain other characteristics of the sound also influence its pitch. For example, experiments have shown that the pitch of a pure tone may be affected by its loudness.[5] Although individuals differ in their responses, most experimental findings show that with increasing level the pitch of low frequency pure tones (below 2 kHz) decreases whereas that of high frequency tones (above 2 kHz) increases slightly. However, tones between 1 and 2 kHz do not show a significant change with level.

Theories to explain the perception of pitch take one of two forms. The "place theory" views the cochlea (within the inner ear) as a frequency analyzer. It suggests that each frequency stimulates a different part of the basilar membrane in the cochlea, thereby stimulating different neurons. The activity of different neurons translates into differences in pitch. In contrast, the "temporal theory" suggests that pitch information is obtained from the timing by which nerve fibers in the auditory system are excited by a particular sound. However, neither of these theories is capable of explaining all aspects of pitch perception. Instead, most experts believe both of these mechanisms contribute to the perception of pitch. The perception of low frequencies (below 5 kHz) can be explained by timing theories, but frequencies above 5 kHz can only be explained by place theory.

Understanding how listeners perceive pitch is important in music and song. This is because the perception of musical scales is related to their pitch. Sounds that differ in frequency by one octave sound similar and are given the same name on the musical scale. Other notes in Western classical music generally hold some simple relationship to the octave, such as 3/2 or 5/4 (although others, such as Indian classical music, may utilize ratios that deviate from the conventional musical scale). Similarly, experiments have shown that when listeners are asked to adjust the frequency of a test tone (F_t) so that it is perceived to be an octave higher in pitch than a standard (F_s), they generally adjust F_t to be *twice* the frequency of F_s. These findings have led some researchers to theorize that musical pitch has two components—"tone height" (which is related to the frequency of the tone) and "tone chroma" (which is related to the musical note assigned to the tone).[6] Interestingly, however, the ability to judge octave relationship between tones has

been found to hold true only when both sounds (F_s and F_t) are below 5 kHz in frequency. Above this frequency listeners are unable to make such judgments consistently.[7] Fortunately, this does not pose serious concerns in singing because the pitch of most songs and musical instruments is well below this range.

A systematic variation of pitch during singing is necessary for the perception of appropriate intonation and vibrato. Intonation is cued by relatively slow changes in pitch that occur over long phrase or sentence boundaries. These changes in pitch generally co-occur with changes in loudness and duration of specific syllables. Appropriate intonation is necessary not only for melody, but also for cueing linguistic information such as syllable stress. On the other hand, vibrato results from relatively faster modulation of pitch. If the rate and extent of the vibrato remain relatively low and if the sung vowel is relatively long in duration, then the modulation of F_0 does not affect the overall pitch of the vowel. This is because the overall pitch of a frequency modulated tone appears to be related to a weighted average of short samples.[8,9] If the rate of vibrato is too slow (below ~ 4 Hz), listeners tend to hear a modulation in pitch.

Loudness

Loudness is the perceptual attribute of auditory sensation in terms of which sounds may be ordered on a scale extending from quiet to loud.[10(p127)] Loudness, like pitch, is generally viewed as a one-dimensional percept. The loudness of a sound is related primarily to the sound pressure level (SPL) of that sound. In general, sounds with greater SPL are perceived to be louder while those with a lower SPL are perceived to be softer. However, loudness is a subjective phenomenon and may be affected by factors other than its SPL alone. Further, the relationship between SPL and loudness is not linear. Therefore, the terms loudness and SPL (or intensity) cannot always be used synonymously.

As loudness is a subjective entity, it cannot be measured directly. Instead, the perception of loudness has been studied using a variety of techniques. The most commonly used methods to study loudness include loudness "scaling" and "matching." In scaling techniques such as magnitude estimation, listeners hear sounds with known acoustic characteristics and assign each a rating on a specific scale. The assigned rating represents the perceived loudness of that signal. In matching techniques, listeners are asked to match the loudness of a sound to that of another sound (called the "standard"). These experiments allow listeners to manipulate the level of the standard until they achieve a match in terms of the loudness of the two sounds. The effects of various acoustic parameters, such as frequency or spectral shape, on perceived loudness can be inferred by systematically varying the sound characteristics during such experiments.

Loudness of pure tones varies as a function of their frequency. In other words, pure tones of different frequency result in different loudness even when these are presented at the same SPL. Although the exact results vary significantly across different experiments, they show the same general tendencies. At low SPL, pure tones in the mid-frequency range (approximately 500–4000 Hz) elicit the greatest loudness. Tones of frequencies below and above this range need significantly greater SPL to elicit the same loudness (for example, see Fletcher and Munson, 1933[11]). However, at higher SPL these differences tend to disappear and tones of all frequencies result in approximately equal loudness at the same SPL. This means that the growth of loudness with increasing SPL varies with the frequency of the tone. The effects of such differences in loudness growth become evident in many practical applications. For example, if a sung vowel is amplified and reproduced at high SLP, the amplified sound often appears to have a "bassy" sound quality. This effect arises from the fact that loudness growth of low-frequency sounds differs from than that of higher frequency sounds, thereby affecting the overall quality of the sound. However, most modern amplifiers minimize this effect by amplifying the low and high frequencies in a manner that preserves the sound quality.

Loudness of pure tones also depends on its duration. If listeners are presented two tones of the same frequency but different durations, then the tone with a longer duration is perceived to be louder than the one with a smaller duration. However, this effect is only seen for tones that are very brief in duration (less than 100–200 milliseconds). For tones greater than about 200 ms, duration appears to have no effect on loudness.[12]

The loudness of complex sounds such as speech and music is related not only to its overall SPL, but also to the spectral shape of the complex signal. Several experiments have studied the change in loudness that occurs when the bandwidth of a signal is increased but its total energy is kept constant. These experiments show that an initial increase in the bandwidth of a broadband noise does not affect the loudness of the sound. However, once the bandwidth of the noise exceeds a certain threshold (called the critical bandwidth), an increase in loudness is perceived. The critical bandwidth has been found to be narrow when the low center-frequency of the noise is low, and it increases with an increase in the center-frequency of the noise.[13] These effects are believed to result from the way sounds are processed by the auditory system. Models to explain such effects have recently been utilized to develop "loudness meters." Such calculations provide significantly better correlates of perceived loudness than older methods that used specific weighing functions with the measured sound pressure level (eg, the A- or C-weighting scale on a sound level meter).

The overall loudness of speech or song is related primarily to the SPL of a few dominant harmonics of the signal.[14,15] Most often, the SPL of the fundamental frequency and/or the harmonics corresponding to the first formant frequency are most closely related to the overall loudness of the vowel. However, as explained above, the best method to quantify loudness is through the use of the critical band concept, which is often implemented in "loudness meters."

Quality or Timbre

Sound quality or timbre is defined as that attribute of auditory sensation in terms of which a listener can judge two sounds having the same pitch and loudness as being dissimilar.[16] Like pitch and loudness, the quality of a sound is a subjective experience. However, unlike pitch and loudness, the quality of a sound cannot be described using a single scale. In other words, when asked to sort a group of sounds or voices based on their quality, listeners cannot organize them using a single scale. Rather, listeners use a larger set of perceptual attributes or descriptors to organize voices in terms of their quality. Therefore, the quality of a sound is considered to be a multidimensional percept.

The quality of a sound is hypothesized to be related to two general properties of the sound. First, quality depends on how energy changes as a function of frequency. This refers to the spectral envelope or the spectral shape of the sound. Second, the quality of a sound also depends upon how energy changes over time. This refers to the temporal envelope of the sound. Most sounds, including speech and music, are characterized by simultaneous variations in their spectral and temporal envelopes. Thus, quantification of vocal quality requires attention to multiple changes that occur in the signal.

In the context of speech and song, the term "quality" is used to describe two different concepts.[14] One aspect, called "vowel quality," refers to the vowel being produced by the speaker. The other, called "voice quality," refers to the personal characteristics of a particular speaker's voice. Vowel quality is a phonemic property and affects the intelligibility of speech. For example, the words "beat" and "boot" differ in terms of their vowel quality and signal a change in the meaning of the word. Voice quality, on the other hand, is relatively unique to individual speakers and allows listeners to obtain paralinguistic information such as the speaker's identity, age, gender, emotional status, and so forth. Although classification of the singing voice appears to be based primarily upon its pitch, voice quality also plays a role in this regard.[14,17]

The quality of steady-state sounds is primarily related to its spectral envelope. Vowel quality, for instance, is cued primarily by the frequency of the first two or three formants. However, in certain instances the vowel spectrum fails to provide information about the vowel formants. For example, vowels sung with a high fundamental frequency are characterized by widely separated harmonics. The vowel formant frequency may not be easily noticeable in the spectrum of such vowels.[14] In such instances, listeners appear to judge the vowel identity based on changes in the formant frequency at the consonant-vowel boundary (this is called the "formant transition").

A speaker's voice quality may be affected by a number of factors that affect its spectral and temporal envelope. The vocal fold vibration affects the spectral envelope of the sound generated at the glottis. For example, voices may differ in terms of their spectral slope and in terms of the level of "aspiration noise" present in the voice. The vocal fold vibration generally has some degree of aperiodicity, which results in changes in the temporal envelope of the voice. The

sound generated at the glottis is further modified by the characteristics of the vocal tract. For instance, differences in vocal tract length and the configuration of the tongue, jaw, lips, pharyngeal cavity, and the velopharyngeal port can affect the formant frequencies considerably, further modifying the spectral envelope of the voice. Although speakers can modify the frequency of the lower formants by manipulating the lips, tongue, and jaw position, it is difficult to manipulate the higher formants as easily. These higher formants are partly responsible for each singer's unique vocal characteristics. The presence of a "singer's formant" in many singers further affects the spectral envelope, thus affecting voice quality.

Figure 7-1 shows the spectrogram of an /ɑ/ vowel produced by a male singing at 233 Hz. The singer's formant is illustrated by the increased energy around 3000 Hz. Figure 7-2 shows the same vowel sung by a female at the same fundamental frequency.

Although we have discussed pitch, loudness, and quality as independent perceptual constructs, these are often interrelated. Changes in one parameter may result in a corresponding change in another. Some of these relationships result from how speech is produced. For example, a change in the F_0 affects how closely a specific harmonic aligns with the formant frequency of the vowel. The resulting "formant tuning," may affect the overall spectral shape, and thereby affect vocal quality. Similarly, attempts to increase the loudness of the voice also affect the spectral shape of the sound generated by the vocal folds. As a speaker increases the loudness of a sung or a spoken vowel, the higher harmonics gain greater energy than the lower harmonics. This results in a decrease in the spectral slope at higher SPL.

Singers rely heavily on auditory feedback during singing. However, the quality of one's own voice when it is heard live (ie, when a speaker hears his or her own voice during singing/speaking) is perceived to be very different from the quality of the same voice when it is recorded and played back to the speaker. There are at least two reasons for this phenomenon. First, when a speaker hears his or her voice live, the sound is being transmitted to the ear primarily through "bone conduction." In effect, the sound travels through the bones of the skull and stimulates the ear directly. In contrast, when listening to a recorded sample of the same voice, the sound reaches the ear primarily through "air

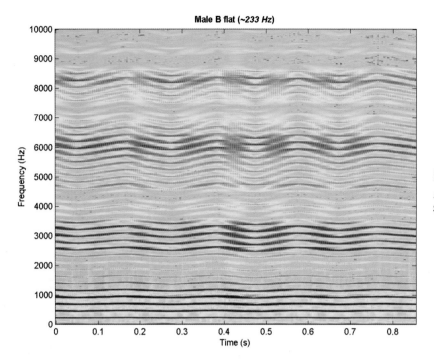

Figure 7–1. Spectrogram of an /a/ vowel sung by a male singer at 233 Hz.

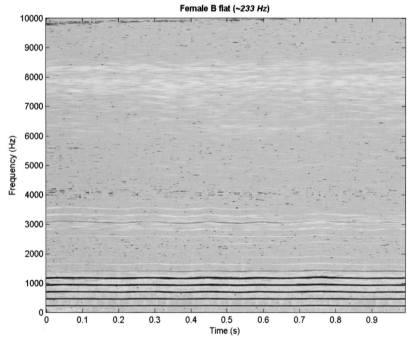

Figure 7–2. Spectrogram of an /a/ vowel sung by a female singer at 233 Hz.

conduction," or by traveling through space in air. As these two mechanisms affect the spectrum of the voice differently, they affect the perceived vocal quality. A second reason for this phenomenon is related to the nature of the sound propagation in air. For a speaker to hear his or her voice live, the sound needs to travel around the head back toward the ears. However, low- and high-frequency sounds do not propagate in all directions equally, thereby affecting the overall-spectrum of the sound reaching the ear. These spectral differences may further result in differences in quality between live and recorded voice.[18] Additionally, it is likely that the characteristics of the recording instrument itself distort the speech signal to some degree.

PERCEPTUAL ASSESSMENT OF THE SINGING VOICE

The following section identifies and defines parameters that should be considered for perceptual assessment of the singing voice. It should be noted that there are no defined standards for perceptual assessment of the singing voice. This creates difficulty as an anchor point of normalcy must be agreed on to compare any voice to the expected normal quality. Therefore, it is not surprising that perceptual assessment is often limited by poor agreement and reliability across different raters. For example, it has been observed that ratings of voice quality made by different listeners show very poor agreement across listeners.[19] However, this variability largely reflects differences in how individual raters interpret and use the rating scale.[20] Although reliability and agreement between raters can be improved significantly in an experimental setup, perceptual evaluation using rating scales in a clinical setting is often limited in terms of the sensitivity and consistency of perceptual judgments. Nevertheless, adequate training and experience can help the clinician in developing the auditory skills necessary to adequately perform a perceptual voice assessment.

In order to assess the voice of a singer, it is necessary to have the singer perform several songs and vocalises. The selections will vary according to the level of the singer and the type of music typically performed. Information should also be gathered on the singer's previous training, their personal goals regarding singing, how often they rehearse, and general vocal hygiene habits. Finally, it is also important to pay attention to any vocal problems noted in the speaking voice.

Intonation

The singer must accurately reproduce a sequence of pitches indicated by the composer during performance. Accurate production of pitch requires excellent auditory skills and constant laryngeal adjustment in response to the auditory feedback. The singer must be aware of the intonation necessary for the sung piece and adjust the pitch accordingly. While instrumentalists must also do this to some degree, singers are required to respond with constant physical adjust-ments to aural and kinesthetic feedback regarding intonation. Singers must match the pitch produced by any accompanying instruments as well as tune to other singers when in an ensemble or choral settings. Intonation is an important factor to consider when assessing the singer, especially in an untrained singer. It is also an important consideration for aging singers that may have loss of hearing acuity, because it may affect their ability to hear their own voices or the accompanying music.

Vibrato

Vibrato is an important component of overall vocal quality and is described as a regular variation around a fundamental frequency of less than a semitone.[21] The current standard for vibrato in classical singing is between 4 to 7 cycles per second.[15,21] Rates slower than this will often be described as a wobble (less than 5.5 Hz) with faster rates (7.5 Hz or higher) being classified as a tremolo. Tremolo and wobble result from emotional state, vocal fatigue, and/or technical problems, especially excessive tension and poor breath support.[21,22] In assessing vibrato, the examiner should look for jaw or chin shaking that occurs simultaneously with the vibrato as these may be indicators of poor technique.

Overall Quality

Voice quality, or timbre, refers to the overall sound of the voice. As described previously, quality is largely related to the spectral and temporal envelope of the signal. It is generally described subjectively, often using contrastive terms such as dark/bright, heavy/light, breathy/pressed, and clear/fuzzy. From a clinical perspective, a prime concern is the consistency of the timbre throughout the range of fundamental frequency. Large inconsistencies in vocal quality may be indicators of: (1) poor technique, particularly if heard in the passagio, (2) tension, if heard in the upper range, or (3) changes in subglottal pressure related to poor breath management. Assessment of voice quality during speaking should also be included during assessment. The overall voice quality observed in singing and speaking should be similar. If not, any incongruities observed may be indicators of potential vocal problems.

Voice Onset

The manner in which the voice is initiated should be considered as part of the evaluation. In general, onsets may be hard or gentle. The hard onset is initiated with increased subglottal pressure and is characterized by a fast intensity rise-time. Such onset is not considered to be healthy as it increases the force of vocal fold impact and is believed to be a contributor to edema and, over time, to vocal fold pathologies. In contrast, an excessively easy onset may result in an extremely breathy sound. The preferred onset pattern is a balanced onset, between these two extremes. Vennard[1] advocates the use of an imaginary aspirate to achieve the preferred onset. This may allow the singer to "sing on the breath" without increasing laryngeal tension. Voice onset in the speaking voice should be examined concurrently. For example, a singer may use a balanced onset in singing but frequent hard voice onsets when speaking. Over time, these hard glottal onsets may lead to vocal fold edema. This, in turn, may lead to difficulties with both singing and speaking.

Classification

Voice classification is discussed at length in the singing literature. The terms used in voice classification have their origins in Italian opera and are termed "Fachs" in German. The Fach designation allowed opera house agents to specify the type of singer needed for a particular role. The Fach terminology is still used and includes terms such as coloratura, lyric, dramatic, and spinto.

These terms are usually combined with the more familiar labels of soprano, mezzo-soprano, contralto, tenor, baritone, and bass.

Classification of the singing voice is generally done by the singing teacher using perceptual means. This classification may not be completed until the voice has completely matured. Classification of the singing voice is based on a number of perceptual factors. These include judgments of voice quality, pitch (based on fundamental frequency), pitch range that can be achieved by the singer (based on the phonation frequency range), passagio demarcation (which is related to the fundamental frequency at which the singer's voice changes from one vocal register to another), and tessitura (or the average pitch of a given song). The range of frequency expected for various voice types is well documented[2,15,21] and generally follow those listed in Table 7-1.

The pitch where the passagio, or the transition from one register to another, occurs is another factor used to determine voice classification. Although the reported frequency of the transition areas differs slightly from one author to another, these tend to follow the general trend shown in Table 7-2.[15] Voice breaks and subtle difficulties in the passagio are frequent indicators of vocal difficulty and should be examined carefully in a perceptual assessment.

The last component to be considered in voice classification is tessitura. This is the area in which the voice performs with special ease.[23] It may also be defined as the average pitch level of a song or part of a song in relation to the overall phonation range.[15] So, the voice classification depends in part

Table 7-1. Range Expectations for Voice Types

Voice Type	Low Note	Frequency	High Note	Frequency
Soprano	G_3	196 Hz	D_6	1175 Hz
Mezzo-Soprano	E_3	165 Hz	A_5	880 Hz
Contralto	D_3	147 Hz	E_5	659 Hz
Tenor	C_3	131 Hz	C_5	523 Hz
Baritone	G_2	98 Hz	G_4	392 Hz
Bass	E_2	82 Hz	E_4	330 Hz

Table 7-2. Passagio Points for Voice Types

Voice Type	First Passagio	Frequency	Second Passagio	Frequency
Soprano	$D\#_4$	311 Hz	$F\#_5$	740 Hz
Mezzo-Soprano	$F\#_4$	370 Hz	F_5	698 Hz
Contralto	G_4	392 Hz	E_5	659 Hz
Tenor	$C\#_4$	277 Hz	$F\#_4$	370 Hz
Baritone	$A\#_3$	233 Hz	$D\#_4$	311 Hz
Bass	$G\#_3$	208 Hz	D_4	294 Hz

on the singer's ability to sustain certain pitch ranges over the course of an aria or an entire opera. For example, the dramatic soprano would be expected to deal with the tessitura of the role of Brunhilde in Wagner's *Die Walkure*.

When assessing the student singer or the elite professional, it is important to determine if the literature being performed is appropriate for the singer's voice classification. If there is a serious mismatch, particularly if the voice is classified in one of the higher categories, the singer may be more prone to strain, and ultimately, to vocal pathologies.[22]

Resonance

Resonance is best described as a reinforcement of specific frequencies in the acoustic spectrum. As described previously, the frequencies that resonate in the vocal tract depend on the size and shape of the vocal tract and affect the overall spectral shape. This varies with vowel positions and typically requires some vowel modification to maintain a consistent vocal quality. The desired quality is a brilliance, or ring to the voice, which correlates with the singer's formant. The singer's formant refers to an emphasis or frequencies around 3000 Hz, which allows the voice to be heard over an orchestra or background noise.[14,18]

The ring of the voice is not to be confused with excessive nasality which may be a problem for some amateur singers. The degree of nasality is typically judged in the singing and speaking voice. Denasality,

the sound that is produced by nasal congestion or stuffiness, if heard in the absence of congestion, should also be considered abnormal.

Dynamics

A healthy singer uses a variety of loudness, or dynamic levels, when singing. These loudness levels are indicated by the composer in most types of music. The loudness levels are relative to each other and will vary depending on the type of performance and the singer's skill. Most trained singers should also be able to perform the messa di voce task throughout their entire singing range.[21] The messa di voce is performed on a sustained pitch with a crescendo followed by a decrescendo. The trained singer can change the loudness level smoothly without changing the pitch level. The messa di voce requires excellent physical control over the voice and may be used as a method of assessing a singer's dynamic control and, to some degree, his or her control of pitch. A singer's inability to vary loudness may indicate poor vocal technique, vocal fold pathologies, difficulty regulating subglottal or breath pressure, or problems with neural control.

Rhythmic Accuracy

Healthy singers can replicate rhythmic patterns indicated by the composer with accuracy. This requires rapid adjustment of the entire mechanism, especially at the laryngeal level and with the articulators. There may be occasional singers who exhibit difficulty with rapid articulation. When they do this consistently, it may be the first sign of a neurologic disease.

Phrasing

Musical phrasing is similar to phrasing for speech in that breaks for breath or for emphasis should occur in linguistically appropriate places. Difficulty with this may indicate poor breath control or vocal fatigue.

Diction

Because singing involves conveying meaning with both text and music, the singer must demonstrate clear, understandable pronunciation across languages. Vowels are often changed in the upper registers, especially by sopranos, to allow for ease of singing and this may sacrifice some intelligibility. As described earlier, the vowel quality in these singers may be cued by formant transitions. Therefore, identification of the vowels may be easier in a sung piece than during production of sustained vowels.

Posture

Because the singer's body is the instrument, it is important to assess posture while singing. Performance usually occurs in a standing position. Therefore, the singer's stance should be assessed for proper spinal alignment with no evidence of excessive tension. Tension in the body, particularly resulting from misalignment of the neck, shoulders, or pelvis will have direct impact on the vocal quality.

Gesture

The singer typically makes use of hand and arm gestures when singing most types of vocal literature. This should be included in the perceptual assessment and is purely subjective. Facial expression is also related and should be congruent with the emotion conveyed in the text.

There is a need for a more formalized scheme for perceptual assessment of the singer, especially in clin-

ical settings. However, few examples of such assessment protocols exist. Some authors have developed checklists that may provide clinicians a systematic method for doing a perceptual evaluation of the singer's voice.[24] Another recent study found that listeners could reliably judge specific perceptual attributes of the operatic voice using both, rating-scales and visual-analog scales.[25] Such research shows that a systematic approach to perceptual evaluation can provide reliable and useful information about a singer's voice. A possible outline for the perceptual evaluation of voice is shown in Figure 7-3.

Self-Perception and the Singer

During all singing, but especially in performance settings, the singer must rely on his or her own perceptions from multiple sources to monitor the vocal production and to make adjustments as needed to maintain the desired quality. Figure 7-4 shows the many different factors that may affect a listener's self-perception of his or her voice. In addition to the auditory feedback of one's own voice, the singer receives some feedback from the audience, which is typically visual. As the singer is communicating via music, the visual feedback from the audience informs the singer that the message is being heard and that the appropriate emotions are being conveyed. Another auditory feedback, typically in the form of applause, allows the singer to know if the product is appreciated. The singer also receives auditory feedback of his or her own voice in the form of reflected sound from the room or perhaps from monitor speakers. This feedback gives the singer information regarding intonation, dynamics, and voice quality. Although singers do not hear themselves as others hear them, the auditory feedback is helpful for many aspects of the performance.

The most important feedback comes from internal sensations such as proprioceptive and kinesthetic feedback. The singer must constantly monitor posture to make sure that it is maintained appropriately. The singer should monitor for sites of tension and make a conscious effort to keep all parts of the vocal mechanism in a state of "active" relaxation. Additionally, vibratory sensations that accompany the "target" voice quality must be monitored and compared to those sensations that have been learned over time as being desirable.

Name: _____ **Date:** _____

Voice Classification: _____ **Evaluator:** _____

Songs performed: _____

Vocalises performed: _____

Messa di voce: _____

Instructions: Rate each parameter based on performance of songs, vocalises, and messa di voce.

Intonation			
	Under pitch ♭	On-pitch	above pitch #

Vibrato			
	Wobble	Normal	Tremolo

Voice Quality			
	Dark	Unremarkable	Bright

Voice Onset			
	Hard	Normal	Gentle

Passagio			
	Rough	Some good transitions	Smooth

Resonance			
	Denasal	Normal	Nasal

Dynamics			
	None	Expressive	Excessive

Rhythmic Accuracy			
	Inaccurate	Semi-accurate	Accurate

Phrasing			
	Poor	Adequate	Appropriate

Diction			
	Sloppy	Moderately pronounced	Articulate

Posture			
	Too relaxed	Balanced	Stiff

Gesture			
	Too little	Adequate	Excessive

Facial Expression			
	Too little	Appropriate	Excessive

Figure 7–3. Perceptual Assessment of Singing Voice. This form may be used to assess the singer's voice after hearing the singer perform songs from her or his repertoire.

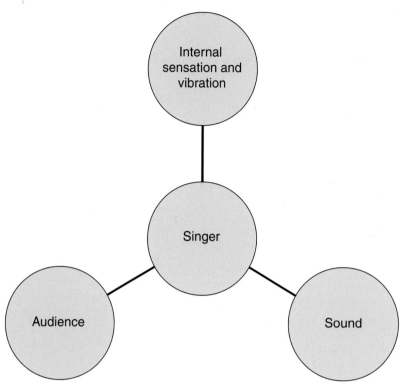

Figure 7-4. Factors that affect a singer's perception of his or her voice.

Another component that a singer must attend to during performance is breath management. While the singer will have practiced appropriate phrasing and breath control in rehearsal, factors such as anxiety, room size, and distraction during performance may all affect breath control. As a result, the singer may run out of breath before the end of an important phrase. Therefore, breath management necessitates conscious attention to placement of an appropriate pause for breath without destroying phrasing and disrupting the musicality of the performance.

As can be seen from the above, the singer must be successful at performing multiple perceptual tasks in a performance setting. So, the singer must be adept at assessing his or her own perceptions and responding accordingly. The ultimate result is a beautiful song, one that both the singer and the audience enjoy.

REFERENCES

1. Vennard W. Singing: *The Mechanism and the Technique.* New York, NY: Carl Fischer, Inc., 1967.

2. Benninger MS, Jacobson BH, Johnson AF. *Vocal Arts Medicine: The Care and Prevention of Professional Voice Disorders.* New York, NY: Thieme Medical Publishing; 1994.

3. Watson CS. Psychophysics. In: Wolman BB, ed. *Handbook of General Psychology.* Englewood Cliffs, NJ: Prentice Hall, Inc; 1973.

4. American Standards Association. *American Standard Acoustical Terminology.* New York, NY: Author; 1960.

5. Stevens SS. The relation of pitch to intensity. *J Acoust Soc Am.* 1935;6:150-154.

6. Bachem A. Tone height and tone chroma as two different pitch qualities. *Acta Psych.* 1950;7:80-88.

7. Ward WD. Subjective musical pitch. *J Acoust Soc Am.* 1954;26:369-380.

8. Feth LL, O'Malley H, Ramsey JJ. Pitch of unresolved, two-component complex tones. *J Acoust Soc Am.* 1982;72:1403-1412.

9. Shonle JI, Horan KE. The pitch of vibrato tones. *J Acoust Soc Am.* 1980;67:246-252.

10. Moore CJ. *An Introduction to the Psychology of Hearing.* 5th ed. San Diego, Calif: Academic Press; 2003.

11. Fletcher H, Musnon WA. Loudness, its definition, measurement, and calculation. *J Acoust Soc Am.* 1933;5:82-108.
12. Buus S, Florentine M, Poulsen T. Temporal integration of loudness, loudness discrimination, and the form of the loudness function. *J Acoust Soc Am.* 1997;101:669-680.
13. Moore BCJ, Glasberg BR, Baer T. A model for the prediction of thresholds, loudness and partial loudness. *J Audio Eng. Soc.* 1997;45:224-240.
14. Sundberg J. Perceptual aspects of singing. *J Voice.* 1994;8(2):106-122.
15. Titze IR. *Principles of Voice Production.* Englewood Cliffs, NJ: Prentice Hall, Inc; 1994.
16. American National Standards Institute. *American Standard Acoustical Terminology.* New York, NY: Author; 1960.
17. Bloothooft G, Plomp R. The timbre of sung vowels. *J Acoust Soc Am.* 1988;84:847-860.
18. Sundberg J. *The Science of the Singing Voice.* Dekalb, Ill: Northern Illinois University Press; 1987.
19. Kreiman J, Gerratt BR, Kempster GB, Erman A, Berke GS. Perceptual evaluation of voice quality: review, tutorial, and a framework for future research. *J Speech Hear Res.* 1993;36(1):21-40.
20. Shrivastav R, Sapienza C, Nandur V. Application of psychometric theory to the measurement of voice quality using rating scales. *J Speech Lang Hear Res.* 2005;48(2):323-335.
21. Ware C. *Basics of Vocal Pedagogy: The Foundations and Process of Singing.* Boston, Mass: McGraw Hill; 1998.
22. McKinney J. *The Diagnosis and Correction of Vocal Faults.* Nashville, Tenn: Broadman Press; 1982.
23. Doscher B. *The Functional Unity of the Singing Voice.* Lanham, Md: The Scarecrow Press, Inc; 1994.
24. Carroll LM, Sataloff RT. The singing voice. In: Sataloff RT, ed. *Professional Voice: The Science and Art of Clinical Care.* New York, NY: Raven Press; 1991.
25. Oates JM, Bain B, Davis P, Chapman J, Kenny D. Development of an auditory-perceptual rating instrument for the operatic singing voice. *J Voice.* 2006;20(1):71-81.

Chapter 8

ACUTE ASSESSMENT OF PROFESSIONAL SINGERS

Josef Schlömicher-Thier
Matthias Weikert

Professional singing must be regarded as a high-performance sport; it requires special training conditions and top physical performance. Singing is an athletic activity and as such requires good physical fitness and coordinated interaction. The vocal mechanism is a finely tuned, complex instrument. Maladies of any part of the body may be reflected in the voice and undermine the power source of the voice. Inappropriate compensation maneuvers result in vocal dysfunction. Stricken by sudden illness, the professional singer is under enormous time pressure, as the première sets him a precise deadline. In case of illness, a variety of individual factors arise. The decision to recast is made more difficult by responsibility toward the other members of the cast, anxiety on the part of the management, exertion of influence by the conductor and the director; recording contracts are tempting, and—last but not least—the audience wishes to see a radiant hero or heroine. In such cases the physician in attendance assumes a high degree of responsibility. It is his or her duty to protect the singer affected by a disorder from further damage which might have a fatal effect on the singer's future career. The physician must also devise an effective treatment algorithm that will enable the patient to make full use of his or her voice again within the shortest possible time. Any unduly prolonged "voice rest for safety" entails unnecessary cancellations. The singer risks losing income and even

further contracts. On the other hand, a rest time that is too short will also constitute a danger. Finding the adequate treatment variables requires knowledge of the performer's world. This chapter presents the findings from a major laryngology practice in Austria where singers come from around the world to perform under demanding conditions. The examinations are often done in the theater or acutely in the office.

Professional singers are expected to meet very special demands. As freelance artists, they may have a full diary of engagements in opera houses and at music festivals all over the world, and only air travel enables them to attend rehearsals in one place and concerts in another. This demands a stable physical and psycho-emotional constitution, a first-class vocal and musical training in a **clearly defined vocal category**, and great flexibility in adapting to new situations in stage-direction and casting.

Demanding roles with text and music to learn require timely (if sometimes brief) preparation before the start of rehearsals. But professional singers are subject to illness from the same causes as other people, such as acute viral and bacterial infection, allergies, faulty diet, environmental influences at work (on stage), side effects of medication, hormonal factors (especially for female singers), psychological strain due to family or social circumstances, personal crises, overwork, and overexertion in the course of working life.

WHAT IS EXPECTED OF A VOICE DOCTOR WHO LOOKS AFTER SINGERS?

The voice doctor has to be aware of the possible causes that can put the singer's voice at risk and damage a singing career. He or she has to know the heavy demands made on the singer in respect of physical and psychological strain, artistic sensibility, individuality, and empathy for the greatest possible expressive capability and interpretation. He or she will know from experience that the ever increasing strain on "jet-setting" singers includes frequent change of location in air-conditioned airplanes, living in dry and often noisy hotel rooms with a variety of allergens, and adverse atmospheric conditions on stage (dust, heat, sensitizing substances). All these factors make the vocal organs particularly susceptible to the harmful influences mentioned above.

THE SITUATION OF THE VOICE DOCTOR—HOW TO PROCEED IN A VOCAL EMERGENCY

The primary concern is the singer's medical history, which must be ascertained even under extreme circumstances and pressure of time. The overall condition of the singer is of prime importance to determine voice capacity. The vocal and physical demands of the performance in question—that is, the theatre, concert hall, or festival must always be taken into account.

Specific Questions

Time of indisposition—gradual or possibly chronic preceding symptoms

Nature and severity of the reaction to the disorder and its effect on the voice

Medication taken

Personal disposition and estimate of current stress

Point in menstrual cycle for female singers under vocal stress

Environmental influences (also on stage) which might lead to acute vocal and physical reactions or decompensation and thus indisposition.

Cancellation Policy

The voice doctor is the mediator between the singer and the manager of the opera house or festival. He must show circumspect empathy for the well-being of the singer, while retaining the confidence of both sides—singer and manager. Overprotective "safety advice" at every incipient infection ("Better stay at home for a week, and then we'll see how you're doing") only causes both sides to lose out: the singer loses his or her fee and the manager has to pay for a replacement.

Only if the physician, the singer, and the manager collaborate in the best interests of the singer's situation, is it possible to find a suitable solution in an emergency. Reorganizing rehearsal schedules, or possibly hiring a "standby" replacement to sing in the orchestra pit while the indisposed singer acts out the complicated movements on stage should be considered. It is also important for the physician to inform the manager as soon as possible that a replacement or a standby may be required. This way, the singer is relieved of the burden of responsibility and the manager is placed under less pressure. On account of the economic pressure of today's concert and festival business, the motto here can be quite realistic: **Save the singer's fee, but avoid health risks.**

THE VOICE DOCTOR'S ROLE IN THE TREATMENT OF SINGERS

Medical care at the workplace (theater stage/concert platform) may be required from time to time. ENT medical examination for the purpose of establishing the vocal constitution and suitability for the part played in the performance may be necessary.

Professional and competent application of vocal physiology for the patient at the workplace, although difficult, must be considered as part of the voice doctor's role. In general, the physician does not make artistic judgments nor influence the singer, but should guide and lead with the greatest possible empathy in emergency situations when decisions have to be made regarding disposition or indisposition. Singers are usually extremely able-bodied and efficient—a "class apart" in health.

PSYCHOPHYSICAL AND PSYCHOSOMATIC BACKGROUND OF THE ENDANGERED ARTIST

If this robust quality of the singer is endangered by acute infection, psychological disturbance, or overtaxing of the vocal capacity, as for instance through a heavy rehearsal schedule or difficult repertoire, then the singer no longer feels able to operate at maximum efficiency, which is necessarily the basic approach to artistic performance. This means that even the slightest disturbance will automatically put the singer in a stress situation in which he or she may show physical and psychological reactions that create additional strain. At this point the professional will immediately ask whether he or she "can sing at all," and is thus in a borderline situation where realistic self-assessment is no longer possible.

Factors Triggering the Stress Situation

These include chronic, initially slight disorders which may decompensate, acute infections, vocal difficulties either occurring acutely during performance or of longer duration. Worrying about domestic circumstances due to frequent changes of venue, and often strenuous travel entailing separation from family also contribute to the singer's stress. Workplace problems on stage or concert platform through conflicts with directors, stage partners, or ensemble colleagues may contribute or increase an already stressed individual.

Factors such as the psychophysical reserves of the patient are important to assess. The patient may activate his or her own physical and psychological reserves sufficiently to feel capable of singing the performance, or may lapse into uncertainty that may affect the voice adversely so that an indisposition threatens, in which case a phoniatrician, or voice specialist, will be required for emergency treatment. The physician must be aware that the singer has doubts about being able to sing the performance, as even a slight cold coupled with the fear of indisposition can lead to considerable feelings of stress. If we look at the increase in these feelings of stress as the performance draws near, we can imagine how nervous the singer becomes, and the consequent increase in physical symptoms, such as muscular tension. The voice—always a highly sensitive indicator of emotion—threatens to fail. Pressure and tension heighten and the singer decides in sudden panic that he cannot sing. The pressure is considerable—the audience is arriving, the curtain will soon rise.

In this crisis, the singer shows signs of regression. He or she feels weakened, exposed, overwhelmed and threatened by the situation. Feeling helpless, he or she relinquishes part of his independence and lapses into regression. This regressive phase projects the patient back into childhood, so that he is prepared to accept help from a parent-figure, in this case the voice specialist.

The **singer in regression** looks for help, security, and guidance; indeed, he or she demands it, though not in so many words. This is now the important task and the opportunity for the voice doctor. The more the singer abdicates his or her independence in this situation, and the more he lapses into crippling regression, the more the physician can assume guidance, which in turn demands great empathy.

The voice doctor has to put him- or herself psychologically in the situation of the singer, whose inner monologue goes something like this: Does the doctor recognize my weakness, does he understand my fear? I'm ashamed and frightened of disgracing myself in my eyes and those of the others and the audience. The physician has to approach the singer at this psychological low point with complete openness and self-effacement, but with a clear mandate for guidance. The doctor shows the singer that he or she understands his helplessness and takes him seriously, that the singer need not feel ashamed, that no one finds him ridiculous. In this extreme situation of having to accept basically undesired medical help, the singer is encouraged to retain his dignity. Thus, in this phase, the singer must feel that the doctor is competent to help, and absolute discretion is necessary.

Once this psychological block is overcome, one can proceed to the actual medical examination, in order to reach a clear evaluation and decision as to whether in this situation sufficient fortification and therapy can be provided in time for the patient to sing the role on stage.

Medical Examination

The voice doctor has to carry out a series of tasks to make the diagnosis and develop a treatment plan that is appropriate for the time. This includes the following tasks:

Ascertaining the patient's medical history;

Obtaining information on symptoms that might point to a general disorder;

Evaluating the singer's psychological and physical situation;

Making a specific ENT-oriented diagnosis with a rapid assessment of vocal problems;

Reaching a clear decision on moderate therapeutic measures appropriate to the situation;

Maintaining contact with those responsible for the impending performance such as manager, conductor, technical team, and possibly other singers and ensemble members.

The medical history often has to be established quickly. An important question here is whether the singer has had similar experiences of singing with this kind of indisposition. How did he or she master the situation? Has he or she ever suffered vocal breakdown on stage in the past? There is often too little time for further diagnosis. The main task is to evaluate the singer's vocal function and the capacity of the voice in relation to the role to be sung. This is done by summing up the symptoms against the possibility of a general acute illness, such as hypertonia, an acute allergic reaction. In this case, a specific ENT examination is necessary, carried out in private so that during questioning and examination the doctor is alone with the singer (who may of course wish to have close friends present) and absolute discretion can be assured. The more quickly and specifically the doctor is able to diagnose the disorder, the more effective the therapy will be. If the vocal function is essentially normal, well-directed and effective treatment of bronchial catarrh or acute nasal obstruction may be sufficient. This is not infrequent in jet-set singers. Both of these disorders can have a disastrous effect on voice production. The larynx is healthy, but the resonance cavities are considerably impaired. These can, however, very often be restored fairly quickly.

In addition to a brief psychotherapeutic intervention, exercises from the field of vocal and respiratory therapy can be helpful. The voice doctor should not adopt a demanding or patronizing attitude, but should remain sympathetic, providing **courteous but authoritative support**, as the singer's unassuming coach. It is important to provide psychological guidance. Skillfully directing and increasing concentration on the approaching performance can mobilize forces in the singer to counteract the indisposition. The doctor must, of course, make a realistic estimate of the role and the singer's vocal potential.

If the singer can be convinced that he is capable of giving an adequate performance, then his biological processes will alter accordingly. Muscular tension will ease, vegetative processes will be influenced for the better. The singer's state of mind and thus his efficiency will be enhanced. Here the singer has abdicated some of his independence to the physician, who should remind him of times when he was singing well, thus creating a positive attitude toward his voice. These are all verbal interventions incorporated in the routine medical rituals of examination and designed to absorb and remedy the singer's regression. The physician provides the singer with a feeling of security.

EQUIPMENT THE VOICE DOCTOR HAS AT THE WORKPLACE (THEATER/CONCERT HALL)

Emergency phoniatric treatment often takes place in the green-room; friends, ensemble members, and theater personnel should generally leave the room. The doctor should develop an instinct for deciding whether close friends or family may stay. The doctor will have his or her ENT emergency equipment case on hand. Nowadays this will contain small LEDs, nasal specula, otoscope, and disposable instruments such as spatulas. Besides the physician's trained eye, the most useful diagnostic instrument is his or her trained ear, for listening to medical history and assessing the voice. He or she also requires manual skills, as specific sensitive manipulation of neck, throat, and larynx can be useful. In addition, the physician should have an assured bearing and a steady voice, in order to inspire confidence and a feeling of security.

THE PROBLEM OF ACUTE MEDICATION AT THE WORKPLACE (THEATER/CONCERT HALL) ONE DAY OR ONLY HOURS BEFORE A PERFORMANCE

The voice doctor must be familiar with the effect of medication on the singing voice. Not only medication, but also environmental factors can influence the extremely complex and highly sensitive equilibrium of the singer. Physical strain, emotional sensibility, and maximum expressive ability must be taken into account. In prescribing medication, the general principles of pharmacodynamics and pharmacokinetics have to be observed. This means that dosage must be individually assessed, according to age, weight, organic functions, lifestyle, and means of application. The physician should ascertain any so-called "initiation rites" of singers—individual habits such as the use of milk, herbal teas, honey, raw eggs, chewing-gum, gargles, grated apple, or even medication before a performance. It is best to avoid expressing contempt or ridiculing these tried and tested "harmless" aids. On the contrary, a moment of reflection on such activities can be important for inducing a stable emotional situation to settle the voice. This is regarded as a vocal rite of initiation. However, the voice doctor must be aware that some of these so called "harmless aids" may actually be harmful if they counteract other prescribed medications or if they unduly change the singer's internal sensations.

CASE REPORTS

Case Report 1: Sensitizing Materials on Stage

During rehearsals, a molding material was used for a stage figure which released aromatic diisocyanate as it dried. The soloists and chorus singers were mostly placed around this figure, and rapidly developed symptoms such as hoarseness, coughing, and breathing difficulties, which abated only after the stage figure was removed.

Case Report 2: Sensitizing Substances on Stage

At an opera rehearsal, cork bark was used to form a stage landscape over which the singers were required to crawl as they sang. To prevent dust forming, the bark was regularly sprayed with water. After a time, the singers complained of coughs and a burning sensation in eyes and mouth. An allergy test showed evidence of mold. The cork bark contained molds, which were activated by humidification, and the symptoms disappeared only after the bark had been removed.

Case Report 3: Reflux Attacks with Case Presentation

A young soprano, singing the role of Pamina in *The Magic Flute*, attended the party following the successful première at 11 PM. As she did not wish to risk harming her voice by eating late in the evening, she drank only two glasses of sparkling wine. During the night she woke with a sore throat and a need to cough. She said that she prefers to sleep prone. The following morning she had a husky speaking voice and a feeling of excessive mucus, and her throat was still sore. When she started her vocal warm-up exercises, her voice responded only to increased pressure, and she had problems with her top register. A videostroboscopic examination showed an inflammation of the arytenoid cartilages, a diffuse glassy texture of the mucous membrane, and streaky vascularization in the vocal folds on both sides, with a mucilaginous coating and slight interarytenoid hyperplasia. The singer was breast-feeding, so initially only inhalations and therapy for protection of the mucous membrane were prescribed. Her sore throat worsened during the night, and a checkup showed edematous vocal folds on both sides. A 4-day PPI therapy with cortisone and Wobenzym brought considerable improvement. She also changed her sleeping position. The next performance, 5 days later, went perfectly.

Case Report 4: Cancellation Policy in a Case of a Vocal Fold Hematoma with Polyps

During a rehearsal, a 47-year-old mezzo-soprano suddenly lost her voice, and came for a consultation. She was cast for two roles during the summer festival: one in a Mozart opera, the other in a modern opera (*Le Grand Macabre*) by Ligeti. Rehearsals were just starting for the premières 3 weeks later. For 4 days she had been taking about 1,000 mg of aspirin daily for repeated migraine attacks. A videostroboscopic examination showed a vocal fold hematoma with a polypoid swelling on the left side. The singer agreed that the manager should be informed. The therapy consisted of prednisolone in decreasing doses, Reparil lozenges, and inhalations. After a voice rest of 10 days, the

hematoma disappeared, but the polyp was still visible on the left side. The question was then whether the singer would have to cancel her appearances in both operas or whether she could still sing the Ligeti. It was recommended that the patient should try some cautious warm-up exercises over a few hours, then an aria from the Ligeti opera. That afternoon, I listened to her singing the Ligeti aria, which required nothing above the middle register, and she managed it beautifully. We decided that she should sing the Ligeti role, but not the Mozart, which had a much higher tessitura. Thus, half the fee was saved, at least.

EVALUATION OF 74 PROFESSIONAL SINGERS AT THE SALZBURG FESTIVAL OVER 5 FESTIVAL SEASONS (2001–2005)

The following figures are derived from an extensive history of caring for singers. They include the main causes necessitating emergency intervention and the treatments given. Although this may not reflect the typical otolaryngologic or voice center practice, it does provide a basis for expectation.

Figure 8–1 shows the distribution of singers according to voice type, with a striking predominance

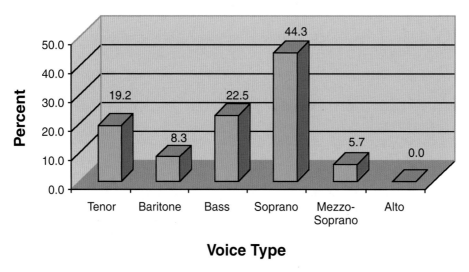

Figure 8–1. The distribution by voice type of 74 singers treated for voice complaints over 5 seasons at the Salzburg Festival.

of soprano voices. Half the singers selected for comparison were male and half were female (Figure 8-2). This leads to the conclusion that, of the female voices, the soprano, is more vulnerable.

A retrospective statistical evaluation of 74 singers was carried out on vocal problems arising during rehearsals and performances over five festival seasons. Figure 8-3 lists the symptoms mentioned by the singers during consultation; there may be several concurrent symptoms. The majority (47.3%) complained of acute cold symptoms; in 40% of cases, the vocal problems were in the upper register. 23% showed distinct hoarseness in the speaking voice. Singers could give more than one answer; hence, the total percentage is more than 100%.

As shown in Figure 8-4, the onset of a disorder is classified as acute (within 1-2 days), intermediate (within 2-5 days), or as a chronic problem (more than 1 week); 64.9% of symptoms occurred as acute The laryngostroboscopic examination showed 70% acute

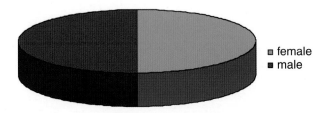

Figure 8-2. Gender distribution of 74 singers treated over 5 festival seasons.

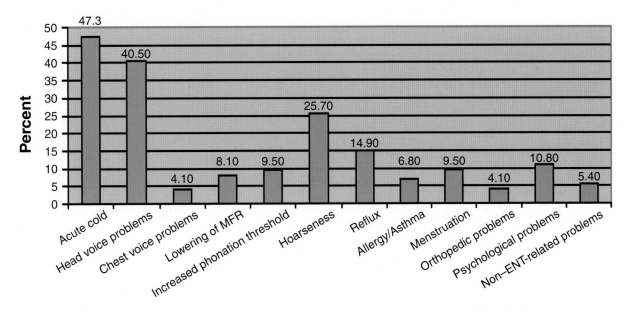

Figure 8-3. Symptoms displayed by the 74 singers who were treated over 5 festival seasons.

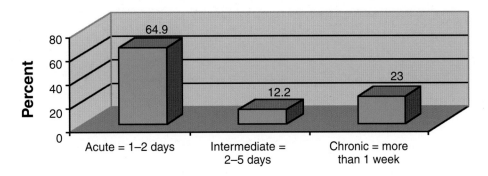

Figure 8-4. Onset of voice problems displayed by the 74 singers who were treated.

change in the mucosa, such as superficial edema or redness, and 32.4% chronic laryngeal changes, such as chronic reflux symptoms, polyps, or nodes (Figure 8-5).

Figure 8-6 displays principal causes of the singers' disorders, with the possibility of several factors occurring together, such as an acute infection exacerbated by rehearsal stress (external factor) or acute infection with previous reflux symptoms and premenstrual tension. It is evident that approximately 48.6% of the disorders reported are caused by rehearsal stress and vocal pressure despite an incipient cold infection. In conjunction with environmental influences on stage (6.8%), rehearsal and performance stress constitute 55.4% of causes; this balances approximately the acute

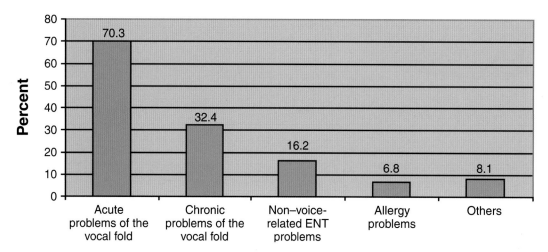

Figure 8-5. Distribution of diagnoses across the 74 singers treated over 5 festival seasons. Because some singers had more than one problem, the total percentage is more than 100%.

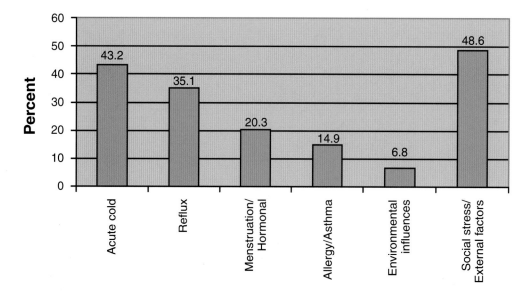

Figure 8-6. Causes of singing-voice disorders for 74 singers seen during the 5 festival seasons (2001–2005). Because some singers had more than one disorder, the total percentage is more than 100%.

causes (infection, allergy, 58%). Reflux (35.1%) is also a prominent cause; this is a lifestyle disorder, and indicates the importance of consistent measures to maintain good vocal health. The question of vocal technique and casting is not significant as a cause of illness, as the singers at the Festival are selected and experienced performers with mature technique and clearly defined vocal category. Figure 8-7 shows that 32.43% of the disorders in the female singers occurred during the premenstrual period or during menstruation. This demonstrates hormonal influence as a significant cofactor in female disorders.

Figure 8-8 underlines the necessity of applying several therapeutic modalities at the same time, such as inhalation together with reflux medication and non-steroid antirheumatic drugs (NSAIDs) or antitussive medication. Sixty percent of therapies consist of 3 or 4 concurrent therapies (multimodal), as opposed to 9.46% monomodal. This indicates the necessity of a synergetic therapy concept.

The frequency of therapies applied is shown in Figure 8-9. Inhalation therapy (78.4%) is of outstanding importance for vocal disorders, followed by NSAIDs (64%) and reflux medication (40.5%). Antibiotics (9.5%) and corticosteroids (16.2%) are prescribed only when their use is clearly indicated.

An evaluation of 74 professional male and female singers (Figure 8-10) showed that, with appropriate therapy for an illness with an acute onset of 1 to 2 days, the average voice rest time needed before the next performance was up to 3 days for more than 55% of the singers. 22% of the singers needed a Voice Rest Time (VRT) of 4 to 7 days; 6.7% of the singers had a VRT of more than 7 days. In the majority of these cases, the symptoms had been sudden and acute. It may be concluded that immediate medicinal intervention in the acute phase of illness achieved a good response relative to a chronic process, which required a longer voice rest time.

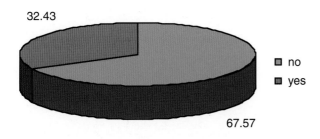

Figure 8-7. Occurrence of singing-voice disorders in female singers in relation to menstruation.

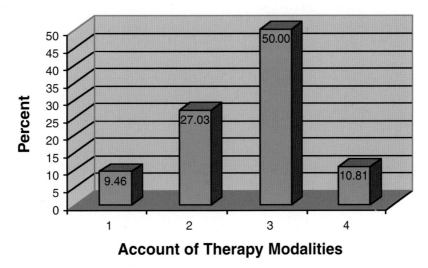

Figure 8-8. Monomodal versus multimodal therapies prescribed for 74 singers over 5 festival seasons.

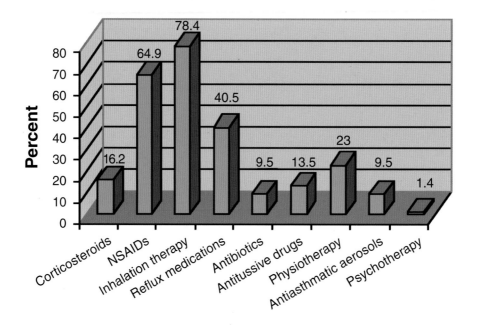

Figure 8-9. Medications prescribed in treating 74 singers over 5 festival seasons. Because some singers had more than one medication, the total percentage is more than 100%.

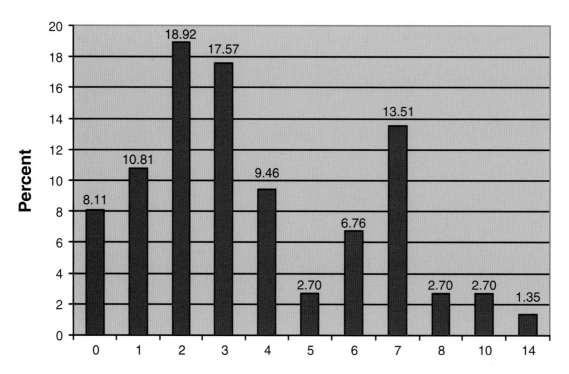

Figure 8-10. Distribution of voice rest prescribed for 74 singers over 5 festival seasons.

SUMMARY

When clarification of a singer's indisposition at the workplace (theater/concert hall) is required, the circumstances are of a special nature. The time available is short. The voice doctor must make a rapid diagnosis and often important decision. The conditions for examination will be emergency ones, in all senses, and the voice doctor must feel comfortable in these situations to put the singer at ease. The singer's reaction to the physician's therapeutic intervention is often unpredictable because the singer is in an exceptionally stressful situation. The voice doctor must be ready to deal with unexpected questions and behaviors. The doctor's task is to emanate calmness and security, and to offer the singer guidance. This can be done only if the physician:

A. Is familiar with the singer's area of work;
B. Is well-informed about opera and concert performances in the relevant venue, or can gather this information quickly;
C. Can assess the difficulties entailed in specific roles (vocal range, passaggio, dynamics, particular movements on stage);
D. Knows the effect of medication on the singing voice; and
E. Communicates well with both singer and management.

SUGGESTED READING

1. Seidner W, Wendler J. *Die Sängerstimme*. Berlin, Germany: Henschel; 2004.
2. Seidner W. Phoniatrische Notbehandlung bei Sängern und Schauspielern. *HNO aktuell*. 2004; 12(4)
3. Richter B. Harmful substances on the opera stage. *J Voice*. 2002;16(1):72–80.
4. Fussi F. *La Voce del Cantante*. Torino, Italy: Omega Edizioni; 2000.
5. Sataloff RT. *Professional Voice: The Science and Art of Clinical Care*. 3rd ed. San Diego, Calif: Plural Publishing, Inc; 2005.
6. Wendler J, Seidner W, Kittel G, Eysholdt U. *Lehrbuch der Phoniatrie und Pädaudiologie*. Stuttgart, Germany: Thieme;1996.
7. Rubin JS, Sataloff RT, Korovin GS. *Diagnosis and Treatment of Voice Disorders*. New York, NY: Igaku-Shoin; 1995.
8. Flach M. Indisposition und akute Dysphonie beim Berufssänger. *Laryngo-Rhino-Otol*. 1992;71:233–235.
9. Joussen K. Wirkung von Medikamenten auf die Sängerstimme. Sprache-Stimme-Gehör. 1999;23: 98–104.

Part III

Treatments

Chapter 9

MEDICATIONS: THE POSITIVE AND NEGATIVE IMPACT ON VOICE

David M. Alessi
Audrey Crummey

*D*rugs can have an effect on laryngeal physiology in a number of ways. These effects are on the mucosa of the vocal folds, the lamina propria, the musculature of the larynx, and its innervation (Tables 9–1 and 9–2).

ANTIHISTAMINES

Antihistamines are commonly prescribed to treat allergies. They include a broad variety of pharmacologic agents, from first-generation H_1-receptor antagonists (eg, diphenhydramine) to the newer, nonsedating H_1 blockers (eg, loratadine). Histamines are compounds that serve as mediators of the allergic response. They are released when allergens interact with surface IgE antibodies on mast cells. Histamines act on H_1-receptors, inducing vasodilation, edema, pain, and other symptoms in affected tissues.

Most H1-receptor antagonists, such as diphenhydramine have significant anticholinergic effects. These agents cause increased viscosity of secretions in the respiratory tract.[1-3] This drying effect leads to decreased vocal fold lubrication, increased throat clearing, and frequent coughing.[4] Furthermore, they also have a sedative effect, which may also decrease the ability for singers to perform successfully. Newer antihistamines such as loratadine, fexofenadine, and desloratadine are highly selective for H1-receptors, and have less of an effect on the central nervous system. They have been reported to have no anticholinergic effect,[2] and cause less drowsiness as well.[5] The drying effect for the newer H_1-blockers appears to be less than older antihistamines, but can still be bothersome. The sedation seen with diphenhydramine is sometimes felt to be beneficial for the insomniac performer. However, it prevents stages 3 and 4 of sleep, and can thus leave the patient more sleep deprived.

Another alternative for singers is a leukotriene-inhibitor such as montelukast. Leukotrienes, like histamines, are released by mast cells and regulate the immune response. Leukotriene inhibitors, like antihistamines, may be effective in treating both asthma and allergic rhinitis.[6-8] However, they do not appear to have the side effects of respiratory dryness and drowsiness.

Singers should be aware that antihistamines have been deregulated by the Food and Drug Administration (FDA), and thus can be found in many common medications. Some over-the-counter sleep aids and treatments for motion sickness such as meclizine contain antihistamines, and should be avoided.[1,3]

Table 9–1. Quick Reference Guide to Recommended Drug Therapy for Singers

Common Complaint	Recommended Drug Therapy
Acid Reflux	Twice-a-day esomeprazole, lansoprazole, omeprazole, pantoprazole, rabeprazole; if no response in 6 weeks, add ranitidine twice, three, or four times per day, or metoclopramide twice or four times per day
Acute Bacterial Laryngitis	cefuroxime, cefdinir, moxifloxacin, gatifloxacin, levofloxacin, telithromycin, high-dose amoxicillin/clavulanate
Asthma	montelukast—AVOID INHALED CORTICOSTEROIDS
Laryngeal Inflammation	For same day performances, oral or intramuscular dexamethasone; for next day performances, prednisone or intramuscular triamcinolone; for more severe problems, methylprednisolone or 5 days of prednisone; AVOID DIURETICS
Dry Mouth (Xerostomia)	Cevimeline and water consumption
Allergies	loratadine, fexofenadine, desloratadine, montelukast; AVOID DIPHENHYDRAMINE
Mucus and Congestion	Expectorants (guaifenesin); AVOID DECONGESTANTS
General Aches and Pains	Acetaminophen; AVOID NSAIDS
Smoking Cessation	Buproprion; AVOID NICOTINE SUPPLEMENTS

DECONGESTANTS

Decongestants act as vasoconstrictors, helping to reduce secretion production by shrinking mucous membranes.[2] Misuse of decongestants like phenylpropanolamine (found in over-the-counter cough medications), as with antihistamines, can cause excessive respiratory dryness.[9] However, some decongestants also contain expectorants, such as guaifenesin.[10] Expectorants act as mucolytics, thinning and increasing secretions. Such agents like high-dose guaifenesin do not have a drying effect on the voice, and may actually help to counteract the drying effects of decongestants. They are often sold as antitussives and may be helpful to singers suffering from overly viscous mucus or postnasal drip.[1] Singers should be mindful that many antitussives may contain antihistamines and other drying ingredients.[3] As with all respiratory dryness, there is no substitute for adequate water consumption, which is the best way to maintain adequate lubrication.

Singers may want to consider using a saliva-stimulating agent to help counteract the effects of respiratory dryness. There has been some success with cevimeline for this purpose. This cholinergic agent with muscarinic agonist activity is often prescribed for severe xerostomia as seen with Sjögren's syndrome. However, it is often useful in performers with dryness issues when simple hydration and mucolytics are not enough.

INHALED CORTICOSTEROIDS

Inhaled corticosteroids (ICSs) are anti-inflammatory drugs often prescribed to treat asthma. They act as vasoconstrictors, reducing respiratory mucosal edema and thickening that follow allergen exposure.[11,12] Long-term use of ICSs may reduce the number of mast cells in the mucosa, and decrease immediate response to allergens.[13] However, inhaled steroids have been known to cause vocal symptoms such as dysphonia, hoarseness, cough, and increased throat clearing.[14] The estimated rate of these symptoms varies widely, and has been reported as between 5 and 50% of

Table 9–2. Drugs That May Induce Dryness

Drug Type	Examples That Induce Dryness	Safe Alternatives
Antihistamines	diphenhydramine	loratadine, fexofenadine, desloratadine, leukotriene inhibitors like montelukast
Decongestants	phenylpropanolamine	Expectorants such as guaifenesin, Antitussives
Inhaled Corticosteroids	Inhalers to treat asthma (eg, fluticasone, budesonide)	Leukotriene inhibitors (eg, montelukast)
Diuretics	Treatments for menstrual fluid retention	Corticosteroids (either oral or intramuscular) can help reduce laryngeal edema
Tricyclic antidepressants	doxepin, clomipramine, amitriptyline	No viable substitutes
Selective Serotonin Reuptake Inhibitors (SSRIs)	fluoxetine, sertraline, paroxetine	No viable substitutes
Antipsychotics	Phenothiazines	No viable substitutes
Major tranquilizers and anxiolytics	alprazolam, diazepam, lorazepam, benzodiazepines, chlorpromazine, thioridazine, haloperidol	No viable substitutes
Antihypertensives	reserpines, agents of the methyldopa group, thiazides, loop diuretics like furosemide, alpha-adrenergic agonists such as clonidine	Ganglionic blocking agents, alpha-adrenergic antagonists
Vitamin C	n/a	No viable substitutes
Anti-influenza drugs	amantadine	oseltamivir, zanamivir, rimantadine
Certain antacids and antispasmodic drugs	phenobarbital, prochlorperazine, isopropamide, propantheline bromide, members of the belladonna alkaloid group	Proton pump inhibitors (esomeprazole, lansoprazole, omeprazole, pantoprazole, rabeprazole)
Lifestyle drugs	caffeine, cocaine, amphetamine	No viable substitutes
Nicotine supplementation	nicotine patches, nicotine gum	bupropion

patients, especially in those susceptible to vocal strain like singers.[11,15,16] This wide reported range of symptom prevalence is probably due to varied methods of data collection, and the higher rates of 50% or more were probably reached through questionnaire rather than through clinical measurement.[13]

ICSs seem to cause dysphonia via local inflammation, but the mechanism of this inflammation is not entirely understood. It is possible that some property of ICSs irritates the airway, leading to the inflammatory response. Such symptoms are probably dose-dependent; in fact, twice-daily regimens show fewer side effects than when ICSs are administered four times daily.[16,17] Furthermore, there is some evidence that the steroid, and not the propellant, is the cause of these symptoms.[17] Generally, once use of the inhaler is withdrawn, dysphonia and other vocal symptoms cease. In certain cases, use of ICSs can induce a vocal fold deformity leading to bowing upon phonation.[18] When bowing occurs, a gap is left between the folds during phonation, leaving room for air to escape. We have seen mucosal thinning on the vocal folds with long-term ICS use that can be severe and may take up to a year to resolve.

In short, ICSs are not a good choice for the professional singer. Alternatives for the treatment of asthma are leukotriene inhibitors.

SYSTEMIC CORTICOSTEROIDS

Systemic corticosteroids are potent anti-inflammatory agents, and can be used to treat laryngeal edema.[2] Thus, they are quite effective in alleviating inflammation caused by acute laryngitis and other laryngeal disorders.[19] Prednisone is a corticosteroid that is administered orally. Methylprednisolone has about the same potency, and can be given either orally or intramuscularly. Dexamethasone is the most potent corticosteroid, having approximately 5 times the strength of prednisone and methylprednisolone. It is the most effective of the corticosteroids in reducing this type of inflammation.[2] However, steroids must be prescribed with great care. If the injection is not given intramuscularly or allowed to seep into surrounding fatty tissue, a deep steroid dimple may occur from the fatty wasting at the site of the injection. This is especially true with triamcinolone injection. The dosage of steroid should be significant, such as prednisone 60 mg daily for the treatment of acute laryngeal edema. The timing of the administration is important also. A shorter-acting but rapid-onset steroid would be used on a performer singing the same evening as opposed to one with a slower onset. The physician should be sure to rule out the presence of vocal fold hemorrhage, acute laryngitis, and ulceration of vocal fold mucosa before steroid treatment. Also, steroids can cause gastric irritation, which could have further negative effects on the voice. Furthermore, as corticosteroids are so effective in treating laryngeal inflammation, singers may have a tendency to overuse them.[1] Thus, use of steroids should be closely monitored by the singer's physician.

DIURETICS

Diuretics are agents that decrease systemic levels of water and can help relieve edema. They are commonly used by women to help counteract the fluid retention that occurs during the premenstrual period. During this time, circulating levels of estrogen and progesterone are decreased, which leads in turn to increased circulating antidiuretic hormone. This is what causes fluid retention in Reinke's space and other tissues.[1] Female singers often request diuretics from their gynecologists in an effort to counteract these effects in laryngeal tissues.[4] However, water in vocal fold tissues is protein bound, and diuretics cannot effectively remobilize this fluid. Rather, diuretics only serve to cause dehydration and increased viscosity of secretions, and in turn make singing an increasingly difficult task.[9,20] Thus, they should not be prescribed to alleviate symptoms of menses, and their use for any other purposes should be closely monitored. An alternative is to use corticosteroids, which affect protein-bound water directly.[3]

PSYCHOACTIVE DRUGS

Psychoactive drugs are commonly prescribed, and many have potentially deleterious side effects for the vocalist. One particularly relevant category is the tricyclic antidepressants. These agents are strongly anticholinergic, and block the reuptake of both norepinephrine and serotonin. They often cause drying of the upper respiratory tract mucosa, and can lead to hoarseness.[2,3,21,22] Another type of antidepressants is selective serotonin reuptake inhibitors (SSRIs). These are some of the most commonly prescribed drugs to treat depression, and include fluoxetine, sertraline, and paroxetine. These are weakly anticholinergic, but are well known to cause xerostomia and can have a dehydrating effect on laryngeal tissues.[2] Monoamine oxidase inhibitors (MAOIs), also prescribed to treat depression, inhibit the breakdown of serotonin and norepinephrine by monoamine oxidase. MAOIs may not have as substantial a drying effect on the vocal folds. However, they can have strong adverse interactions with many medications, including decongestants and nasal sprays.[1] Therefore, use of MAOIs should always be monitored closely by a physician.

In addition to antidepressants, there are also some antipsychotic drugs that can have adverse effects on the voice. The phenothiazines, which are prescribed to treat conditions such as schizophrenia and mania, almost always lead to dryness of the vocal tract mucosa.[2,3] Furthermore, patients taking phenothiazines and other antipsychotics, are occasionally known to exhibit tremor, which can affect the vocal fold muscles. Approximately 14% of patients who take antipsychotic agents for longer than 7 years will develop tardive dyskinesia, especially of the head, neck, and tongue.[1] Of course, such conditions would be quite detrimental to a vocalist's career.

Major tranquilizers are another type of medication that can lead to vocal fold dryness. These agents are often prescribed for pain management and for sedative purposes. One type of the major tranquilizers is the benzodiazepines, which include aprazolam, diazepam, lorazepam, and others. Other common tranquilizers are chlorpromazine, thioridazine, and haloperidol.[3]

Many vocalists may try to use anxiolytic drugs to help alleviate performance anxiety, commonly known as "stage fright." Use of these drugs should be considered very carefully by both the singer and his or her physician. For one, some anxiolytics, particularly major tranquilizers like benzodiazepines, should be avoided because they induce vocal fold dryness. In addition, anxiety can serve a crucial role for vocalists. Extreme anxiety can be debilitating, but mild anxiety can actually enhance performance. There is some evidence that small doses of beta-adrenergic stimulators (commonly known as beta-blockers) can effectively treat performance anxiety, but in high doses detract from performance.[23] It seems that some degree of nervousness is what gives singers a competitive edge, and can be necessary for a successful performance. Generally, preperformance anti-anxiety medicines should be avoided. It is preferred that both the laryngologist and the vocal coach instill confidence in the performer that everything is fine.

ANTIHYPERTENSIVE AGENTS

Antihypertensives are commonly prescribed, and most types have the potential to negatively affect the voice.

Antihypertensives vary considerably in their mechanism of action, so it is usually possible to find a type that minimizes adverse side effects for the singer. Almost all the current agents have some parasympathomimetic action, and thus result in dryness of mucous membranes in the upper respiratory tract.[3] This effect is seen in particular for reserpines and agents of the methyldopa group.[23]

Diuretics are also commonly used to treat high blood pressure. As previously discussed, diuretics can cause increased viscosity of secretions secondary to systemic decrease in water. Thiazides cause a decrease in sodium, potassium, and water.[2] Loop diuretics, such as furosemide, have a similar effect.

Alpha-adrenergic agonists, such as clonidine, act centrally to reduce blood pressure.[2] They act on presynaptic neurons to inhibit norepinephrine activity. As a result, they can have drying effects on the respiratory tract secretions similar to those of other anticholinergic agents.

There are some antihypertensive agents that have minimal side effects for the voice. For example, angiotensin-converting enzyme inhibitors do not cause drying of mucosal secretions.[2] However, they can induce coughing, which may be caused by the release of prostaglandins. Coughing can lead to vocal fold trauma, and in turn may cause Reinke's edema. Beta-blocking agents are also used to treat high blood pressure. They are sympatholytic agents; consequently, they do not affect the vocal tract. However, as previously discussed, anxiolytics can have adverse effects on a singer's ability to sing at his or her best during a performance. Finally, ganglionic blocking agents and alpha-adrenergic antagonists are options to treat hypertension without drying effects on the vocal fold.

HORMONES

Hormones can have significant impact on a singer's voice. These changes in voice can be brought on by either endogenous or exogenous causes.[24] Endogenously, tumors of the ovary or adrenal gland can produce androgenic hormones that lead to masculinization of the voice. However, these are quite rare. More commonly, virilization is caused exogenously by the administration of androgens for medical purposes.[2,3] The effects of androgens can cause lowering of fundamental frequencies, huskiness, hoarseness, and coarsening of the voice.[24,25] Furthermore, these effects are often permanent, depending on the subject's age, the treatment duration, and the amount of drug given.[26,27] It seems that the female voice is most sensitive to virilization during puberty and menopause, when hormonal levels are already in flux.[28] Voice changes are found to accompany hormonal treatment in 5 to 10% of patients.[25] In particular, this effect has been found with danazol, but is also applicable to other agents similar in structure to testosterone. Anabolic steroids, which are often abused for the sake of enhancing athletic performance, have been shown to cause an often irreversible deepening of the voice in women.[28-30]

Hormonal agents are prescribed to treat a variety of conditions. Nandrolone decanoate (Decadurabolin) is an anabolic steroid often prescribed as a treatment for osteoporosis, and it too has been shown to irreversibly lower vocal pitch of female patients.[28,31] Androgen therapy is often prescribed by gynecologists as a treatment for endometriosis and dysmenorrhea.[2,3,25] Chemotherapy for women with breast cancer can also include androgenic hormone therapy as part of the treatment.[3]

In the past, oral contraceptives were seen as a threat to a singer's voice.[32] Earlier formulations of birth control pills contained relatively high amounts of progesterone, and were thus more likely to lead to masculinization of the voice.[3,33] In fact, some types of birth control from Europe may still have significant dosages of anabolic steroids. However, most modern oral contraceptives in the United States have tended toward lower hormone levels, and voice side effects are seen in only about 5% of patients.[1] These changes tend to be temporary, and normal voice is usually restored when use of birth control pills is discontinued. The "morning-after pill" is becoming more commonly used in the United States and abroad, and mifepristone (RU-486) is an antiprogestin that may also have an androgenic effect on the voice; however, the effects of these substances have not been clearly studied.

When a female singer reaches menopause and hormone levels begin to change, she may notice adverse changes in her voice. Such changes are quite typical. Estrogen replacement therapy is often helpful in counteracting these changes, and should be offered by the physician at the time of menopause.[1]

Men may also experience voice changes as a result of exogenous hormones, although these scenarios are less common. Estrogens in men can lead to feminization of the voice. In particular, this situation can arise in men who are being treated palliatively with diethylstilbestrol for prostatic carcinoma.[2]

Dysfunction in endocrine function can cause vocal changes, and hormone therapy is often successful as a remedy for these effects. Hypothyroidism causes mucopolysaccharides to accumulate in tissues, including the vocal folds.[2] This leads to a decrease in vocal efficiency and "ring."[1] Thyroid hormone replacement therapy helps counteract this process, thereby restoring normal vocal function. Men with impaired pituitary secretion of gonadotropins tend to have higher than normal fundamental vocal frequency because gonadotropins regulate the production of sex steroids. There is some evidence that this can be ameliorated by testosterone treatment.[34]

Thyroid hyper- or hypofunction can have a deleterious effect on laryngeal function. Mucosal thinning or thickening can occur as well as increased dryness, to name a few of the known effects. Thus, testing for thyroid function is a key part of any dysphonia workup. This is especially important when a patient is already on thyroid supplementation. The appropriate amount of exogenous thyroid hormone needs to be adjusted carefully with the use of serial thyroid function tests.

VITAMIN C

It is quite common for physicians to encounter singers who are taking large quantities of ascorbic acid (vitamin C) in an effort to prevent colds or shorten their duration.[3] There is evidence that vitamin C (at 4000 milligrams per day) can be useful in limiting the duration of the common cold.[35,36] There is evidence that the rhinovirus receptor in the nasal mucosa (ICAM receptor) is inhibited by ascorbic acid. However, in some of these patients there has been found a drying effect of too high dosages of vitamin C.[1,3] These effects are diuretic in nature, and are comparable to the effects of a mild antihistamine. Therefore, the use of high-dose vitamin C should be limited to exposure to or the onset of a cold.

TREATMENTS FOR ACUTE LARYNGITIS

Upper respiratory tract infections (URTIs) are frequent complaints of singers. In particular, singers tend to suffer from laryngitis as a result of excessive voice use.[19] Acute laryngitis is defined as inflammation of the larynx and vocal fold lasting less than 3 weeks.[37] Acute laryngitis is generally viral in nature, particularly due to viruses like parainfluenza, rhinovirus, influenza, and adenovirus. Symptoms usually resolve on their own within 3 to 8 days.

It is important for physicians to be discriminating in prescribing antibiotics. This can be difficult because many patients with URTIs expect to be prescribed antibiotics, and may pressure their physicians to do so. However, antibiotics are normally not necessary, as most cases of laryngitis are of viral origin.[38] There is a vast quantity of evidence showing that antibiotics have no effect on most cases of laryngitis.[37,39,40] Furthermore, overuse of antibiotics can lead to superinfection of *Candida*.[2] The physician should educate vocalists as to why antibiotics are not useful, and seek other solutions to alleviate the patient's discomfort.

When laryngitis is bacterial in origin, species most commonly encountered with acute bacterial laryngitis are similar to those found in acute maxillary sinusitis, such as *Streptococcus pneumoniae*, *Haemophilus influenzae*, *Moraxella catarrhalis*, and *Staphylococcus aureus*.[39-41] Because of significant emergence of resistant organisms, we prefer to adapt the Allergy Health Partnership recommendations for the treatment of sinusitis. High-dose amoxicillin, normal or high-dose amoxicillin/clavulinate acid, cefuroxime, cefdinir, moxifloxacin, gatifloxacin, levofloxacin, and telithromycin are all effective antibiotic treatments. Corticosteroids can be helpful in treating the resulting inflammation, but should be used sparingly. Also, as influenza is a common cause of laryngitis, physicians can offer the singer a prophylactic influenza vaccine. However, these should not be administered before a performance, as side effects can result.

Amantadine is often prescribed to treat certain strains of the influenza virus, but this is not suggested for singers. Amantadine, which is also prescribed to treat Parkinsons's disease, has anticholinergic side effects and can induce xerostomia and xerophonia.[1] The newer viral neuramidase inhibitors (oseltamivir, zanamivir, rimantadine) have no significant drying effects and are generally more effective against the influenza virus.

TREATMENTS FOR REFLUX LARYNGITIS

Chronic laryngitis is often caused by gastroesophageal reflux disease (GERD). There are many different methods of treating acid reflux including antacids, H2-blockers, and gastric proton pump inhibitors (PPIs).[1] Aluminum-magnesium antacids are beneficial, but need to be used frequently. Calcium preparations may also be helpful, but they can eventually result in increased acid production.[2] Other commonly used antacids include phenobarbital, prochlorperazine, isopropamide, and propantheline bromide. All of these may have drying effects on the larygeal mucosa.[1,3] H2-blockers (eg, cimetidine) are quite useful in treating acid reflux. Generally, drying of the vocal mucosa is not a major side effect, but it can occur on occasion.[1,3] H2-blockers inhibit the secretion of acid from gastric parietal cells, but do little to affect the rate of acid production. Some antispasmodic drugs such as members of the belladonna alkaloid group (eg, scopolamine, atropine) have been widely prescribed for those with stomach ulcers. These, however, have an anticholinergic function and thus lead to dryness of the vocal tract.[1] Gastric proton pump inhibitors (PPIs) are a newer, very effective way of managing acid reflux, and have few adverse side effects for singers.[1,2] They have quickly become the preferred method of treatment for laryngopharyngeal reflux disease.[42] As laryngeal reflux is a more difficult disease to treat then gastroesophageal reflux disease marked by dyspepsia, most laryngologists start their patients on twice-a-day dosing. It must be emphasized that no treatment will be effective unless accompanied by a strict antireflux protocol (early dinner, elevation of the head of bed, etc).

ANALGESICS

Pain can serve an important function for the singer. Laryngeal sensation informs the singer of the degree of pressure being applied to the vibrating vocal cords.[43]

Pain in this region alerts him or her when the voice is being overstressed and helps maintain good vocal discipline. Thus, any agent that decreases proprioceptive input from the larynx and vocal folds should be discouraged.[1,44] In particular, topical anesthetics such as benzocaine, lidocaine, and analgesic throat lozenges, are potentially quite dangerous. Although use of these agents is tempting for the singer suffering from pain as a result of pharyngitis, it could cause the singer to unknowingly inflict vocal damage.[2,3]

Nonsteroidal anti-inflammatory drugs (NSAIDs) are particularly pernicious analgesics for singers. NSAIDs include common over-the-counter agents such as acetylsalicylic acid (aspirin) and ibuprofen. The anticoagulant effect of such drugs increases the risk for vocal fold hemorrhage, which can be devastating to a singer's career.[1,2,45] NSAIDs should thus be avoided, particularly before strenuous performances. If a singer absolutely must alleviate nonlaryngeal pain, acetaminophen may be a good substitute. It is not an NSAID, and therefore probably does not put the singer at risk for mucosal hemorrhage.

"LIFESTYLE" DRUGS

The stressful nature of a singer's career may cause him or her to self-medicate in a variety of ways. For one, many singers may use caffeine to help them keep up with a busy rehearsal schedule. Caffeine is a mild diuretic, and a stimulant of the central nervous system. The sympathomimetic properties of caffeine combined with its effect as a diuretic make it a potentially dehydrative agent. There is some evidence that caffeine may have detrimental effects on a singer's voice, and for this reason its use should be discouraged.[46]

Other stimulants may also have adverse effects for a singer. They can become particularly damaging when combined with raised adrenaline levels during a performance.[3] Cocaine is a stimulant that is used frequently among singers. Its use can cause serious damage to the nasal mucosa and induce vasoconstriction. It also may decrease sensorium, which can decrease voice control and lead to abusive vocal habits.[4] Amphetamines are strong adrenergic agonists, and frequently lead to vocal tract dryness.[2] "Diet pills" also often have a stimulating effect, and should be avoided.[3]

Central nervous system depressants, such as alcohol, barbiturates, and marijuana, may also have detrimental effects on a singer's voice. Any agent that inhibits a singer's sensorium can lead to poor, and potentially damaging, vocal technique.[3] Alcohol is one of the more common depressants that a singer may ingest. Alcohol intoxication results in decreased awareness, which impedes vocal discipline.[4] The effects of small amounts of alcohol, such as a glass of wine, are still debated among experts. Some maintain that because alcohol causes vasodilation, it necessarily leads to mucosal alteration, but this effect seems to vary considerably among individuals.[4]

Smoking is exceedingly damaging to the larynx. However, nicotine supplementation can have drying and stimulating effects. Antidepressants have been particularly successful in smoking cessation with performers. Bupropion is a selective blocker of central nervous system dopamine uptake. With motivated patients (which most singers are), the smoking cessation period is made significantly easier. Although many performers are concerned about any psychoactive drug affecting their stage psyche, most will find there is no effect (or even a beneficial effect).

SUMMARY

The use and misuse of medications with subtle effects may not be as important to a non-performer as it is to a singer. Minor amounts of dryness can cause a loss of the singer's passagio or high register. Undertreatment of laryngopharyngeal reflux disease can lead to disabling granulomas in a professional voice user. Forgetting to elicit use of all prescription and nonprescription drugs may allow for long-term laryngeal injury. A thorough understanding of drugs and their effect on the larynx is essential for any practitioner treating performers.

REFERENCES

1. Spiegel JR, Hawkshaw M, Sataloff RT. Voice disorders and phonosurgery I. *Otolaryngol Clin North Am.* 2000;33:771–84.

2. Thompson AR. Pharmacological agents with effects on voice. *Am J Otolaryngol.* 1995;16:12–18.

3. Lawrence VL. Common medications with laryngeal effects. *Ear Nose Throat J.* 1987;66:318–322.

4. Sataloff RT, Spiegel JR, Hawkshaw MJ. History and physical examination of patients with voice disorders. In: Rubin JS, Sataloff RT, Korovin GS, eds. *Diagnosis and Treatment of Voice Disorders.* 2nd ed. San Diego, Calif: Singular Publishing Group; 2003:137–158.

5. Wilken JA, Kane RL, Ellis AK, et al. A comparison of the effect of diphenhydramine and desloratadine on vigilance and cognitive function during treatment of ragweed-induced allergic rhinitis. *Ann Allergy Asthma Immunol.* 2003;91:375–385.

6. McMillan RM. Leukotrienes in respiratory disease. *Paediatr Respir Rev.* 2001;2:238–244.

7. Baena-Cagnani CE, Berger WE, DuBuske LM, et al. Comparative effects of desloratadine versus montelukast on asthma symptoms and use of beta 2-agonists in patients with seasonal allergic rhinitis and asthma. *Int Arch Allergy Immunol.* 2003; 130:307–313.

8. Meltzer EO, Philp G, Weinstein SF, et al. Concomitant montelukast and loratadine as treatment for seasonal allergic rhinitis: a randomized, placebo-controlled clinical trial. *J Allergy Clin Immunol.* 2000;105:917–922.

9. Verdolini K, Min Y, Titze I, et al. Biological mechanisms underlying voice changes due to dehydration. *J Speech Lang Hear Res.* 2002;45:268–281.

10. Jackson-Menaldi CA, Dzul AI, Holland RW. Hidden respiratory allergies in voice users: treatment strategies. *Logoped Phoniatr Vocol.* 2002;27:74–79.

11. Hanania NA, Chapman KR, Kesten S. Adverse effects of inhaled corticosteroids. *Amer J Med.* 1995;98:196–208.

12. Ihre E, Zetterström O, Hammarberg B. Voice problems as side effects of inhaled corticosteroids in asthma patients—a prevalence study. *J Voice.* 2004;18;403–414.

13. Roland NJ, Bhalla RK, Earis J. The local side effects of inhaled corticosteroids. *Chest.* 2004;126: 213–219.

14. Stead RJ, Cooke NJ. Adverse effects of inhaled corticosteroids. *Br Med J.* 1989;298:403–404.

15. Lavy JA, Wood G, Rubin JS, Harries M. Dysphonia associated with inhaled steroids. *J Voice.* 2000; 14:581–588.

16. Williamson IJ, Matusiewicz SP, Brown PH, Greening AP, Crompton GK. Frequency of voice problems and cough in patients using pressurized aerosol inhaled steroid preparations. *Eur Respir J.* 1995;8:590–592.

17. Toogood JH, Jennings B, Greenway RW, Chuang L. Candidiasis and dysphonia complicating beclomethasone treatment of asthma. *J Allergy Clin Immunol.* 1980;65:145–153.

18. Williams AJ, Baghat MS, Stableforth DE, Cayton RM, Shenoi PM, Skinner C. Dysphonia caused by inhaled steroids: recognition on a characteristic laryngeal abnormality. *Thorax.* 1983;38:813–821.

19. Sataloff RT. Professional singers: the science and art of clinical care. *Am J Otolaryngol.* 1981;2:262–266.

20. Verdolini K, Titze IR, Fennell A. Dependence of phonatory effort on hydration level. *J Speech Hear Res.* 1994;37:1001–1007.

21. Rhoads JM, Lowell SH, Hedgepeth EM. Hoarseness and aphonia as a side effect of tricyclic antidepressants. *Am J Psychiatry.* 1979; 136:1599–1600.

22. Lyskowski JC, Dunner FJ. Hoarseness and tricyclic antidepressants. *Am J Psyichiatry.* 1980;137:636.

23. Gates GA, Saegert J, Wilson N, Johnson L, Shepherd A, Hearne EM. The effect of β blockade on singing performance. *Ann Otol Rhinol Laryngol.* 1985; 94:570–574.

24. Damste PH. Virilization of the voice due to anabolic steroids. *Folia Phoniatr.* 1968;16:10–18.

25. Pattie MA, Murdoch BE, Theodoros D, Forbes K. Voice changes in women treated for endometriosis and related conditions: the need for comprehensive vocal assessment. *J Voice.* 1998;12:366–371.

26. Schlondorff G. Anabolic hormones and voice disorders. *Dtsch Med Wochenschr.* 1966;91:555–557.

27. Boothroyd CV, Lepre F. Permanent voice change resulting from danazol therapy. *Aust N Z J Obstet Gynaecol.* 1990;30:275–276.

28. Gerritsma EJ, Brocaar MP, Hakkesteegt MM, Birkenhäger JC. Virilization of the voice in postmenopausal women due to the anabolic cteroid nandrolone decanoate (Decadurabolin). The effects of medication for one year. *Clin Otolaryngol.* 1994;19:79–84.

29. Baker J. A report on alterations to the speaking and singing voices of four women following hormonal therapy with virilizing agents. *J Voice.* 1999;13: 496–507.

30. Talaat M, Talaat AM, Kelada I, Angelo A, Elwany S, Thabet H. Histologic and histochemical study of effects of anabolic steroids on the female larynx. *Ann Otol Rhinol Laryngol.* 1987;96:468–471.

31. Need AG, Durbridge TC, Nordin BE. Anabolic steroids in postmenopausal osteoporosis. *Wien Med Wochenschr.* 1993;143:392–395.

32. Wendler J, Siegert C, Schelhorn P, et al. The influence of Microgynon and Diane-35, two sub-fifty ovulation inhibitors, on voice function in women. *Contraception.* 1995;52:343–348.

33. Schiff M. The "pill" in otolaryngology. *Trans Am Acad Ophthalmol Otolaryngol.* 1968;72:76–84.

34. Akcam T, Bolu E, Merati A, Durmus C, Gerek M, Ozkaptan Y. Voice changes after androgen therapy for hypogonadotrophic hypogonadism. *Laryngoscope.* 2004;114:1587–1591.

35. Douglas RM, Hemila H, D'Souza R, Chalker EB, Treacy B. Vitamin C for preventing and treating the common cold. *Cochrane Database Syst Rev.* 2000;4:CD000980.

36. Van Straten M, Josling P. Preventing the common cold with a vitamin C supplement: a double-blind, placebo-controlled survey. *Adv Ther.* 2002;19: 151–159.

37. Reveiz L, Cardona AF, Ospina EG. Antibiotics for acute laryngitis in adults. *Cochrane Database Syst Rev.* 2005;1:CD004783.

38. Turnidge J. Responsible prescribing for upper respiratory tract infections. *Drugs.* 2001;16:2065–2077.

39. Schalén L, Christensen P, Eliasson I, Fex S, Kamme C, Schalén C. Inefficacy of penicillin V in acute laryngitis in adults: evaluation from results of double-blind study. *Ann Otol Rhinol Laryngol.* 1985;94:14–17.

40. Schalén L, Eliasson I, Kamme C, Schalén C. Erythromycin in acute laryngitis in adults. *Ann Otol Rhinol Laryngol.* 1993;102:209–214.

41. Hol C, Schálen C, Verduin CM, Van Dijke EE, Verhoef J, Fleer A. *Moraxella catarrhalis* in acute laryngitis: infection or colonization? *J Infect Dis.* 1996;174:636–638.

42. Koufman JA. Laryngopharyngeal reflux 2002: a new paradigm of airway disease. *Ear Nose Throat J.* 2002; 81:2–6.

43. Wyke BD. Laryngeal reflex mechanisms. *Phonation.* 1976; 528–537.

44. Proctor DF. *Breathing, Speech, and Song.* New York, NY: Springer-Verlag; 1980.

45. Neely JL, Rosen C. Vocal fold hemorrhage associated with coumadin therapy in an opera singer. *J Voice.* 2000;14:272–277.

46. Akhtar S, Wood G, Rubin JS, O'Flynn, PE, Ratcliffe P. Effect of caffeine on the vocal folds: a pilot study. *J Laryngol Otol.* 1999;113:341–345.

Chapter 10

COMPLEMENTARY AND ALTERNATIVE MEDICATIONS AND TECHNIQUES

Michael D. Seidman

Complementary and integrative medicine (CIM), also known as complementary and alternative medicine (CAM) is defined as any practice that can be used for the prevention and treatment of diseases, but not taught widely in medical schools, not generally available in hospitals, and not usually covered by health insurance. Similarly, Andrew Weil, MD, defines integrative medicine as a healing-oriented medicine that draws upon all therapeutic systems to form a comprehensive approach to the art and science of medicine.[1]

Generally speaking the amateur, semiprofessional, or professional singer often realizes benefits and accepts CIM more readily than the average population. Surow and Lovetri speculate that singers tend to be highly conscious of their bodies and frequently turn to CIM to optimize their health.[2] In their survey they found that 71% of the respondents admitted to using CIM therapies, on a fairly frequent basis. Prior to delving into the different possible CIM modalities pertinent to the singer, it is relevant to discuss the evolution of CIM.

Some of the more common and widely accepted therapies originated in Asia centuries ago; others were developed in Europe or America over the past several centuries. There are many examples of CIM therapies, as noted in Table 10–1. Conventional medicine started approximately 200 years ago, whereas alternative therapies have been present since civilization began. There are references, for example, to the healing applications of aloe vera in the Bible. During the mid-20th century, there was a rapid elimination of CIM, and it was often branded quackery or charlatanism. As a result, physicians tend to disregard practices that are not validated by double-blind, randomized, placebo-controlled studies. But clearly it is difficult if not impossible to randomize and placebo-control every type of therapeutic intervention.

In spite of the general lack of scientific research, there has been an astounding increase in the use of CIM therapies. Americans spent approximately $27 billion in 1998 and $32 billion in the year 2000 on alternative therapies. Roughly 40 to 50% of all Americans

Table 10-1. Examples of CIM Therapies

Acupuncture	Massage therapy
Alexander technique	Megavitamin therapy
Biofeedback	Naturopathy
Chiropractic	Neuromuscular therapy
Energy healing	Prayer
Feldenkrais technique	Reflexology
Folk remedies	Relaxation
Homeopathy	Remote healing
Herbal supplements	Rolfing
Hypnotherapy	Self-help groups
Imagery	Spiritual healing by others
Magnet therapy	Therapeutic touch

have tried some form of alternative therapy, according to a report in the *Journal of the American Medical Association.* Another report suggests that more than 60% of Americans are now using CIM therapies.[3]

The disturbing aspect of this is the fact that of the Americans using CIM, 70% do not tell their physicians.[4] This is quite alarming, as many of the herbal as well as some nutritional supplements can interfere with common medications, at times with potentially life-threatening effects. Increasingly, patients insist on seeing a physician who is at least open to considering CIM therapies, particularly where conventional therapies may be less effective. Currently, approximately 75% of medical schools are offering courses on alternative medicine. It is becoming increasingly clear that physicians must learn about CIM. In the best circumstances, we should utilize expertise from a variety of practitioners and collaboration between physicians and people who practice CIM is to be encouraged. Currently, this is frontier territory, but it might be the best case scenario for our patients.

CIM philosophy emphasizes prevention and wellness rather than "fixing." Generally speaking, CIM may be less costly than the use of expensive high-technology testing, surgeries, and drugs, as less invasive options typically demand less health care resources. People are beginning to ask for alternatives incorporating mental and spiritual aspects. This is based on a belief in the unity and importance of the body, mind, and spirit—essentially, these three elements cannot be separated when trying to treat someone or to maintain or improve their health. CIM professionals attempt to mobilize and enhance the healing ability inherent in each person. Furthermore, a CIM professional establishes a partnership with the patient, and treatment is directed toward the unique goals and values of each individual.

In the 17th century, the philosopher René Descartes initiated the thinking of distinct domains of human construction and the exactness of science (Figure 10–1). The pre-Descartes era shows the body, mind, and spirit as integral components of health, whereas post-Descartes these elements were separated. The conventional Western paradigm dictates that diseases are caused by internal cellular and organ dysfunction (Figure 10–2). As a result, more than 99% of all research funding in the United States is aimed at therapies focused on the body, whereas the mind and spirit are rarely investigated. Conversely, the holistic or integrative medicine paradigm (Figure 10–3) suggests that the domains of the body, mind, and spirit are inseparable and disease signals an imbalance. Optimal treatment involves addressing all domains together. Clearly, the effects of structural movement patterns, hormonal, nutritional, and genetic forces, as well as personal past, emotion, stress, and behavior patterns all play a role in the body, mind, and spirit, and should never be separated. In the holistic paradigm, it is felt that imbalances of the body, mind, and spirit are the cause of cellular and organ dysfunction. Then the real question becomes when are cellular and organ changes the result of disease rather than the cause and are both hypotheses possible?

It is becoming evident that the best practices involve providing patients with healing options. Even the most open-minded provider cannot be an expert in all therapies, or be aware of everything that is available, what the research supports, and where to refer people. Providers must be honest with patients, especially if they do not know about a treatment modality. It is important to avoid stating that something is harmful or has no evidence behind it if you have not actually investigated the subject, just as it is essential above all to do no harm.

To help singers find solutions to health problems, to provide strategies to enhance their performances, and to optimize their health, it is necessary to discuss the orchestra of therapeutic modalities available. The discussion begins with nutraceuticals and herbs, and then delves into several other potential therapeutic options.

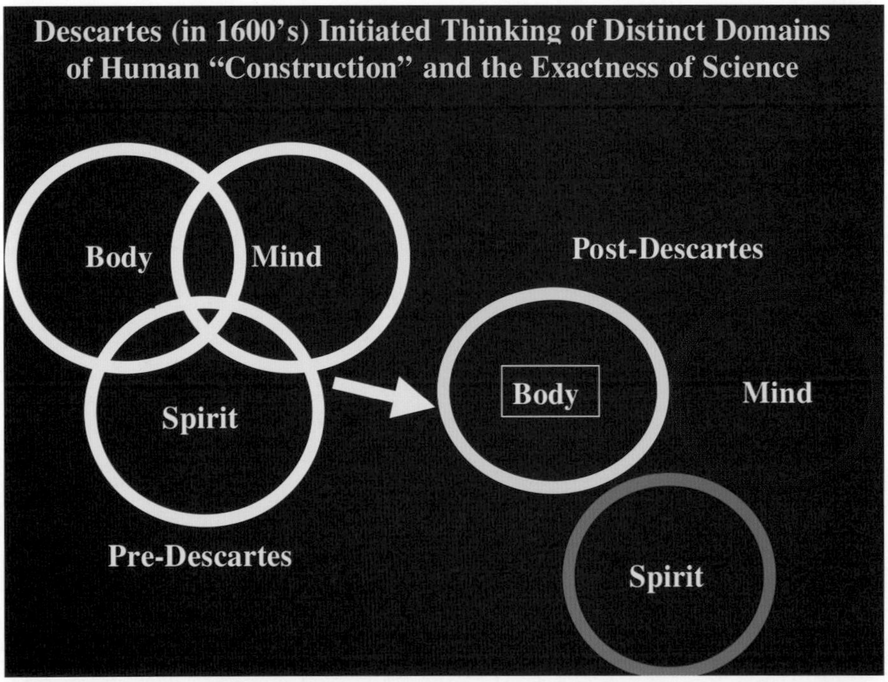

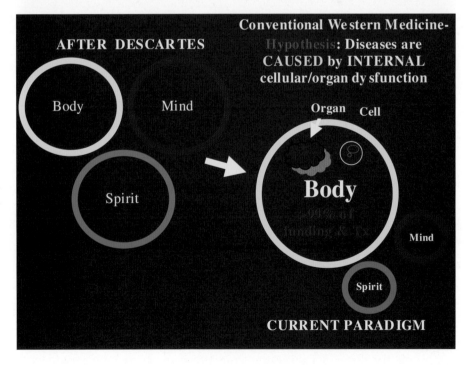

Figure 10–1. Comparison of pre- and post-Descartes thinking about the relationship of the human body, mind, and spirit. (Courtesy of Robert Levine, PhD)

Figure 10–2. Illustration of the current paradigm of Western medicine regarding the disease process.

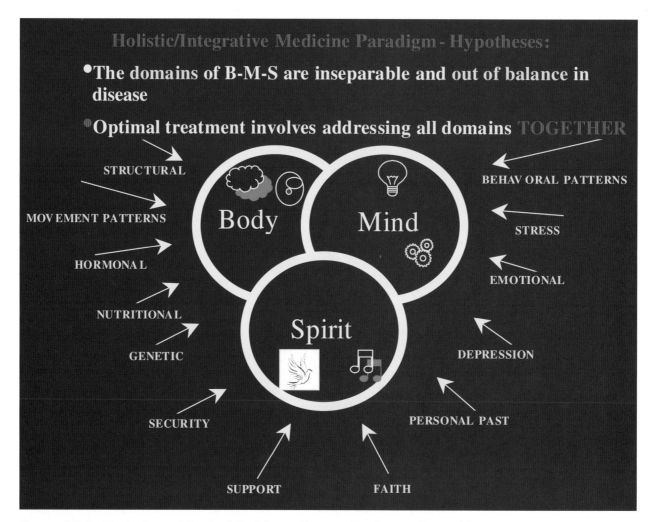

Figure 10–3. Illustration of the holistic/integrative medical paradigm of the disease process.

NUTRACEUTICALS, VITAMINS, AND HERBS

Many herbs can be used for medicinal purposes and many of them are extremely relevant to the singer. Some of the more commonly used herbs are listed in Table 10–2, where we have provided details, such as claims information, specific actions when known, contraindications, potential side effects, interactions, and dosages, when available.

There is always concern about whether a specific supplement contains precisely what the manufacturer claims. Unfortunately, there have been many examples suggesting that this is not always the case. However, herbal remedies are increasingly being sold with standardization information included on the labels. For the time being, we must take the manufacturers at their word, because this area is not regulated by the Food and Drug Administration (FDA).

One of the most reputable references with regard to the medicinal use of herbs is the Complete German Commission E. This commission provides monographs on hundreds of herbs, rating them as either positive or negative. Typically, an herb that is rated positively has reasonable scientific support and data to validate its use. An herb with a negative rating may be ineffective, unsafe, or simply not studied to the extent that sufficient information is available.

Table 10-2. Herbs Used for Medicinal Purposes

Herbal Supplement	Indications	Actions	Contraindications	Side Effects	Interactions	Dosage
Echinacea	Treatment and prevention of the common cold and flu	Immunostimulant Enhances phagocytosis	Autoimmune or chronic illness Allergy to flowers of the daisy family	Minor gastrointestinal irritation Increased urination Mild allergic reactions	Immune suppressants (ie, Neoral prednisone Imuran methotrexate	As powder extract: 300 mg cap/TID Alcohol tincture (1:5): 3–4 ml TID Juice: 203 ml TID Whole dried root: 100–200 g TID
Goldenseal	Topical antibiotic for wounds that are not healing well Mouth sores and sore throats	Strong activity against a wide variety of bacteria and fungi	Pregnancy	Gastrointestinal distress Increased nervousness		As cream, cover entire surface of the wound Tincture: swished or gargled Tea: 0.5–1g in a cup of water
Kava Kava	Mild to moderate anxiety Insomnia	Anti-anxiety Mild analgesic Muscle relaxant Anti-convulsant	Pregnancy Nursing mothers Endogenous depression	Mild gastrointestinal irritation Drowsiness Yellowish skin discoloration Balance disturbance Skin rash Enlargement of pupils	Benzodiazepine Buspirone Alcohol Barbiturates Anti-depressant Anti-psychotic	Standardized extract: 140–240 mg in 2–3 divided doses (30–70% kava-lactones)
Ginseng	Tonic Stimulant Diuretic Diabetic impotence	Physiologic effects Lower blood pressure Depress CNS activity Stimulates immune system	Coagulopathy Diabetes Insomnia Schizophrenia Cardiac disease	Bleeding Hypotension Hypoglycemia Insomnia	Medications for: Psychosis Diabetes MAO inhibitors Stimulants Coumadin Caffeine	American: Root: 0.25–0.5 po BID Asian (Panax): 0.6–3 gm 1–3 times daily

continues

Table 10-2. continued

Herbal Supplement	Indications	Actions	Contraindications	Side Effects	Interactions	Dosage
Gingko Biloba	Dementia Improve cognitive, sexual, and GI functions Dizziness/Tinnitus	↑ CNS blood flow Neuroprotective Free Radical ↓ capillary fragility	If the patient is on anticoagulants	Spontaneous bleeding (rare) Headache and gastrointestinal irritation	Cyclosporin SSRIs MAO inhibitors Thiazide diuretics Anticoagulant properties may induce seizures, infertility	120–480 mg/day in 2–3 divided doses
Saw Palmetto	Anti-inflammatory ↑ urinary flow ↓ symptoms of BPH	Inhibits dihydro-testosterone Diuretic Anti-androgenic	Do not take while on prescription BPH treatment	None	Caution with diuretics	160 mg BID
Pygeum Africanum	Symptoms of BPH Anti-inflammatory Diuretic ↓ cholesterol	Anti-poliferative effect on fibroblast	None reported	Nausea and abdominal pain	None known	50–200 mg stand ext/day
Guarana	Stimulant headache ↑ energy	Sympathomimetic Caffeinelike activities	Cardiac problems Renal disease HTN or hyperthyroidism	↑ heart rate HTN Anxiety Arrythmias	Avoid other stimulants	Not specified
Feverfew	Migraine Rheumatoid arthritis	Inhibits serotonin release	Aster family allergies Avoid during pregnancies	GI upset 6–15% 1st week of use	Anticoagulants (inhib cycloxygenic)	50 mg–1.2 gm/d equivalent to 0.2–0.6
Hawthorne	Atherosclerosis Arrhythmia	Improves cardiac output and coronary blood flow	Do not use with other inotropes	Mildly sedative	Digitalis Fox Glove	160–900 mg/day

Herbal Supplement	Indications	Actions	Contraindications	Side Effects	Interactions	Dosage
Black Cohosh	Menopause Astringent Diuretic Expectorant Vertigo Tinnitus	Estrogenlike action Oxytocic Luteinizing hormone suppression Binds to estrogen receptors	None known	Occasional GI upset Nausea, headache and dizziness in high doses	None known	Extracts w/alcohol: 40–60% (v/v) corresponds to 40 mg drug
Garlic	Reduces levels of lipids in blood Prevents age-dependent vascular changes ↓ Cholesterol 10–12%	Antibacterial Antimycotic Lipid-lowering Inhibition of platelet aggregation Prolongation of bleed and clotting time Enhances fibrinolytic activity	None known	GI upset Allergic reactions Odor may pervade breath and skin	Anticoagulants Hypoglycemics	4 g fresh garlic (minced bulb and prep is taken orally)
Pulsatilla	Sedative, headaches Fluid in the ears	Antispasmodic Increases circulation Antibacterial	Avoid during pregnancy	GI upset Topically—skin irritation Mild renal and urinary tract irritation	None known	120–300 mg TID
St. John's Wort	Dizziness, Tinnitus Mild to mod depression Viral infections Wound healing	Antidepressant Weak MAOI SSRI & dopamine agonist	Avoid in pregnancy	Photosensitivity	Anti-depressants MAOI Anti-seizure meds Birth control	300 mg TID
Ma Huang	Asthma Bronchial edema (weight loss—not an approved use) Stimulant	Sympathomimetic-Bronchodilator	Cardiac problems Anxiety Hypertension Angle closure glaucoma Pheochromo-cytoma Thyrotoxicant	Hypertension, neurosis, insomnia, palpitations, hyperglycemia Death	Halothone Cardiac glycosides MAOI Guanethedine Oxytosh	15–30 mg total alkaloid or 300 mg herb/day

The herb *Echinacea* provides us with a good example of some of the issues involved in herbal remedies. *Echinacea* is a very popular herb with a reputation for combating the common cold and flulike illnesses. It is a commonly used herb by professional singers at the first sign of a sniffle, cough, or general malaise. What most people do not realize is that there are nine different subtypes of echinacea, including *Echinacea purpurea*, *Echinacea pallida*, and *Echinacea angustafolia*. Not only does each subtype have different health benefits, but those benefits vary depending on the part of the plant used. The leaf of *Echinacea purpurea*, for example, has been shown to enhance T and B cell functions, whereas the root of that same plant does not. Conversely, *Echinacea pallida* root has been shown to enhance T and B cell function but the leaf of that same plant does not. Meanwhile, *Echinacea angustafolia* is rated as a negative herb by the German Commission E. Yet while visiting numerous health food stores, there were more than 100 bottles of echinacea on the shelves and 95% of them contained *Echinacea angustafolia*![5]

Why would the market be filled with *Echinacea angustafolia* if it is a negatively rated herb? One explanation is that manufacturers are not doing their homework. Another possibility is that it is a much less expensive or more available herb. Nutritional products that contain *Echinacea purpurea* leaf and *pallida* root are to be considered, both of which have been clearly shown in scientific studies to enhance and activate T and B cell functions, to encourage phagocytosis, and to have antibacterial and antiviral properties. Unfortunately, if a study is conducted with a product made from *Echinacea angustafolia*, the results are likely to indicate that it does not work in treating cold or flu symptoms. Studies like this cast doubt on all herbal remedies.

Drug/herb interactions pose another reason for concern. *Echinacea*, for example, may interfere with Neoral, prednisone, Imuran, and methotrexate. Furthermore, consumers and physicians should understand that immunostimulants, like *Echinacea* and the herb goldenseal, should not be used for prolonged periods of time. There are also contraindications for patients who have immune disorders or severe infections, such as tuberculosis. St John's wort is a commonly used herb for mild to moderate depression, yet it can interfere with commonly used anesthetics and the results can be deadly. Thus, it is critical to learn about the potential for interactions.

The professional singer needs to be aware of the potential benefit of other supplements as well. When singers get an upper respiratory tract infection (URI), anxiety and fear set in, particularly when a show is scheduled later that day or in the next couple of days. Many professional singers turn to specific supplements. Given the plethora of choices, this paper briefly discusses only a few of the more commonly used supplements.

Ionized zinc has been demonstrated to have direct antiviral activity. In order to achieve this antiviral activity the concentration required is 0.1 mmol/L to suppress rhinovirus activity. Zinc lozenges provide approximately 4.4 mmol/L. Zinc has been shown to protect cells from damage by viral toxins, and inhibit the rhinovirus's ability to attach, enter, and infect human nasal cells. Interestingly, studies have shown both efficacy and lack of efficacy. Some of this discrepancy can be accounted for by the compounds coupled with the zinc. These additives, specifically citric and tartaric acid, mannitol, and sorbitol, are used to enhance the flavor. However, these compounds can chelate the zinc and make it ineffective.[6-12]

There is a product called Zicam that is a homeopathic gel consisting of zinc gluconate. The mechanism of action is that the zinc gel binds to viral intercellular adhesion molecule (ICAM) attachment sites, stops the spread, and inhibits viral replication. However, in some cases it may cause burning and there have been some reports of anosmia, but it is suspected that the anosmia is more than likely secondary to the upper respiratory tract infection itself (Hensley et al, unpublished data).[13]

Another product that has been noted to be extremely helpful at rapidly eradicating the common cold and flu is a proprietary formula developed by the author and marketed by Body Language Vitamin Co (http://www.bodylangvitamin.com). This product utilizes the synergistic activity of multiple herbs and supplements, including *Echinacea purpurea* leaf, *pallida* root, goldenseal, zinc, quercetin, citrus bioflavanoids, and so on. It has been shown to reduce the duration of cold and flu by 70 to 85% in 85% of users, provided it is started at the onset of symptoms (Seidman, unpublished data). The ingredients have been shown to enhance T and B cell function and phagocytosis. It, like other herbals, should not be used in patients with active autoimmune processes or patients on immunosuppressant drugs.

Uncaria tomentosa has been shown to increase T and B cell lymphocytes, and phagocyte and lymphoblast function. Its effects appear to be mediated by the activity of the constituent pentacyclic oxindole alkaloids (POAs). It has also been shown to contain quinovic acid, which reduces inflammation. There are no specific contraindications, side effects, or interactions.[14,15]

Pulsatilla (Anemone pulsatilla) acts as a sedative and an antispasmodic and can be used to treat headache, neuralgia, laryngitis, mild dizziness, and tinnitus. The herb has been demonstrated to have relaxation properties and to enhance circulation. *Pulsatilla* is not recommended for use during pregnancy. There are no known interactions although a fresh *pulsatilla* plant can cause blistering or a rash.

Aconite *(Aconitum napellus)* can be beneficial in the treatment of upper respiratory infections, influenza, facial neuralgia, arthritis, and gout. The alkaloids activate sodium channels, which have been shown to affect neural function. Aconite should not be used in conjunction with any other alkaloids such as quinine or morphine, or tryptophan. The side effects can include nausea, vomiting, dizziness, parasthesia, and palpitations.

Cordyceps sinensis enhances immunity and reduces coughing by increasing lung "chi." It acts as a bronchodilator increasing the function of natural killer and B cells. There are no specific contraindications, interactions, or side effects.[16]

Astragalus membranaceus has been known to enhance energy, by increasing resistance to disease while increasing "chi" and circulation. Additionally, it has anti inflammatory properties. It has been demonstrated to enhance the body's ability to adapt to stress, stimulates proliferation of stem cells, macrophages, and lymphocyte cells, and increases the production of interferon. Although its use is to be questioned in the presence of active autoimmune diseases, there are no significant known contraindications, side effects, or interactions.[17,18]

Ginseng *(Panax ginseng)* has been useful in the treatment of fatigue, depression, stress, sexual energy, and digestion and promotes general well-being. It is an adaptogenic stimulant that promotes secretion of adrenocorticotrophic hormome, causing a release of endorphins and enkephalins. It should not be taken during pregnancy and may interfere with anticoagulant therapy. In high doses it may cause insomnia, anxiety, and gastrointestinal upset. It should not be taken with other anticoagulants, stimulants (such as caffeine), monoamine oxidase inhibitors (MAOIs), or antipsychotics.

Goldenseal *(Hydrastis canadensis)* has been shown to be beneficial for mucosal inflammation, diarrhea and gastritis, wound healing, immune function, URI, and the flu. It is believed to act as an adaptogen (enhances body defenses) and may increase circulation. The herb should not be used during pregnancy. In high doses, it may cause nausea, vomiting, diarrhea, CNS stimulation, and respiratory failure. There are no known significant interactions. There are many more herbs that can be considered but this should provide the reader with a great start. Additionally, Table 10-2 lists additional commonly used herbs.

It is critical for health care providers to question patients specifically about the use of nutraceuticals and herbs. Proven therapeutic options should be discussed. If a viable alternative exists, it can be considered, bearing in mind, of course, that natural does not necessarily mean safe. As always, one needs to be diligent about quality control and standardization, and realize that herbal/pharmaceutical interactions do occur with some frequency. Health care professionals should also consider nutraceutical safety issues and keep an objective perspective. According to one study, the average annual mortality rates over the past 12 years show that deaths related to vitamin use occur at approximately 1 death per year and herbs cause 2 deaths per year, whereas smoking is responsible for more than 400,000 deaths per year, poor diet is linked to 300,000 deaths per year, and pharmaceutical errors contribute to more than 100,000 deaths per year.[19] Thus, it is not very likely that anyone will be harmed with nutritional or herbal therapies.

Vitamins and minerals are crucial for many different bodily functions. A number of multivitamins provide the standard vitamins and minerals, but there is really no such thing as one pill that can provide everything the body needs. Typically, it takes 4 to 10 pills a day to obtain the necessary nutrients. It is always best if the ingredients are natural and minerals are chelated. Chelating a mineral means an amino acid is bound, to the mineral. Thus, when physicians recommend Tums as a good source of calcium, this is a fallacy. Tums is calcium carbonate; the same chemical formula as stone. The absorption of calcium carbonate is approximately 2 to 4%. Thus, for my patients, I always recommended the use of a chelated calcium such as calcium glycinate, gluconate, or citrate. Furthermore, it is an added benefit if the supplement is produced in an FDA-inspected laboratory. In addition, antioxidants should have powerful molecular and cellular antioxidants that are well absorbed. Obtaining sufficient antioxidant protection could require an additional two to four pills a day.

Many nutrition experts believe that our current vitamin and mineral guidelines are too low. The recommended dietary allowances (RDA), or dietary reference intakes (DRI), were established by the Food and Nutrition Board in 1941. They are considered the best scientific judgment on nutritional allowances and are designed to meet the nutrient needs of practically all healthy people. Although the RDAs are safe and adequate nutrient levels, they are neither minimal requirements nor optimal levels. This then raises the question of whether or not we need to take supplements. There is a considerable body of evidence suggesting that the answer to this question is yes. Although conflicting results can be confusing for the general public, health care practitioners should be aware of the important role played by vitamins, minerals, and other supplements in overall health. Although the public is encouraged to adopt a healthy lifestyle, engage in stress reduction, eat a nutritious diet, and obtain adequate exercise, few people actually follow those guidelines. As a result, vitamin, mineral, and antioxidant supplements are not only necessary but recommended by an increasing number of health authorities. They play a very important role in the health and maintenance of all people and certainly professional voice users should consider some of these strategies.

Aside from nutraceuticals, many other CIM therapies warrant further discussion. Traditional Chinese medicine (TCM) encompasses both acupuncture therapy and Chinese herbal therapy. It is a system of medicine that also looks at how diet, lifestyle choices, and emotions affect a person's overall health.

ACUPUNCTURE AND CHINESE HERBAL THERAPY

Beth Kohn and Susan Jakary are well-known acupuncturists for the Center for Integrative Medicine at Henry Ford Health System. They note that TCM is based on the concept that a vital life force, or energy (called "qi," which is pronounced "chee") is what fuels all of the functions of our bodies, including respiration, digestion, elimination, and reproduction. Symptoms and chronic disease patterns reflect an imbalance in this energetic system. Traditional Chinese medicine strives to alleviate or eliminate the symptom (also called the branch manifestation) while at the same time balancing the underlying cause (called the root). This allows the body to change the course of any underlying imbalance thus giving way to alleviating chronic health issues.

The energy, or qi, moves through the body along pathways known as meridians. These meridians have names that are similar to our Western organs such as the lung, spleen, and heart meridian. Each meridian relates to certain functions and processes within the body as well as to different emotions. Each meridian also connects and relates to other meridians creating a unified system of energy within the body. One example of this is the lung meridian being closely related to respiration, health of the skin, perspiration, protection against colds and flu, and voice quality and strength. Symptoms that may reflect an imbalance in the lung meridian might include cough, hoarse voice, or laryngitis, asthma, allergies, sore throat, and the common cold to name a few. Specific acupuncture points and herbal formulas can be used to resolve the symptoms and restore balance.

Acupuncture needles are very fine, thin needles that are gently tapped into the surface of the skin. Typically, they are about 10 times thinner than conventional needles and are not considered painful when inserted. Their insertion stimulates a physiologic healing response in which endorphins and enkephalins are released into the bloodstream. The patient often senses a feeling of extreme relaxation.

Performers who need to strengthen their voice quality may find acupuncture and herbal therapies extremely effective. Chinese medicine can provide a strong foundation to support performers by protecting their voices during times when they may be more vulnerable. This may be when they are asked to perform multiples shows in a short period of time or during the cold and flu seasons. Acupuncture and herbal therapy may also be used to speed up recovery time for patients suffering from the common cold or just from the rigors of frequent voice use.

When a performer feels a sore throat or some slight fatigue signaling the onset of an upper respiratory infection (URI), they can use TCM to help prevent the progression of the illness. Chinese herbals are classically plant, mineral, or animal based and are prescribed specifically for the individual and what his or her needs are. No two patients are identical, so their acupuncture and herbal therapies are tailored to their specific needs.

Acupuncture has been demonstrated to relax and release muscle tension. It is the ease of movement by expansion and contraction of the diaphragm and surrounding external intercostals muscles that allows the lungs to inflate to capacity. In addition, it is especially beneficial to relax the muscles in the jaw, neck, shoulders, back, and abdomen. The technique of cupping is quite effective for relaxing muscles and increases circulation to these areas. Even the base of the tongue can tense, causing surrounding structures to contract, distorting voice clarity, pitch, and timbre. Lastly, acupuncture is calming and centering for the emotions. Sometimes unconscious thoughts or past emotional trauma create habitual holding patterns inside the body. Not only can this affect mental state, but could negatively affect the skeletal alignment, breathing, muscle performance, and the healthy functioning of the organ systems.

HYPNOTHERAPY AND NEUROIMMUNOPSYCHOLOGY

Donna May, a licensed hypnotherapist, notes that in her practice mind body therapies such as hypnotherapy or neurolinguistic programming (NLP) are helpful adjuncts to the professional singer. Hypnotherapy has been used for many years to facilitate relaxation and to envision a perfect performance. Many professional singers use this form of therapy. Initially, they experience several sessions with a professional hypnotherapist and then can learn to do this on their own.

It is clear that our beliefs and perceptions strongly influence behavior. You are much less likely to suc-

ceed if you are not convinced that you will. A classic example, is before Roger Bannister ran 1 mile in less than 4 minutes, it was believed to be impossible. Within the same year of Roger's landmark record, other athletes also ran the mile in less than 4 minutes because they now believed it to be possible. Similarly, Paula Radcliffe recently set a new world record by running the marathon in just under 2 hours and 16 minutes. These successes set the stage for further accomplishments. Beliefs are so powerful that they can affect our neuroimmunopsychology, and they are an invaluable asset to assist a person in achieving his or her goals.

NLP is essentially the science of how to run your brain in an optimal way to produce the result you want. An example of the power of NLP is depicted in the book, *Unlimited Power* by Anthony Robbins. In chapter 4 there is a story of one of the great musicians of the 20th century, Pablo Casals, the cellist, told by Norman Cousins, author of *Anatomy of an Illness*.[20] At 90 he was frail, arthritic, with emphysema and swollen clenched fingers. He walked with a shuffle, stooped over, his head pitched forward. Yet when he sat himself on the piano bench to play each morning, something quite miraculous happened. Casals suddenly transformed himself and went into a resourceful state, and as he did, his physiology changed to such a degree that he began to move and play producing both in his body and on the piano results that should have been possible only for a healthy, strong, flexible pianist. The story goes on to say that his fingers seemed to race above the keyboard and his entire body seemed fused with the music. "By the time he walked away from the piano, he seemed entirely different from the person who sat down to play. He stood straighter and taller and he walked without a trace of a shuffle to the breakfast table and then went out for a stroll along the beach." As Anton Chekhov said, "Man is what he believes."

NLP addresses the mind and allows the individual to form positive images that are the foothold for success. These strategies include: success strategies, modeling excellence, utilizing past successes and resources, anchoring for success, and structure and physiology body posture, breathing, facial, expression, gestures, and others.

A brief example of what a vocalist might do to harness the power of NLP is as follows: It is critical that the singer envision a past performance when they had the perfect delivery of their tonal aspects and their ability to work the crowd. It is then necessary to elicit that resourceful state of being by discovering their success strategy. What did they see, hear, say to themselves? How did they use their physiology (stand, breathe, etc)? An anchor for success could then be established and utilized for the future. By being able to put themselves in the resourceful state through anchoring, they can again achieve excellent results.

These powerful techniques can also be used to assist patients with a variety of disorders including overcoming fears and phobias, anxiety, depression, and limiting beliefs. A hypnotherapist can also utilize the above strategies by incorporating them into a hypnosis script and using the techniques with the client during hypnosis. The power of the mind is a grossly untapped area of holistic health that has real opportunity to enhance the overall outcome.

NEUROMUSCULAR THERAPY

It is important to have a brief understanding of skeletal and muscular situations that can facilitate the voice or lead to its downfall. Kyrras Conrad, an authority on the techniques of St. John neuromuscular therapy (NMT) notes that there are numerous mechanisms to support the vocalist by maximizing voice quality and endurance and by addressing vocal dysfunctions. Many of the same muscles will be treated for both wellness care and to correct abnormal or suboptimal function. Maximizing voice quality in the well person will usually involve treating all the muscles of phonation and air exchange. Vocal dysfunctions are treated by assessing the individual's particular problem and, in addition to the muscles treated in wellness care, will more specifically and thoroughly treat the muscles involved with that problem.

Voice quality, range, texture, resonance, and endurance are all affected by the tone of the associated musculature. Areas of hypertonicity are generally considered to be hypoperfused or even ischemic; ischemic areas have diminished range of motion and are believed to create trigger points. Trigger point referral sites may also develop reduced circulation, and this may manifest as pain, parasthesia, numbness, itching, and/or diminished range of motion.[21,22]

Hypertonicity of the muscles that affect the voice can occur as a result of direct trauma, such as sudden deceleration injuries, manual strangulation, and so forth; indirect trauma, such as injuries to other parts of the body that result in uneven muscle tone of the neck and shoulders; or microtrauma from repetitive use or poor posture. Practicing or performing in areas with exceedingly dry air, the presence of smoke, and so forth can also cause excessive and uneven muscle contraction.

Vocal dysfunctions are often related to muscles of the larynx, the lips, and the tongue. Movement of the tongue, resonance, and clear articulation are directly affected by the condition of the muscles of the oropharynx, nasopharynx, and laryngopharynx. The hyoglossus, palatoglossus, genioglossuss, styloglossus, the pharyngeal constrictors, palatopharyngeus, palatines, levator labii, zygomaticus, risoris, obicularis oris, buccinator, and platysma, as well as many other superficial and internal muscles, often require treatment. Endurance and air volume are also issues and are related to muscles of the thorax, such as the intercostals, pectoralis major and minor, the rhomboids, serratus anterior and posterior musculature, and the diaphragm. Mandibular range of motion is most profoundly affected by the temporalis, masseter, and medial and lateral pterygoid muscles.

Treatment strategies are developed after assessing for imbalances of muscle tone. Therapy applied to the hypertonic areas will improve circulation and allow muscles to return to normal resting length and so allow the muscles to flex and extend freely for full expression of the voice. St. John neuromuscular therapy uses several techniques such as friction, static pressure of 8- to 12-seconds duration, and trigger point therapy to externally and internally treat the bodies, origins, and insertions of all affected muscles where those muscles are entirely accessible, and treats as much as possible of those muscles to which access may be limited. Only the upper 2 to 3 inches of the pharyngeal constrictors, for example, can be treated internally in most individuals.

St. John neuromuscular therapy is a low-cost, non-invasive method to correct vocal dysfunction related to soft tissue problems and should be considered for therapy before more invasive solutions are attempted. In addition to effectively treating soft tissue pathology, this therapy will maintain good vocal health in the healthy individual as well as help perfect the voice of the vocal professional. This leads us to a brief discussion of massage therapy. Massage therapy has been demonstrated to have strong beneficial physiologic effects, including the ability to enhance immune system function[23-26] and provide a sense of relaxation and well-being. Many professional performers find benefit to the healing properties of massage.

SUMMARY

In summary, although many CIM remedies have been in existence for thousands of years, there is a general lack of randomized, double-blind, placebo-controlled studies supporting their efficacy. As a result, many health care professionals are skeptical and hesitant to recommend CIM modalities. The care of the professional voice clearly involves utilizing strategies categorized as CIM. There is tremendous public interest in alternative therapies, particularly in areas that are difficult to treat with conventional medicine. Statistics show that the amount of money being spent on CIM by the public is increasing rapidly each year. And, with increased funding now available from the NIH, preliminary research is showing that certain CIM remedies are appropriate for treating a number of acute and chronic health conditions. In view of this, it is imperative that medical professionals familiarize themselves with these options. In addition, we should be aware that modalities we may consider to be "alternative" are mainstream and accepted practices elsewhere in the world.

Because anecdotal evidence outweighs proof from clinical trials in the area of CIM, it is not always easy to determine what works and what does not. This results in products and therapies of varying quality and effectiveness.

Above all, as health care professionals, we need to remove our blinders and consider the options, without jeopardizing our patient's health. With both public interest and scientific research in CIM on the rise, our profession is certain to experience a further increase in the use of CIM therapies. For the sake of both our patients and our profession, it is essential that health care practitioners remain current in this increasingly evolving field.

REFERENCES

1. Weil Lifestyle LLC. (2005). About Dr. Weil, Available at: http://www.drweil.com/u/Page/About/. Last accessed December 2005.
2. Surow JB, Lovetri J. Alternative medical therapy use among singers: prevalence and implications for the medical care of the singer. *J Voice.* 2000; 14(3):398–409.
3. Barnes P, Powell-Griner E, McFann K, et al. Complementary and alternative medicine use among adults: United States, 2002. *CDC Advance Data Report #343.* May 27, 2004.
4. Eisenberg DM, Davis RB, Ettner SL, et al.. Trends in alternative medicine use in the United States, 1990–1997: results of a follow-up national survey. *JAMA.* 1998;280:1569–1575.
5. Blumenthal M, Busse W, Goldberg A, et al. *The Complete German Commission Monographs: Therapeutic Guide to Herbal Medicine.* Austin, Tex: American Botanical Council; 1998.
6. Korant BD, Kauer JC, Butterworth BE. Zinc ions inhibit replication of rhinoviruses. *Nature.* 1974; 12:248(449):588–590.
7. Korant BD, Butterworth BE. Inhibition by zinc of rhinovirus protein cleavage: interaction of zinc with capsid polypeptides. *J Virol.* 1976;18(1):298–306.
8. Kelly RW, Able MH. Copper and zinc inhibit the metabolism of prostaglandin by the human uterus. *Biol Reprod.* 1983;28:883–889.
9. Novick SG, Godfrey JC, Godfrey NJ, et al. How does zinc modify the common cold? Clinical observations and implications regarding mechanisms of action. *Med Hypotheses.* 1996;46(3):295–302.
10. Mossad SB, Macknin ML, Medendorp SV, et al. Zinc gluconate lozenges for treating the common cold: a randomized, double-blind, placebo-controlled study. *Ann Intern Med.* 1996;15;125(2):81–88.
11. Jackson JL, Peterson C, Lesho E. A meta-analysis of zinc salts lozenges and the common cold. *Arch Intern Med.* 1997;10;157(20):2373–2376.
12. Jackson JL, Lesho E, Peterson C. Zinc and common cold: a meta-analysis revisited. *J Nutr.* 2000; 103(Suppl S5):1512S–1515S.
13. Hirt M, Nobel S, Barron E. Zinc nasal gel for the treatment of common cold symptoms: a double-blind placebo-controlled trial. *Ear Nose Throat J.* 2000;79(10):778–780, 782.
14. Reinhard KH. *Uncaria tomentosa* (Willd.) DC: cat's claw, una de gato, or saventaro. *J Altern Complement Med.* 1999;5(2):143–151.

15. Keplinger K, Laus G, Wurm M, et al. *Uncaria tomentosa* (Willd.) DC.—ethnomedicinal use and new pharmacological, toxicological and botanical results. *J Ethnopharmacol.* 1999;64(1):23–34.

16. Li Y, Chen GZ, Jiang DZ. Effect of *Cordyceps sinensis* on erythropoiesis in mouse bone marrow. *Chin Med J (Engl).* 1993;106(4):313–316.

17. Chu DT, Wong WL, Mavligit GM. Immunotherapy with Chinese medicinal herbs, II. Reversal of cyclophosphamide-induced immune suppression by administration of fractionated *Astragalus membranaceus* in vivo. *J Clin Lab Immunol.* 1988; 25(3):125–129.

18. Zhao KS, Mancini C, Doria G. Enhancement of the immune response in mice by *Astragalus membranaceus* extracts. *Immunopharmacology.* 1990; 20(3):225–233.

19. Seidman M. Nutrition and health: fact or fantasy? Paper presented at the Annual Meeting of the American Academy of Otolaryngology-Head and Neck Surgery; September 20, 2004; Los Angeles, Calif.

20. Robbins A. *Unlimited Power.* New York, NY: Simon and Schuster; 1986:chap 4.

21. Alvarez DJ, Rockwell PG. Trigger points: diagnosis and management. *Am Fam Physician.* 2002;65(4): 653–660.

22. Simons DG, Travell JG, Simons LS. *Myofascial Pain and Dysfunction: The Trigger Point Manual.* Vol I. 2nd ed. Baltimore, Md: Williams & Wilkins; 1999.

23. Zeitlin D, Keller SE, Shiflett SC, et al. Immunological effects of massage therapy during academic stress. *Psychosom Med.* 2000;62(1):83–84.

24. Birk TJ, McGrady A, MacArthur RD, et al. The effects of massage therapy alone and in combination with other complementary therapies on immune system measures and quality of life in human immunodeficiency virus. *J Altern Complem Med.* 2000;6(5):405–414.

25. Von Adrian UH. A massage for the journey: keeping leukocytes soft and silent. *Proc Natl Acad Sci USA.* 1997;13(94):4825–4827.

26. Hernandez-Reif M, Ironson G, Field T, et al. Breast cancer patients have improved immune and neuroendocrine function following massage therapy. *J Psychosom Res.* 2004, 57(1):45–52.

Chapter 11

VOICE THERAPY FOR BENIGN VOCAL FOLD LESIONS AND SCAR IN SINGERS AND ACTORS

Mara Behlau
Thomas Murry

The singer depends on precise voice production and on a specific vocal quality for his or her professional subsistence. What separates singers and actors from other voice professionals is the artistic demands of the performance. As described in chapter 1, the universe of professional voice users includes clerics, teachers, lawyers, salesmen, secretaries, telemarketing agents, and stockbrokers. Although these groups of people may use their voices more than singers and actors, they do not have the artistic demands of performers. The primary distinction between singers and other voice professionals is with the artistic nature of their voices.[1] In order to identify the needs of the professional singer and actor, it is important to understand the demands of vocal quality and artistic delivery.[2] Singers as well as other professional voice users may be compared to professional athletes, who are more likely to suffer muscular injuries than the general population due to their high physical demand.[3]

> Singers, like professional athletes, need specific and often intense rehabilitation in order to return to their top performance form.

It is important to understand the concept of preferred voice in the modern life, as proposed by Behlau.[4] This requires a different dimension of vocal analysis that encompasses options of respiratory, vocal, articulatory, psychodynamic, and behavioral parameters used both by the individual and by the group in which he or she fits. The professionals may or may not be aware of these options, which are usually acquired by modeling, imitation, and training, throughout the years of their professional practice. In addition to being acquired through modeling, a professional vocal pattern or style can also be specifically trained. People who do voiceovers and singers frequently admit that they started their careers imitating a successful professional until they found their own vocal output. Those vocal choices sometimes match the professional activity in ways that become the vocal markers of the profession itself. The use of a particular voice style often allows immediate identification of the profession, for example, the voice of priests, lawyers, and newscasters. Some of the vocal options are not necessarily healthy and may lead to a potential or real risk for vocal health. For example, preparing for an audition that requires new repertoire or that requires singing and dancing may lead to habits not often used.

Expansion of repertoire for a particular show or even a particular song may result in acquired patterns not consistent with previous training.

Injuries to the singer's voice are not unusual. Singing places demands on the vocal folds and the entire vocal system that are at times excessive. Singing styles often require specific voice qualities, which may be considered as a preferred voice for a particular role. Understanding the dynamics involved is crucial to determining whether or not the changes proposed to the performer and the training program required to achieve it will be acquired without injury.

Singers acquire benign lesions and scars of vocal folds for many reasons. The diagnostic and treatment considerations for the singer go beyond the habitual references of the voice clinic. Situations for the singer and actor are very diverse and extend from the desire of having an unusual voice of success. Rock singers may have edema and leukoplakia for special effects. If not careful, however, they risk the possibility of restricted professional activity due to a vocal fold scar. Pop singers or musical theatre performers are unable to sing in tune due to scarring after surgical excision. When the singer with a scar attempts to reach certain notes, further injury is likely to occur.

> There is a preferred voice for a particular singing style, as well as a preferred voice for each singer.

The choices are not always conscious choices. Many times the required voice is simply the singer's natural voice produced in a melodious and controlled way; at other times, the required voice is adapted to meet a performance requirement. The evaluation of the dysphonia may be difficult, as no voice-related quality of life and handicap instruments are sensitive enough to measure these aspects. Besides, many singers have the ability to develop muscular compensations that mask (at least partially) real difficulties. There is even a risk of not evaluating the original problem and focusing on the secondary compensation that sometimes draws more attention.[5]

A complete analysis of the vocal problem involves the identification of factors both predisposing and contributing to the dysphonia. Individual aspects, vocal technique problems, general health, and environmental issues must be addressed. Individual factors consist of anatomo-functional predisposition, personality traits, allergies,[6] and gastroesophageal reflux.[7] General health factors are related to the use of medications,[8] and self-medication is a particular concern. Environmental factors[2] include room acoustics, sound amplification, air quality, noxious fumes and chemicals,[9,10] or other aspects related to the work environment, including rehearsal schedules, tours, and interviews.

Information obtained by observing a performance or listening to a CD may reveal aspects that are not identified in the clinical setting. For example, the posture used during singing, acting, or performing with a stage band or a large orchestra may reveal strain or excessive effort not seen in the voice clinic.

The clinician must learn to recognize that different dynamics are required for different styles and types of singing. The evaluation and treatment for each different style of singing must be accurate, objective, and timely. Care of the singer's voice must include considerations about the next auditions, number of rehearsals, and types of performances. The voice clinician must be aware of various methods, techniques, exercises, and strategies depending on the singer's needs. Some singers have already been through previous therapies that did not work or with which they were not comfortable, and new approaches may provide better results. However, the sense of urgency should not compromise the clinical sensitiveness, welcoming care, and support that the dysphonic singer needs. Artists are human beings with great susceptibility and sensitivity about their work. They react deeply to comments and observations about their art.[11]

THE SINGER'S VOICE EVALUATION

The speech-language pathologist who works with singers and actors must have knowledge about medical speech-language pathology, skills to work with a team, and specific knowledge of the vocal arts. Some general knowledge about music and the lifestyle and activities of performers is also important. However skilled the general clinical speech-language pathologist may be for treating language problems, he or she may not have the primary prerequisites for the care of singers. A voice clinician is the professional that understands his or her own responsibilities as well as those of the laryngologist, recognizing the limits of both specialists and the possibilities of the contributions of each.

The comprehensive voice evaluation begins with a detailed history, including the type and quality of singing training and the use of other voice modalities, such as teaching and liturgical. When possible, a review of voice recordings made before the current problem may be useful, as singers sometimes assign substantial importance to their last event, not recognizing the existence of earlier voice changes. The clinician should highlight the conditions surrounding the individual's present search for help and the vocal history of the singer. The contribution of specific factors that triggered the voice problem must be clarified, and other factors that may be responsible for maintaining it or for changing it since its onset must be identified. A clear understanding of the onset factors allows the singer to replace the guilt feelings associated with the problems and helps reduce the emotional overload connected to the voice disorder. Precise complaints such as "I cannot reach the A4"; "after the fourth song I notice that I lose the metal of my voice"; I notice that I sometimes sing off tune, however the others say I'm doing fine"; "I don't feel the resonance on the palate" should be specifically considered. Otherwise the patient may not adhere to the suggested recommendations or he or she may look for another clinician who will listen to and understand the importance of the specific problem.

Although the primary symptoms are usually manifested in the singing voice, the speaking voice must also be evaluated. Singing and speaking are as different as swimming the backstroke versus the butterfly. Many singers are so concerned with singing that they forget that the speaking process utilizes the same organs, but with different muscular adjustments. Moreover, while singing is usually a result of training, speaking is the result of behavioral habits acquired during a lifetime combined with emotional factors related to one's personality in the speaking situation. The clinician should always remember that most singers and actors usually talk more than they sing and talk more off stage than when acting or rehearsing.

There is no agreement on the minimum battery of tests to evaluate singers; however, ideally it should include a perceptual voice analysis, a three-point modified voice range profile (VRP), an acoustic spectrographic analysis of speaking and singing, and observations of the vocal folds during speech and singing.

The perceptual analysis of the vocal quality should be performed with several phonatory tasks. An open sustained vowel, such as "a" like in "accent" or "e" like in "egg," should be used to evaluate the sound resource characteristics and connected speech. An evaluation of voice quality, tune matching, and register changes should also be included. Clinician rating scales may also be used, such as GRBAS[12] or CAPE-V[13] (see Appendix 11–1). However, neither scale fully addresses the singer's needs. The CAPE-V enables a more comprehensive description of voice quality as it relates to severity and to the number of deviated vocal parameters.

The Voice Range Profile (VRP) is commonly employed in Europe but rarely in other places, probably due to its difficulty and the amount of time it takes to complete. However the 3-dimensional VRP graph consisting of the mean, lowest, and highest fundamental frequency and minimum and maximum loudness helps to analyze the singer's vocal pliability.

The acoustic analysis by the extraction of measures of fundamental frequency, jitter, shimmer, and noise measures may not be reliable in some situations because of irregularity in the acoustic signal.[14] Nevertheless, the descriptive spectrographic analysis is greatly valued and serves as a powerful visual feedback for the singer.

The stroboscopic evaluation,[15] and particularly the phonoscopic analysis[16] is essential to the singer, not only to establish the diagnosis, but also to show small deviations that may have been overlooked by other less comprehensive evaluations. During the phonoscopic examination, the clinician obtains information about the laryngeal behavior during high and low pitch, soft and loud volume, whisper and sound, intermittent voice production, and so on.

Investigation of the impact of the singer's dysphonia on his or her professional activities can be done by means of a set of questions checking on rehearsal and show cancellations, contract breaks, reduction of singing activities, increase of warm-up time, and fatigue after a performance. The use of established instruments may help in this task.[17-22] No specific protocols to evaluate singers have been validated to do this; however, as one spends more time with singers and actors, a standard set of questions usually evolves.

To summarize the evaluation, it is interesting to note that there is generally no direct relationship between the size of the lesion and the vocal deviation or between what is perceptually observed and acoustically measured or between the visual analysis of the vocal folds and the vocal output. Most significantly, there is little or no relationship between the dysphonia impact evaluation and self-perceived severity.

THE SINGER'S VOCAL REHABILITATION PROGRAM

> Voice therapy is the primary management strategy for the treatment of benign laryngeal lesions in singers because of its conservative nature and because it potentially lowers the risk for future problems.

The ideal situation for most singers with a vocal injury is to take part in a voice therapy program that includes vocal education, psychodynamics and voice training with the help of a singing specialist.[23] There are major differences among singers, however, in voice training and vocal rehabilitation (see chapter 4). It is necessary to differentiate the vocal intervention with a short-term purpose, such as placing the voice on a CD track in 2 days or performing in a show the next day, from interventions with long-term purposes, such as helping a rock singer to find alternative muscular adjustments in order to have a less aggressive voice production. The behavioral model can be used for most singers' problems. The medical model may be used in certain cases. In this model, the patient plays a more passive role initially. He or she must be active in voice rehabilitation.[24] Some lesions can be reabsorbed and some voices can definitively improve even in the presence of a lesion. The plasticity of the voice can be checked to give a more precise evaluation on the benefit of vocal rehabilitation.[25]

Whenever possible, the vocal education, psychodynamic, and training tripod should be employed.[26] Vocal education and vocal hygiene guidelines must be viable and include alternative strategies to change maladaptive habits. The clinician must be realistic and understand that it is easier to execute a series of exercises than to comply with changes in habits or behavior. Psychodynamic therapy goes beyond analysis of the emotions. However, analysis of the emotional impact of the deviated singing voice to the public may help to define schedule, rehearsal, and shows issues.

Vocal training options are wide-ranging[27] and can either include more schematic and predefined treatment, such as vocal function exercises,[28] confidential voice therapy,[29] and the Lessac-Madsen resonance method[30,31] or adapted exercises.[26,32] However, due to the urgent characteristic of the management of these professionals, varied exercises are usually employed and are combined and modified according to the pathophysiology of the condition, the reported complaint, and the observed vocal deviation, which represents a combination of philosophic, physiologic, and symptomatologic education and counseling. An eclectic approach described by Behlau[26] consists of the seven categories for the treatment of dysphonia shown in Table 11–1.

Many singers succeed very well with an expedient treatment focused on their complaint and diagnostic findings. Others will have recurrent lesions that must be followed up for a long period of time. The majority do not accept a surgical procedure, although it may ultimately be the best treatment. Even then, the singer can benefit from voice rehabilitation.

Table 11–1. The Seven Categories of Treatment for Dysphonia

1. Body Method
2. Speech Organs Method
3. Auditory Method
4. Speech Method
5. Facilitating Sounds Method
6. Phonatory Competence Method
7. Voice Activation Method

BENIGN VOCAL FOLD LESIONS AND VOCAL FOLD SCARS IN CLASSICAL AND COMMERCIAL CONTEMPORARY MUSIC (CCM) SINGERS

The main benign vocal fold lesions seen in singers and actors are: nodules, cysts, polyps, Reinke's edema, and leukoplakia. In addition, a particular challenging condition is the vocal fold scar, which usually has an iatrogenic nature and can bring devastating consequences to the singer's life. Figure 11–1 shows a vocal fold scar in a 31-year-old female singer who developed a voice problem while rehearsing for a CD.

Diagnostic accuracy and a detailed evaluation of vocal behavior will allow specific treatment planning. However clear the relationship between a certain causal factor and the vocal deviation may be (for instance, gastroesophageal reflux and hoarse voice with limited singing range), a complete evaluation is indispensable, because the co-occurrence of several events is very common. More often, the voice disorder is not related to one factor, event, or time period. Voices that do not change with trial therapy have reduced possibilities for voice rehabilitation. Many therapeutic strategies may be utilized, such as changing the vocal quality by modifying the respiratory pattern, glottic closure, resonance, and articulation. Voice monitoring may also be employed, for example, visual monitoring using laryngeal or spectrographic instrumentation, auditory monitoring via auditory feedback, or vocal amplification and proprioceptive monitoring, such as identification of regions of tension or muscular biofeedback.

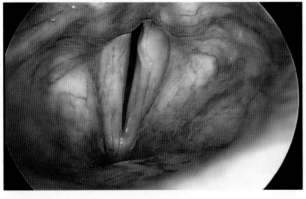

Figure 11–1. Vocal fold scar with sulcus on the left vocal fold of a CCM singer.

In this chapter, two categories of singers are described, classical and commercial contemporary.[33] This categorization may be simplistic and overlapping, but it facilitates understanding the major differences found between the two groups. Although there may be exceptions and singers may not fit in either category, for comparison we can generalize two different profiles.

Classical singers usually have a long history of singing classes, greater knowledge of vocal production, and systematic practice and training. They look for help early when having a voice problem as even minor deviations in the vocal quality can compromise a performance. They usually do not smoke or consume significant amounts of alcohol. They do not sing with amplification and rarely use sound technology resources except in the recording studio. Classical singers are initially more responsive to suggestions made than commercial contemporary singers as they are used to following vocal practice schedules and specific singing exercises.

In contrast, the commercial contemporary singers typically have a short history of singing lessons or no professional voice training. They may not appreciate the voice production mechanism as readily as a classical singer. In fact, some singers even believe that singing classes and vocal knowledge may hinder voice spontaneity. Whether this idea evolves from colleagues or is just due to their repertoire is uncertain, but untrained singers have a less systematic approach to vocal warm-up and rehearsal and generally take longer to look for help. This may be because small deviations in their vocal repertoire may not compromise performances but actually add to their appeal. For some singers, voice modification or stylistic changes are, at least in part, accepted in the singing styles of commercial contemporary singers. There is a greater likelihood that they smoke and drink alcohol, even during performances (one can recall classic videos of cabaret singers with a cigarette). They sing with a microphone and with sound technology that can minimize some vocal deviations. Contemporary singers tend to be less adherent to the suggestions made due to a more unstable schedule and irregular life habits. They often sing in more than a single style and they feel that experimentation with styles may actually increase their popularity.

A review of 30 singers classified according to their singing style, recently seen by both authors, is presented in Tables 11–2 and 11–3.

Table 11–2. Review of 15 Consecutive CCM Singers Presenting with Voice Complaints

Contemporary Singer	Style and Training	Complaint	Type of Lesion	Management	Outcome
1. Female, 36y-old Nonsmoker Allergy	Pop singer 4 years classical training	1½-year vocal complaint Local show	VF nodules Similar episode 6 years ago	Vocal rehabilitation High compliance	Dismissed Reabsorption of lesion and adapted voice
2. Male, 34y-old Smoker	Pop singer No singing training	2-year vocal complaint Local show	VF polyp	Vocal rehabilitation Noncompliant Refused surgery	Follow-up Lesion with better voice, but fatigue
3. Female, 32y-old Smoker	Gospel singer 2 years classical training	1-year vocal complaint Recording CD	Epidermoid cyst + mucosal bridge	Vocal rehabilitation Moderate compliance	Follow-up Lesion with better voice and less fatigue
4. Female, 28y-old Nonsmoker GE reflux	Gospel singer No singing training	1-month vocal complaint After a 4-day festival	Hemorrhagic polyp	Surgery and vocal rehabilitation pre and post-op	Dismissed No lesion and adapted voice
5. Female, 34y-old Nonsmoker	Latin music (salsa and mambo) singer + musical theatre Irregular 10 years classical training	Vocal complaint after 1 month intense rehearsals	VF nodules	Vocal rehabilitation High compliance	Dismissed Reabsorption of lesion and better voice
6. Male, 42y-old Smoking GE reflux	Brazilian pop music No singing training	1½-year vocal complaint Touring with show	Leukoplakia and edema	Vocal rehabilitation Surgery programmed High compliance	Follow up Lesion but better voice and less fatigue
7. Male, 43y-old Smoker	Brazilian country music No singing training	2-year vocal complaint Several similar episodes during past 15 years Touring with show	Epidermoid cyst	Refused surgery Vocal rehabilitation Low compliance	Follow up Lesion and some vocal improvement (did not cancel shows)
8. Male, 29y-old Smoker	Rap singer No singing training	1-year vocal complaint Touring with show	Leukoplakia and edema	Vocal rehabilitation Low compliance	Abandoned Lesion and vocal improvement

Contemporary Singer	Style and Training	Complaint	Type of Lesion	Management	Outcome
9. Male, 31y-old Smoker Reflux	Heavy rock singer Pop and rock training	6-month vocal complaint Preparing for recording CD	Edema	Vocal rehabilitation High compliance	Dismissed No lesion and adapted voice, no fatigue
10. Female, 39y-old Nonsmoker	Romantic singer No training	8-month vocal complaint Recording CD Previous episode 3 years ago	Epidermoid cyst	Vocal rehabilitation	Dismissed Lesion but adapted voice
11. Female, 16y-old Nonsmoker	Broadway shows 1 year training	3 months Can't produce high notes New teacher 4 months ago	Bilateral VF. lesions Vocal nodules	Voice therapy 6 visits New singing teacher Moderate compliance	Dismissed Nodules reduced but not completely Began show rehearsal
12. Male, 34 y-old Non Smoker Reflux	Broadway show and pop singer 8 years lessons B.A. Music	1½ years range reduced since recording in a studio	Right VF stiff Possibly old hemorrhage	4 sessions voice therapy surgery Epidermal cyst Voice therapy post-op High compliance	Full voice use 6 months later after voice therapy and singing lessons
13. Male, 28y-old Nonsmoker Reflux	Pop singer No training	1-year complaint Sings in rock band	Granuloma Edema	Reflux therapy Voice therapy Singing teacher	Dismissed Edema No granuloma Continue performing
14. Female, 24y-old Nonsmoker	Broadway show singer 6 years classical training	4-month complaint After singing sick	Vocal polyp Reactive lesion	Voice therapy Refused surgery High compliance	Polyp remains No reactive lesion Dismissed to new singing teacher
15. Female, 31 y-old Past history of smoking Moderately obese	Pop singer 8 years classical training M.A. Music Education	3-month complaint after making new CD	Bilateral VF nodules Reflux	Voice therapy Stop singing 6 weeks Moderate compliance	6 sessions—stopped Returned 4 months later 6 additional sessions Weight loss—mild edema

Table 11–3. A Review of 15 Consecutive Classical Singers Presenting with Voice Complaints

Classical Singer	Style and Training	Complaint	Type of Lesion	Management	Outcome
1. Female, 49y-old Nonsmoker	Dramatic soprano + Brazilian pop (crossover) 33 years classical training	1-week vocal complaint Wagner Festival	VVFF edema Previous episode of VF glandular cyst, removed by surgery 15 years ago	Vocal rehabilitation High compliance	Dismissed Reabsorption of lesion and adapted voice
2. Female, 34y-old Nonsmoker GE reflux + stomach polyp	Lyrical soprano + choral singing 16 years classical training	6-month vocal complaint During choral singing	VVFF edema	Vocal rehabilitation High compliance Stomach polyp removal	Dismissed Adapted voice
3. Female, 28y-old Nonsmoker	Lyrical soprano 3 years classical training	2-month vocal complaint Post-touring with concert	Edematous VVFF nodules	Vocal rehabilitation Moderate compliance	Dismissed Reduced lesion with adapted voice
4. Male, 42y-old Nonsmoker GE reflux	Baritone + choral director 13 years classical training	1-month vocal complaint Post-chorus festival	Edema + VVFF hemorrhage	Vocal rest and vocal rehabilitation	Dismissed No lesion and adapted voice
5. Male, 39y-old Smoker GE Reflux	Tenor + choral singing 11 years classical training	Vocal complaint after 2 months intense rehearsals	Leukoplakia	Vocal rehabilitation Moderate compliance	Follow up Reduced lesion and better voice
6. Female, 46y-old Nonsmoker GE reflux	Lyrical soprano + Brazilian pop (crossover) 20 years classical training	3-month vocal complaint During pop music CD recording	Epidermoid cyst	Vocal rehabilitation High compliance	Dismissed Lesion but better voice
7. Female, 37y-old Nonsmoker	Lyrical soprano 10 years classical training	4-month vocal complaint	VVFF nodules	Vocal rehabilitation High compliance	Dismissed Lesion reabsorbed
8. Male, 39y-old Nonsmoker GE reflux	Baritone 17 years classical training	2-week vocal complaint After concert abroad	VF polyp	Microsurgery + pre and post-op vocal rehabilitation High compliance	Dismissed Lesion removed and adapted voice

Classical Singer	Style and Training	Complaint	Type of Lesion	Management	Outcome
9. Female, 26y-old Nonsmoker	Soprano Chamber music 1 year classical training	2-year vocal complaint	VVFF nodules	Vocal rehabilitation High compliance	Dismissed No lesion and better voice
10. Female, 25y-old Nonsmoker	Lyrical soprano + choral singing + wedding singer 2 years classical training	6-month vocal complaint After tight agenda	VF nodules	Vocal rehabilitation Moderate compliance	Follow up Lesion but better voice
11. Female, 21y-old Nonsmoker	Lyrical soprano 4 years classical training	9-month complaint after change of teachers	VF polyp reactive lesion	Vocal hygiene Voice rest modified High compliance	Reduced edema Normal voice
12. Female, 31y-old Nonsmoker	Soprano 18 years classical training	3 months after extensive auditions	Bilateral edema	Vocal hygiene Voice rest modified High compliance	Reduced edema Normal voice
13. Male, 18y-old Nonsmoker	Tenor 3 years classical training	1-year complaint after school show	Unilateral lesion	Voice therapy Microsurgery	Dismissed No lesion Voice improved after 6 months
14. Female, 27y-old Nonsmoker	Coloratura soprano 11 years classical training	2 years narrowing range	No lesion Strained speaking voice	Voice therapy New singing teacher Moderate compliance	Dismissed to singing teacher after 6 sessions of voice therapy
15. Female, 37y-old Nonsmoker	Soprano—University faculty 19 years classical training	12 months weak upper range	Unilateral VF paresis LPR	Voice therapy	Reduced performance schedule Continue teaching

Vocal Nodules

Vocal nodules (see Figure 11–2) in classical singers are predominantly seen in females. They occur in young women 25 to 35 years of age. They are bilateral lesions and symmetric in position although they can be asymmetric in size. Perhaps, vocal nodules are the most common laryngeal lesions in young female singers, just as they are in nonsingers.[34] Vocal nodules occur in sopranos and sometimes represent only an adaptation of the system to high mechanical demands. In many cases, there is neither a vocal complaint nor apparent deviation of the speaking and singing voice. Others, however, complain of loss of pitch range or excess breath at low frequencies.

Vocal nodules associated with a vocal complaint may occur in female classical singers at the beginning of their careers or after singing demanding roles. Vocal nodules in those conditions are likely to be edematous and respond very well to voice treatment. The voice of the patient with vocal nodules is generally rough with varied degrees of breathiness, a probable frequency change to a lower pitch, and the loss of high notes in the vocal range. In these patients, a program of vocal conservation may be used to reach an immediate effect that is short lasting, with voice use limited to essential situations to speed up the lesion recovery.

Vocal nodules in commercial singers may occur at the beginning of their careers; however, they usually report a long history of dysphonia with fluctuating vocal quality. A particular event may represent the reason for medical consultation.

Vocal nodules in these patients can be either edematous or fibrotic with involvement of the laryngeal vestibule and tension in the extrinsic laryngeal musculature. Those lesions may not always respond positively to voice treatment. It may be more difficult to make these singers sensitive to a program of vocal conservation.

In addition to vocal instruction and conservative voice use, there are three main avenues of management: (1) confidential voice therapy, (2) resonance therapy, and (3) varied exercises of tongue, lips, and tongue-lip trills. The confidential voice therapy may be employed as an initial strategy of treatment when there is enough time to do so. Resonant voice therapy and/or varied vocal exercises may be added later. Environmental or schedule changes, if possible, should be immediately considered to maintain maximum vocal hygiene.

Vocal Fold Cysts

Vocal fold cysts are significantly different from vocal nodules in terms of diagnosis and treatment. Cysts may be either unilateral or bilateral. In case of bilateral cysts, the diagnosis is more difficult to establish. Vocal fold cysts occur in both sexes and all ages. They can be associated with edema, contralateral reaction (nodular lesions), and with other benign lesions such as polyps and leukoplakia. Cysts may be either epidermoid or glandular and the latter have easier outcome, with less chance of postoperative dysphonia. Singers with cysts may have profoundly deviated voices, depending on the location and the adherence of the cyst to the vocal ligament. The occurrence of cysts in popular singers seems to be more common than in classical singers. It may be that classical singers have a great need of a superior vocal quality and therefore seek help sooner. The nonclassical singer, on the other hand, often tolerates minor deviations in voice quality allowing structural changes to develop.

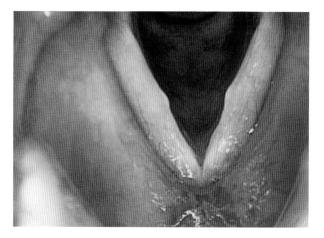

Figure 11–2. Vocal nodules seen in a young female singer.

> The treatment for vocal fold cysts is voice therapy prior to and after surgery.

Exophytic cysts surrounded by flexible mucosa are lesions of relatively easy surgical management. Vocal fold cysts that are subepithelial are more difficult to treat surgically and behaviorally. They can potentially produce scars, causing significant dysphonia that is difficult to reduce with any kind of treatment. The singer's voice with a cyst can vary, but roughness and tension are the most common elements.

Vocal rehabilitation should be directed to the reduction of secondary lesions and to the search for a vocal balance as cysts do not reduce with exercises. Facilitating sounds and varied exercises that make the mucosal wave more flexible (such as tongue and lip trill with scales, nasal sounds, and voiced fricatives) have a positive response. Laryngeal manipulation exercises to reduce tension in the neck, throat, larynx, and shoulders are often suggested. Surgery must be carefully planned[25,35-37] and vocal rehabilitation after surgery is mandatory to optimize results.[38,39]

Vocal Fold Polyps

Vocal polyps are generally unilateral lesions (10% of bilateral presentation), and are more characteristic of the male sex, occurring at any age. A change in voice quality is evident, with roughness and fundamental frequency bifurcation. Singers may note a loss of high frequency especially at pianissimo. Polyps may be associated with a history of recent dysphonia, intense phonotrauma, nonhabitual violent physical activity such as an extensive recording session, cheering at a football game,[40] gastroesophageal reflux conditions,[7,41] and use of the voice in noisy environments.[42]

The occurrence of polyps in classical singers is lower than in CCM singers. Popular singers, particularly in the most vocally aggressive styles such as heavy rock and gospel music singers, may reflect a tissue response to excessive glottic compression. The presence of a polyp may help the singer to compose his or her image up to the moment that vocal fatigue, limitation of vocal range, and loss of tune control take the singer to the voice clinic. Although the indicated approach is usually surgical removal, there are anecdotal reports of progress with voice therapy. Voice rehabilitation may reduce the size and shape of the polyp resulting in an acceptable voice for a pop singer.

Rehabilitation options include tongue and lip trill associated to musical scales to improve vocal fold flexibility and to provide a better distribution of the impact during voice production. Control of vocal attack and a better use of resonance may also be tried, especially in the speaking voice. Digital manipulation of the larynx and postural change exercises (with movements of head and neck) may offer tension relief. It should be pointed out that changes that modify or diminish the vocal image may be rejected by the singer.

Reinke's Edema

Reinke's edema is a superficial and diffuse tissue change, which can be either unilateral or bilateral and symmetric or not. It generally occurs in singers over 45 years of age and it is strongly related to smoking,[43] gastroesophageal reflux,[41] and hormonal problems in women.[44] The occurrence in classical singers is rare due to good vocal hygiene, no smoking, and good vocal education. The voice is typically low and may interfere in the identification of sex; the history is quite long and the vocal change is usually reported to be slowly progressive over a long period of time.

Reinke's edema is common in commercial singers, such as in night club, jazz, R&B, and soul music singers. The low voice may be considered a positive differential feature for the singer, who is also going to reject any treatment that compromises his or her vocal signature. Nevertheless, signs and symptoms of fatigue and lack of pitch and loudness control may make the singer look for assistance. It is interesting to note that, even after surgical removal of the lesion, there is a partial return of the edema about 2 to 3 months later[45] and, thus, the voice remains low (but not as low as before treatment), with easier vocal production. Patients must be properly instructed, and if the indication of treatment is surgery, voice education and preoperatory intervention should be carried out to optimize the results after surgery.[46] The options of voice therapy include tongue and lips trills, stretching and shortening of vocal folds exercises, vocal tract semioccluded exercises, and massage on the neck region when the extrinsic musculature is involved. For the postoperative phase of treatment, trills and musical scales will offer the recovery of the high regions of the voice range.

Leukoplakia

Leukoplakia is a condition in which white lesions are seen on one or both vocal folds. The organic causes include smoking, alcohol consumption, gastroesophageal reflux, and genetic predisposition. Leukoplakia is more frequently found in males and less likely to occur in women. When the leukoplakia is diffuse with ample and shallow lesions and nondefinite border on both vocal folds, it may represent an irritation response due to phonotrauma or gastroesophageal reflux[47]; in those cases, vocal rehabilitation should be tried instead of surgery. Classical singers may present with leukoplakia that is often associated with gastroesophageal reflux[41] or caused by genetic predisposition. On the other hand, for most people and popular singers, the lesion is probably due to the influence of smoking,[48] alcohol, and vocal behavior.[49] The voice is rough with fluctuating deviation and greater severity due to the lesion rigidity. Moreover, strained vocal quality is frequently present. Singers with leukoplakia may suffer great disarray in their vocal image and usually look for immediate assistance. However, when leukoplakia is associated with Reinke's edema, it may compose and characterize the singer's voice.

> Of all benign laryngeal lesions, leukoplakia is the one that deserves greater attention as far as the risk to develop a cancer is concerned.

Concerns about health should come before any consideration of vocal style and preference. Thus, surgical biopsy is usually the first choice, especially in patients who smoke. Vocal rehabilitation following surgery may be required. Redistribution of the phonatory impact along the vocal folds with exercises helps to reduce glottal attack and increase respiratory-phonatory control.

Vocal Fold Scar

Vocal fold scars usually have an iatrogenic nature,[50] due to either an undesirable consequence of benign lesion removal or traumas during intubation or extubation of other surgery. They may also be a result of recurrent laryngitis or a residual consequence of an acute vocal trauma. Scars represent buildup of rigid tissue, whose consequences may be career-threatening to a singer. The vocal quality may be polyphonic, with breathiness, strain, fundamental frequency bifurcation, frequency breaks, voice breaks, and evident phonatory effort. There may be vocal compensatory mechanisms that include ventricular phonation, compensatory nasal resonance, lifted rib cage, and increased subglottic pressure. There is no ideal treatment. Medication, surgical modification, or voice rehabilitation are usually attempted. Some case reports suggest good long-term results with voice rehabilitation. The treatment regimen differs from that employed for benign lesions. The management of vocal fold scars may last longer than 1 year, with periodic vocal and laryngological follow-up. Improvement may be gradual, which demands careful documentation in order to observe the small changes that occur over time. Use of the Voice Handicap Index may be the best guide to changes that occur.

The rationale for voice rehabilitation for vocal fold scars can be summarized as follows:

1. Initially, there should be an attempt to separate what is compensatory or secondary to the scar from the original deviation itself. To do that, supraglottic and vocal tract adjustments should be addressed, reducing excessive extrinsic muscular activity that may include high larynx, mandibular stiffness, tongue displacement, and body posture deviation.
2. Voice assessment should evaluate whether the main complaint is related to the vocal quality deviation, fatigue, or lack of constant and acceptable phonation.
3. If the problem resides in voice quality changes, all possible mechanisms that lead to the voice previously obtained should be tried. If changes in the source are not possible, the manipulation of the tract (resonance) is indicated as an attempt to get closer to a desired vocal quality.
4. If the vocal endurance is the main problem, glottic closure must be re-evaluated endoscopically. An extensive closed phase is often responsible for vocal fatigue. Treatment to reduce vocal fatigue can be done with vocal function exercises[28] chant talk, vocal tract semioccluded exercises such as glottal stability—hand over mouth or finger-kazoo, and maximum phonation time exercises with vocal quality control.

5. If glottic phonation/sonority is acceptable, a widening of the dynamic vocal range should be pursued using variation of pitch and loudness exercises and maximum phonation time exercises using voice quality control.

6. If there is not enough glottic tone in the voice, treatment with phonation triggering should be specifically carried out by means of short phonatory bursts. To achieve enough sonority, the selected exercises must be intensely repeated. Initially, the volume of the voice may be increased slightly to help phonation during the first few days. Some of the indicated exercises are the sequential repetition of a nasal sound (eg, "m-m-m-m" or "n-n-n-n-n") or

a voiced fricative (eg, "z-z-z-z"). These sounds must be short, produced in a series, on an average of 6 to 8 times a day. As soon as sonority/phonation is produced for at least 50% of the voice production, the individual must go back to his or her habitual loudness. When sonority/phonation is constant, a widening of the dynamic vocal range should proceed.

Although the vocal rehabilitation of vocal fold scars has not been submitted to controlled clinical research yet, there are reports in the literature that the intervention may last up to a year.[26, 37]

An example of voice quality change with vocal rehabilitation is shown in Figure 11–3A and 11–3B.

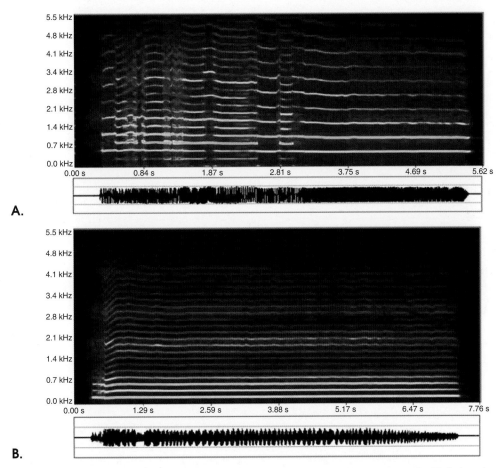

Figure 11–3. Postsurgical scar in a 46-year-old female teacher after removal of bilateral vocal fold cysts. **A.** Before vocal rehabilitation: Spectrographic analysis (narrow band filter, 45 Hz) of the sustained vowel æ, as in apple. Notice effort to initiate phonation, instability of vocal quality, and fundamental frequency bifurcation on the trace (presence of subharmonic), high fundamental frequency (from 255 Hz to 276 Hz), and reduced maximum phonation time (4.83). **B.** After vocal rehabilitation: Spectrographic analysis (narrow band filter, 45 Hz) of the sustained vowel æ, as in apple, after 4 months of intensive vocal rehabilitation. Notice instability at glottal attack but a better stability of trace, a lower fundamental frequency (212 Hz), and a larger maximum phonation time (7.04).

Following use of exercises such as nasal prolongations and fricative buzz using the /z/ onset of phonation and maintenance of stability can be seen. Both voice quality and duration of phonation improved in this patient.

SUMMARY

Vocal rehabilitation is the most important treatment modality for benign lesions of the vocal folds in singers. Although surgery is indicated in some cases, voice therapy which begins as trial therapy may be the primary rehabilitation program for many singers. Awareness of the preferred voice for the musical style and the desired voice for the singer is essential for the proper management of performers. A clear and projected vocal quality is not necessarily desired by heavy rock and gospel singers. The voice clinician should consider the singer's preferred style and respect personal options, when vocal health and career longevity are not compromised.[51] The voice specialist clinician combines his or her medical knowledge with an understanding of the artistic realm of the singer.

REFERENCES

1. Fussi F, Magnani S. *L'arte vocal. Fisiopatologia ed educazione della voce artistica*. Itália: Omega; 1994.
2. Vilkman E. Voice problems at work: a challenge for occupational safety and health arrangement. *Folia Phoniatr Logop*. 2000;52:120–125.
3. Stemple J. Management of the professional voice. In: Stemple J., ed. *Voice Therapy. Clinical Studies*. St. Louis, Mo: Mosby; 1993:155–171.
4. Behlau M. Vozes preferidas: considerações sobre opções vocais nas profissões. *Fono Atual*. 2001;4:10–14.
5. Hsiung MW, Hsiao YC. The characteristic features of muscle tension dysphonia before and after surgery in benign lesions of the vocal fold. *ORL J Otorhinolaryngol Relat Spec*. 2004;66:246–254.
6. Cohn JR, Spiegel JR, Hawkshaw M, Sataloff RT. Allergy. In: Sataloff RT. *Professional Voice: The Science and Art of Clinical Care*. 2nd ed. San Diego, Calif: Singular Publishing Group; 1997:369–374.
7. Sataloff RT, Castell DO, Sataloff DM, Spiegel JS, Hawkshaw M. Reflux and other gastroenterologic conditions that may affect the voice. In: Sataloff RT. *Professional Voice: The Science and Art of Clinical Care*. 2nd ed. San Diego, Calif: Singular Publishing Group; 1997:319–329.
8. Spiegel JR, Hawkshaw M, Sataloff RT. Dysphonia related to medical therapy. *Otolaryngol Clin North Am*. 2000; 33:771–784.
9. Herman Jr, Rossol M. Artificial fogs and smokes. In: Sataloff RT. *Professional Voice: The Science and Art of Clinical Care*. 2nd ed. San Diego, Calif: Singular Publishing Group; 1997:413–427.
10. Williams NR. Occupational voice disorders due to workplace exposure to irritants—a review of the literature. *Occup Med (Lond)*. 2002;52:99–101.
11. Sapir S, Mathers-Schmidt B, Larson GW. Singers' and non-singers' vocal health, vocal behaviors, and attitudes towards voice and singing: indirect findings from a questionnaire. *Eur J Disord Commun*. 1996;31:193–209.
12. Hirano, M. *Clinical Examination of Voice*. New York, NY: Springer-Verlag; 1981:81–84.
13. American Speech-Language Hearing Association. (ASHA). 2003. *Consensus Auditory-Perceptual Evaluation of Voice (CAPE-V)*. 2003 document text available from: http://www.asha.org.
14. Titze I. Workshop on acoustic voice analysis. Iowa City, Ia: National Center for Voice and Speech; 1995.
15. Elias ME, Sataloff RT, Rosen DC, Heuer RJ, Spiegel JR. Normal strobovideolaryngoscopy: variability in healthy singers. *J Voice*. 1997;11:104–107.
16. Leonard R, Kendall K. Phonoscopy. a valuable tool for otolaryngologists and speech-language pathologists. *Laryngoscope*. 2001;111:1760–1766.
17. Sataloff RT. Voice and speech impairment and disability. In: Sataloff RT. *Professional Voice. The Science and Art of Clinical Care*. 2nd ed. San Diego, Calif: Singular Publishing Group; 1997:795–800.
18. Jacobson BH, Johnson A, Grywalski C, Silbergleit A, Jacobson G, Benninger M, Newman CW. The voice handicap index (VHI): development and validation. *Am J Speech Lang Pathol*. 1997;6:66–70.
19. Hogikyan ND, Sethuraman G. Validation of an instrument to measure voice-related quality of life (V-RQOL). *J Voice*. 1999;13:557–569.
20. Benninger M, Sataloff RT. The evaluation of outcomes and quality of life in individuals with voice disorders. *J Singing*. 1999;56:34–43.
21. Murry T, Rosen, C. Voice handicap index in singers. *J Voice*. 2000;14:370–377.

22. Ma EP-M, Yiu EM-L. Voice activity and participation profile: assessing the impact of voice disorders on daily activities. *J Speech Lang Hear Res.* 2001;44: 511-524.

23. Emerich K, Baroody M, Carrol L, Sataloff R. The singing voice specialist. In: Sataloff RT. *Professional Voice: The Science and Art of Clinical Care.* 2nd ed. San Diego, Calif: Singular Publishing Group; 1997:735-754.

24. Stone Jr RE. The speech-language pathologist's role in the management of the professional voice. In: Benninger MS, Jacobson BH, Johnson AF, eds. *Vocal Arts Medicine: The Care and Prevention of Professional Voice Disorders.* New York, NY: Thieme; 1994:291-317.

25. Dejonckere PH, Lebacq J. Plasticity of voice quality: a prognostic factor for outcome of voice therapy? *J Voice.* 2001;15:251-256.

26. Behlau M, Madazio G, Feijo D, Azevedo R, Gielow I, Rehder MI. Aperfeiçoamento vocal e tratamento fonoaudiológico das disfonias. In: Behlau M, ed. *Voz. O livro do especialista.* vol 2. Rio de Janeiro, Brazil: Revinter; 2005:409-564.

27. National Center for Voice and Speech. *A Vocologist's Guide: Voice Therapy & Training.* Iowa City, Ia: Author; 1994.

28. Stemple J, Lee L, D'Amico B, Pickup B. Efficacy of vocal function exercises in the practice regiment of singers. *J Voice.* 1994;3:271-278.

29. Colton R, Casper J. *Understanding Voice Problems: A Physiological Perspective for Diagnosis and Treatment.* Baltimore, Md: Williams & Wilkins; 1990.

30. Lessac A. *The Use and Training of the Human Voice: A Biodynamic Approach to Vocal Life.* Mountain View, Calif: Mayfield; 1997.

31. Verdolini K, Druker DG, Palmer PM, Samawi H. Laryngeal adduction in resonant voice. *J Voice.* 1998;12:315-327.

32. Casper J, Murry T. Voice therapy methods in dysphonia. *Otol Clin North Am.* 2000;33:983-1002.

33. Lovertri JL, Weekly EM. Contemporary commercial music (CCM) survey: who's teaching what in non-classic music. *J Voice.* 2003;17:207-215.

34. Herrington-Hall BL, Lee L, Stemple J, Nieme KR, McHone MM. Description of laryngeal pathologies by age, sex and occupation in a treatment-seeking sample. *J Speech Hear Disord.* 1998;53:57-64.

35. Bastian RW. Vocal fold microsurgery in singers. *J Voice.* 1996;10:389-404.

36. Sataloff RT. *Professional Voice. The Science and Art of Clinical Care.* 2nd ed. San Diego, Calif: Singular Publishing Group; 1997.

37. Zeitels SM, Hillman RE, Desloge R, Mauri M, Doyle PB. Phonomicrosurgery in singers and performing artists: treatment outcomes, management theories and future directions. *Ann Otol Rhinol Laryngol Suppl.* 2002;190:21-40.

38. Casper J, Behlau M. Vocal rehabilitation before and following phonosurgery. In: *Proceedings of 25th World Congress of the International Association for Logopedics and Phoniatrics.* Montreal, Canada: IALP; 2001:361.

39. Murry T. Pre- and postoperative phonotherapy. *J Singing.* 2001; 57:39-42.

40. Roch JB, Cornut G, Bouchayer M. Mode d'apparition des polypes des cordes vocales. *Rev Laryngol Otol Rhinol (Bordeaux).* 1989;110:389-390.

41. Koufmann J. Gastroesophageal reflux and voice disorders. In: Rubin JS, Sataloff RT, Korovin G, Gould WJ. *Diagnosis and Treatment of Voice Disorders.* New York,NY: Igaku-Shoin; 1995:161-175.

42. Rontal E, Rontal M, Jacob HJ, Rolnick MI. Vocal cord dysfunction—an industrial health hazard. *Ann Otol Rhinol Laryngol.* 1979;88:818-821.

43. Matsuo K, Kamimura M, Hirano M. Polypoid vocal folds: a ten year review of 191 patients. *Auris Nasus Larynx.* 1983;10(suppl):37-45.

44. Abitbol J, Abitbol B, Abitbol P. Sex hormones and the female voice. *J Voice.* 1999;13:424-446.

45. Bouchayer M, Cornut, G. *Phonosurgery for Benign Vocal Fold Lesions* [videotextbook]. Gibraltar: The 3 Ears; 1994.

46. Koufman J, Blalock PD. Is voice rest never indicated? *J Voice.* 1989;3:87-91.

47. Gadelha ME, Pontes P, Guidugli J, Gregorio LC. Morphological aspects of vocal fold leukoplakias. Correlation with histopathological classification. In: Isshiki N, ed. *Proceedings 3rd International Symposium of Phonosurgery.* Kyoto, Japan: International Association of Phonosurgeons; 1994.

48. Gillis YM, Incze J, Strong MS, Vaughan CW, Simpson GT. Natural history and management of keratosis, atypia, carcinoma in situ, and microinvasive cancer of the larynx. *Am J Surg.* 1983;146: 512-516.

49. Perrin C, Long FX, Mariel P, Barthelme A, Prokopik JD. Leucoplasies et dysplasies des cordes vocales. *J Français d'Oto-rhino-laryngol (Audiophonl Chir).* 1983;32:487-491.

50. Rosen, D. Vocal fold scar: evaluation and treatment. *Otolaryngol Clin North Am.* 2000;33:1081-1086.

51. Miller R. Voice skill and vocal longevity. *J Singing.* 1998; 54:35-37.

Consensus Auditory-Perceptual Evaluation of Voice (CAPE-V)[13]

Name: _____   **Date:**_____

The following parameters of voice quality will be rated upon completion of the following tasks:
1. Sustained vowels, /a/ and /i/ for 3-5 seconds duration each.
2. Sentence production:
   a. The blue spot is on the key again.   d. We eat eggs every Easter.
   b. How hard did he hit him?   e. My mama makes lemon muffins.
   c. We were away a year ago.   f. Peter will keep at the peak.
3. Spontaneous speech in response to: "Tell me about your voice problem." or "Tell me how your voice is functioning."

```
┌─────────────────────────────────────────────────┐
│ Legend:  C = Consistent   I = Intermittent        │
│          MI = Mildly Deviant                      │
│          MO =Moderately Deviant                   │
│          SE = Severely Deviant                    │
└─────────────────────────────────────────────────┘
```

SCORE

Overall Severity _____   C   I   ____/100
                    MI   MO   SE

Roughness _____   C   I   ____/100
                    MI   MO   SE

Breathiness _____   C   I   ____/100
                    MI   MO   SE

Strain _____   C   I   ____/100
                    MI   MO   SE

Pitch   (Indicate the nature of the abnormality): _____
               _____   C   I   ____/100
                    MI   MO   SE

Loudness   (Indicate the nature of the abnormality): _____
               _____   C   I   ____/100
                    MI   MO   SE

_____   _____   C   I   ____/100
                    MI   MO   SE

_____   _____   C   I   ____/100
                    MI   MO   SE

COMMENTS ABOUT RESONANCE: NORMAL   OTHER (Provide description):_____

_____

ADDITIONAL FEATURES (for example, diplophonia, fry, falsetto, asthenia, aphonia, pitch instability, tremor, wet/gurgly, or other relevant terms):

Clinician:_____

Chapter 12

STRATEGIES FOR DEALING WITH VOCAL TENSION

Janet Madelle Feindel

As a young acting student, studying at the Royal Academy of Dramatic Art, in London, England, I was fortunate enough to witness two performances by an actor named Michael Pennington at the Royal Shakespeare Company. He played the role of Berowne in Shakespeare's *Love's Labours Lost* and the Duke in *Measure for Measure*. In the first instance, I was seated in the uppermost balcony and in the other, the middle orchestra. In each case, I experienced this actor's voice as if he were sitting next to me, speaking in my ear in spite of the fact the theater seated over a thousand people. His voice effortlessly revealed the nuances of the character. In May 2003, I attended the New York City Broadway production of Eugene O'Neill's *Long Day's Journey Into Night* at the Plymouth Theater. Vanessa Redgrave played Mary Tyrone. Ms. Redgrave's voice emitted from her whole being and exposed the character's innermost thoughts and emotions. She connected the thought with the breath and her intention in her portrayal in a seemingly effortless and translucent manner; in the same way a dancer makes the *jeté* look easy. This ease of speaking takes huge talent and years of practice.

HEALTHY, EXPRESSIVE, AND EFFECTIVE VOICE USAGE

An important premise frequently overlooked by actors and directors is that healthy voice usage is expressive voice usage. People often mistake phony emotion, or what Patsy Rodenburg refers to as "bluff acting," for a genuine relationship to the text.

The voice mechanism should be free enough to reflect the needs of the character. The actor's psychophysical awareness should be such that the actor's voice and body respond to the thought with spontaneous changes in the pitch, rhythm, dynamic, and tonal variety, rather than following a prescribed approach. Tension impedes this possibility, creating a multitude of vocal tension issues.

As part of the curriculum at Carnegie Mellon's School of Drama, students learn to identify healthy, effective, and expressive voice usage and unhealthy, ineffective, and inexpressive voice usage. This is done through discussion and examples of film and stage acting. To identify healthy voice usage, all the following characteristics should be evident:

- Physical ease.
- Clear unobstructed tone.
- Resonant sound; that is, the sense that the actor fully embodies the voice and one has the sense as stated earlier that the voice emits from the whole body, not just the mouth.
- A sense of release as the person expresses heightened emotions rather than a sense of constriction and pulling down in the body.
- A precise relationship with the thoughts and intentions that the actor wishes to communicate, resulting in clear crisp articulation that does not sound affected but yet is vigorous. The actor uses the language to fully carve out the ideas to impact another human being.
- The person is "in his or her back," which means the person is supporting the voice with the use of the back part of the rib case and, hence, utilizing the full capacity of the diaphragm as opposed to squeezing and "pulling down" on the release of breath and thought.

The rib swing is a useful way for performers to think about the breath support. Too often the actor squeezes from the diaphragm, pushing the ribs together, which actually causes constriction in the shoulder, neck, jaw, and larynx areas, hence weakening support rather than aiding it. This habit also tends to produce a forced sound rather than a free sound, because the actor is attempting to find power through pushing rather than release. It is also important to remember that the diaphragm is not a pouch below the sternum but extends across the whole torso, like a flexible parachutelike drum.

To identify unhealthy voice usage, some or all of these characteristics will be evident:

- Tension around the neck, face, and shoulder muscles.
- Poor alignment; that is, the neck pushing out or the chin pulling too far to the chest.

- Unbalanced breath support, which is either a too breathy and "off voice" vocal quality or not enough breath support for the effort of the sound, causing a hoarse, forced, and/or crackling sound.
- A tendency to pull down and tighten when speaking, pushing the words and ideas out, with extra tension at the ends of lines "squeezing the meaning out" rather than letting them release effortlessly.
- At times, an overemphasis on articulation rules, with the actor "playing the voice" rather than playing the scene, thereby obscuring the meaning rather than integrating clear articulation to communicate ideas with clarity.

TRAINING

The physical aspects of voice training follow a progression much like the training of an athlete, with exercises to develop vocal flexibility, stamina, and strength similar to exercises used in singing training. Voice training also involves aspects of movement and alignment or postural awareness (such as the Alexander technique), because muscular tension constricts sound vibration and full expression in the actor.[1]

> As a trainer of the speaking voice for actors, I strive to teach students to achieve the same vocal freedom and expression Michael Pennington and Vanessa Redgrave demonstrated.

Voice training differs from the training of the athlete, however, in an important aspect. The actor needs to coordinate the physical aspects of the training with the impulse of the thought, the imagination, the intention of the character as written, and the need to communicate to affect another on stage. All the aspects of speaking voice training must therefore be connected to the speaking of text, as the actor needs to incorporate the principles of voice into his acting, finding the "ladder of the thought."[2]

This delicate interplay of goals challenges voice/speech trainer and student alike: making these connections becomes a unique process in many respects. The vocal mechanism involves all facets of the individual: psychological, physiologic, spiritual, as well as anatomic. The study of the speaking voice becomes intensely personal in many respects, even more than other aspects of actor training such as movement and facial expressions. The teacher provides a map but the actor takes the internal journey. The physical voice in its ease, dynamic, and flexibility reflects the inner workings of the individual, what Cicely Berry refers to as "That Secret Voice."[3] This personal aspect of voice makes it important to create a positive, supportive atmosphere while still maintaining a sense of purpose and discipline in both teaching and coaching situations. Training of the voice may, therefore, incorporate personal writing and therapeutic techniques as tools to open up the full range of the actor's vocal experience both in the practical and in the metaphorical sense. Addressing vocal tension requires a solid understanding of vocal mechanics and sensitivity to acting concerns as well as the emotional make-up of the actor.

CHANGING HABITS: ALIGNMENT AND THE ALEXANDER TECHNIQUE

Voice development involves changing habits. Tensions in the voice often stem from habits established in early life so that the elimination of such tensions is not something that happens overnight. Often students have breakthroughs and can deliver a whole speech with considerable freedom, but the real challenge is the ability to sustain that freedom over the course of a month of performances. However, habits persist and the unconscious resists change. Often, when change in the voice occurs the habit seems to rear its head even more stubbornly than before. So the old adage "three steps forward, two steps behind" definitely applies to the learning curve in voice training. It takes hours of practice and acceptance of the emotional self to allow full vocal freedom precisely because the voice reflects our emotional landscape. This is where the application of the principles of the Alexander technique proves useful because the principles address habitual response.

Alignment refers to the way an actor stands and moves, allowing for maximum ease and appropriate breath support. On a deeper level, alignment refers to the delicate interplay of the actor's thought, breath, and movement impulses. The actor needs to move with ease, finding the most flexibility without excess tension. If an actor plays Richard III, requiring uneven carriage, he or she must still find an inner kinesthetic freedom within the posture that allows the actor the vocal relaxation necessary to deliver heightened text for 3 hours. If the actor does not achieve this balance, the posture itself can create the potential for vocal tension and possible vocal damage. The incorporation of proper alignment, as part of training the voice, provides a challenging task for the actor.

The Alexander technique deals specifically with the alignment principles developed by Frederick Mathias Alexander, born in Australia in 1869. He specialized in "recitations" of Shakespeare. When he began performing, he continually lost his voice. When he was unable to find a medical remedy, he studied his movement patterns in front of a mirror for a decade. Alexander analyzed the "habits" that were causing the vocal misuse. He noticed the following as he began to recite:

1. He tightened his neck muscles;
2. This caused his chin to lower;
3. This resulted in his larynx tightening and pulling down; and
4. His breath support became shallow.

He discovered that he was not able to stop these habits at will. What he was able to do, however, was prevent pulling back his head, which resulted in the disappearance of the other two habits. As he began to master this new approach, his hoarseness discontinued.

He began to understand that patterns of use were not just physical but involved mental conceptions as well. He coined the idea of "inhibition" from these observations. Before he started a habitual movement, he stopped and "inhibited" the tense habit before it began. He then gave himself new thought directions related to the movement: let the neck be free, to allow the head to go forward and up, and to allow the back to lengthen and widen. He named these the "means whereby."[4]

Voice training involves changing habits. The Alexander technique helps enormously to effect that change. Most respected acting schools include the Alexander technique in the core curriculum. Sessions are individual and/or group classes. The student is taken through a series of "procedures" exploring "positions of maximum mechanical advantage." These involve getting in and out of a chair, using the movement as a way to discover and apply the principle of inhibition. Teachers of the Alexander technique also teach "constructive rest" done on the floor or on a massage table. (See the end of the chapter for a description of constructive rest and other resource material on the Alexander technique.) The student can often make more sense of the principles in a lying down position then apply these principles in standing activity. The teacher guides with gentle touch, directing the student to become more aware of her or his habitual tensions and how "inhibiting" (or "stopping to observe") the habitual response can help the student bypass these tensions. The important component here involves the fact that the teacher must also utilize and incorporate the principles of the directions in order that the teacher's touch can guide the student.

Voice and speech trainers have the ability to diagnose what is not working effectively. It is much more challenging to actually give the student constructive ways to improve his or her voice. One of the challenges of voice work involves guiding the student to consciousness about one's habits while eschewing self-consciousness, which is the enemy of all good acting. Voice training involves awareness of habits and looking for ways to release tension to allow the organic freedom of the voice to emerge. To achieve this, effective voice training takes about 3 to 4 years to build a foundation and as much as 10 years to master. Any good actor, worth his or her salt, will continue voice work throughout his or her career.

THE PSYCHOPHYSICAL CONNECTION: VOICE IS MORE THAN JUST A SOUND

The overall psychology of the individual is extremely important in tackling any vocal tension issue, as voice tension is generally a symptom of the individual's tension. If at all possible, it is generally more effective to address any issue by guiding the actor to a deeper understanding and kinesthetic relationship to language. Once this is addressed at least to some extent, dealing with more specific manifestations of tension, such as soft palate tightness, jaw tightness, tension in the shoulder and neck muscles, poor articulation, and so forth, will prove easier. That said, every individual is different and one needs not only good diagnostic skills but also many approaches at one's fingertips as well as flexibility. Each person responds differently and even the same person responds differently at different times. The process involves exploration, and the journey is not necessarily logical. This is why the interdisciplinary approach to dealing with vocal issues proves so effective. Sometimes one must start where one observes the problem and then attempt, with the collaboration of the actor, to unravel what the source of the issue is. When a massage therapist finds a tension spot, sometimes it is harmful to massage that spot immediately. It is more effective to tend to the muscles around the knotted muscle first. The same is true in voice work. Sometimes tackling the issue head-on only causes self-consciousness in the actor and compounds the problem. It can prove useful to take a different tack all together and then this can lead to an indirect solution to the immediate problem.

Some tension issues may only involve a minor technical adjustment or change of perception. For example, the actor's first response to moving into a bigger space often is to shout when, in fact, shouting creates the exact opposite to the desired effect. The text becomes less clear and the actor more difficult to understand. The adjustment that does have to happen, however, is that the actor must perceptually *include* the entire audience and speak more clearly. Then the voice will carry. The ability of the voice to carry stems from the actor's thought, rather than the actor consciously pushing for volume. The paradox is that when the actor listens to him or herself, attempting to modify the sound, volume, or pitch in some way, it creates a disconnect between the actor's natural impulse to the language and results in less volume and a less convincing performance.

From 1994 to 1999, I served as Voice and Dialect Coach at the Canadian Stage Company's Dream in High Park, in Toronto, Canada. The Canadian Stage Company in Toronto produces an outdoor Shakespeare program every summer. When the company moved to the outdoor space, the actors became nervous and began shouting the text, which made it unintelligible. The vocal coach asked the actors to work in partners, one actor speaking the text on the stage and the other moving gradually farther and farther toward the back of the audience space. The goal was to let the actor on stage know when he or she was being clear and heard and when not. What invariably happened was that as the partner got farther away, into the house, the actor on stage would begin to push and the partner in the audience would communicate that he could not understand the actor on stage. This would go on until the actor on stage was guided or discovered the necessary adjustment on his or her own, to speak slightly more slowly, using the consonants more and let "the thought propel the sound," that is, striving to communicate the text as clearly as possible, including the large row of the amphitheater. When they regained their composure by putting their attention back onto the thought and clarity of the ideas, speaking slightly more slowly, and using their consonants more crisply, the actors would regain intelligibility and the ability to fill the space. Until each partner experienced this exercise, it was difficult for the actors to believe that the effort was in the clarity of the thought, rather than physically pushing the sound out.

Technique involves a balance of technical freedom, a "clear channel" and the psychokinesthetic mechanism's ability to respond spontaneously to the thought and to the requirement of the space. Therefore, if the space is larger, and the actor includes this fact into his or her awareness, the voice will naturally fill the space, as an extension of the thought. Pushing for volume, on the other hand, will not have the desired effect but result in garbled text.

One cannot separate the person from the voice; the voice reflects the person's intention, need, and thought. Tension in the voice, unless caused by some malfunction, generally reflects tension in the person or at least a lack of thorough understanding of the text. Unless one fully takes into account the specifics of each thought, one cannot realize his or her vocal potential. It is not enough to free the sound, but the actor must sculpt the ideas with precision, commitment, and a full kinesthetic relationship to the language. This is one of the most important issues in tackling voice tension.

GETTING THE WHOLE PICTURE AS A COACH

Effectively addressing vocal issues involves awareness of the psychology of the actor and the interplay between the director's vision and the actor's execution of that vision or at least how the actor perceives the director's vision. The coach needs to discern the vocal mechanics that interfere with vocal ease of delivery. One must bear in mind that dealing with the actor's voice is an extremely individual process; therefore, no one exercise works identically in each instance. One has to diagnose the difficulty based on the sound, the physical manifestation of tension and then analyze how this impacts the acting process. The process can prove quite complex.

The actor is, ideally, the best judge of when vocal tension occurs; however, occasionally the actor denies the problem. When actors develop voice problems, there is loss to the theaters in terms of time and money as well as the inconvenience of rescheduling performances or rehearsing an understudy. Unfortunately, some directors communicate in a way that can inadvertently create vocal tension as well.

Certain psychological limitations at times do not allow an actor to admit and to deal with vocal problems, even though these issues are clearly causing the actor professional difficulty.

In the context of a production, vocal problems emerge in a variety of ways. The audience may complain of not "hearing the actor." In reality, this usually means not "understanding" the actor rather than the actor not being loud enough, as described in the previous section. Sometimes actors are too low, often because the scene requires delicacy and an intimate sentiment, but the actor needs to share that with the audience. Or an actor plays the role with a dialect so strong that the actor cannot be understood because he or she focuses more on the dialect than on the character's intentions. Or the actor speaks with so much hoarseness that it is unpleasant to listen to and becomes distracting to the audience. Or an actor screams without proper support, going for a generalized emotion, rather than a specific intention. All these situations are recipes for vocal fatigue, misuse or—worst-case scenario—vocal injury, the most common of which being the occurrence of vocal nodules.

As a coach, one has to comprehend the goals of both the director and the actor. Sometimes the director asks for something but due to lack of vocal understanding does not know how to guide the actor to it in a vocally healthy way. Actors are under tremendous pressure to produce results. When a director asks for a particular effect, the actor tends to attempt without any regard for the healthiest way to achieve it. The freelance nature of the actor's work creates a tension in itself and the actor is always on display, frequently wondering where and when the next contract for employment will come. This can create in the actor a need to please the director and, therefore, a pressure to perform whatever is requested of the actor, sometimes to his or her detriment. Often, in attempting to go for a result requested by the director, the actor forgets to maintain and incorporate the principles of healthy voice use and alignment. Considering these factors, anyone working with the actor on vocal issues needs to understand the pressures the actor is under, the vision of the director, and the needs of the overall production.

APPLYING THE PRINCIPLES OF THE ALEXANDER TECHNIQUE

The Alexander principles help actors enormously. An actor can learn to "inhibit" or "stop" the tension habit and thereby free his or her performance. Alexander used the word "inhibition," which in some respects is a little unfortunate in acting training, as it evokes the idea of repression, which does not help the actor. This is not the way in which Alexander meant it, however. He meant that by stopping, we then have the opportunity to make a choice to do something different. This allows us to stop the offending habit long enough to figure out ways to prevent it. The most obvious benefit is that once the actor frees her or his head, neck, and torso relationship, this minimizes tension in the neck muscles, which allows the larynx to function more effectively.

Many of the principles of voice training do include the idea of "inhibition" or "stop" (though the voice teacher may not necessarily refer to the idea in quite the same way). Alexander found if he concentrated on the end result, his habitual tension returned. However, if he focused on the steps to get there, "the means

whereby," he was able to perform the given task without the tension returning. In so doing, the Alexander technique trains the mind to bypass its initial response to specific stimuli.

The Alexander technique should be integrated with all aspects of both directing and acting training. The actor should be blocked in ways that allow for proper alignment and easy breath support. If an awkward position is unavoidable, the actor wants to think of the neck lengthening and the shoulders releasing (not pushing) apart as much as possible. The position itself may look constricted but the job of the artist is to find an inner release in that position. The actor should search for the most efficient movement, using the least amount of tension possible. The beauty of the Alexander technique is that the principles can be applied to any position.

In a production of *Uncle Vanya*, directed by a well-known European director, the final scene was dramatically weakened by the director and actor not understanding the Alexander principles of alignment and body mechanics. The final scene in which Sonya speaks so eloquently about life's purpose was all but lost on the audience because the poor actress was so collapsed on the table, one could barely hear or understand her, due to her lack of breath support and positioning of her neck, causing constriction in the larynx. Had she only moved forward from the hip joints, thereby keeping her back open, which would have allowed her to use the swing of her back ribs and give her the support she needed, we would have experienced the extraordinary moving quality of this monologue, and been given the same physical impression. If only both director and actor had received training in the voice and the Alexander technique and applied this knowledge in that setting!

The idea of not "end gaining" that Alexander spoke of plays an important part in the development of character within a play. An actress playing Blanche in *Streetcar Named Desire*, for example, has to play her objective strongly to arrive at the end of the play in the appropriate emotional state. If she focuses on achieving the emotional state during the course of the play, her performance appears forced and unbelievable. Through text analysis, she explores her objectives and plays those thoroughly. When the character does not achieve her goals (ie, Mitch does not marry Blanche and she has no route to survival), Blanche finds herself desperately attempting to make her situation more tolerable. She fights against the obstacles presented to her, which creates the appropriate emotional response. This is the equivalent of the "means whereby" in the Alexander technique sense; she does not attempt to create an emotional response but it stems from her not achieving her goal.

> In a workshop with Cicely Berry, O.B.E., Voice Director of the Royal Shakespeare Company, England, and Andrew Wade, Voice Coach at the Guthrie Theatre and formerly Head of Voice at the RSC, the following occurred: A woman delivered a piece of text, a performance which might be described as histrionic. It was extremely tight vocally, overemotional, forced, and difficult to listen to. Berry asked the actress to pick up all the shoes (of the participants in the workshop) in the room, sequentially. The actress walked around the room, picking up the shoes, putting them into a pile, as she spoke her text. The actress's vocal delivery suddenly became like quicksilver and her delivery animated, charming, and engaging; all this while she was organizing the shoes. Her voice resonated with ease and full support as she utilized her full range.

What happened? The task of putting the shoes in order took her attention off the end result, that is, "inhibited" her habitual response to the delivery of text, and allowed her to discover the inherent freedom within the energy of the text. One might say she got out of the way of the text, letting it play her. Instead of imposing her own preconceived idea of the way the text should play and manipulating her delivery, she found a more intuitive connection to the language. By taking the attention off the result, ironically, the outcome proved far more interesting to the listener. There exist many similar exercises to "take the weight off the text."

During rehearsals of *Love's Labours Lost,* directed by Robin Phillips at the Stratford Festival in 1979, the following occurred. The scene was going reasonably well, but the actresses involved were becoming overly concerned with the language, which was causing a heaviness and self-consciousness in delivery. Mr. Phillips asked the actresses to repeat the scene and mime pinning their hair up with bobby pins at the same time. The scene became quite lively, more animated but in a relaxed, rather than pushed, way. The voices became freer and more expressive as the relationships of the characters became more playful. This simple exercise enabled the actresses to "take the weight off the words" and find a more natural delivery of the lines as well as a lighter approach to the scene. The act of miming pinning up the hair "inhibited" the habitual tendency to "push" the meaning out of the text and the voice, rather than allow them to flow naturally.

"YOU'VE GOT TO BELIEVE THEY CAN DO IT"

The Hidden "s"

An excellent bit of guidance is from Cecily Berry, who said, "You've got to believe they can do it." Invariably, this idea relaxes the actor and sometimes literally in the next minute the actor will actually achieve the very thing that overcomes the problem. If the actor does not achieve it immediately, often he or she masters the specific challenge by the next tutorial or class.

> While coaching at the Stratford Festival in Canada, the director of one of the productions expressed concern about a particular actor because of his sibilant "s," an "s" that hisses and catches our ear more than one would like. I was searching for a solution that would help this soft-spoken young man. We worked with traditional ways to "fix" the "s," with mild success: working on tongue placement, reading drills, and so on.
>
> The sibilant "s" in the case of this man was the result of faulty support

and what seemed to me a kind of vocal mannerism. My instinct told me a clue was missing but I did not know what. Finally, I asked him if English was the mother tongue of his parents. He told me they were Serbian. This was during the war in former Yugoslavia. I asked him to imitate his father. The actor then spoke with a thick Serbian accent and his voice became strong and full and his delivery extremely clear. Then I asked him then to speak his Shakespeare text in that same accent and again, the voice was full, strong and the sibilant "s" was completely gone. Then I asked him to speak the text again, with his father's "voice" but without the Serbian accent. He managed to speak the text clearly, with full voice and the "s" issue was completely nonexistent. Clearly, the "s" issue was a byproduct of an overall voice use issue. The man had seemingly cut himself off from his roots in some way, causing a lack of overall support in his speaking. This lack of support impacted him both physically and psychologically, creating a disconnect that resulted in a breathiness and the sibilant "s." The traditional exercises had not effectively solved this actor's sibilant "s" problem, because it was merely a symptom of a more complex issue.

Sometimes in the training of an actor, teachers insist that the tongue placement for the "s" be at the alveolar ridge. In point of fact, everyone has a differently shaped mouth and sometimes this tongue placement does not work. Rather, placing the front of the tongue against the back of the lower front teeth is more effective in some cases. It is important to make sure the individual actor knows where he or she should say an "s" or a "z." Voiced sounds (ie, d, n, l, r, ch, g, dg, etc) preceding "s" generally require the sound "z," whereas unvoiced sounds (ie, t, st, b, k, etc) require an "s" sound. One challenge in dealing with articulation issues such as the production of "s" or "z," is that the poor actor can become so focused on the production of the s or z, that the rest of the vocal process comes to a halt, producing tension in the neck and shoulders, jaw, tongue root, and the rest. The actor must include physical ease and breath support when dealing with articulation issues.

A similar example came up at Stratford with an actor of Asian descent. It was assumed that the young actor could never master Shakespeare, that "it just wasn't in him." The young actor came to tutorial quite distraught, as he had been getting negative feedback about his voice use, not to mention the unspoken feedback about his perceived inability with Shakespeare. He was also told that he spoke Shakespeare in a "monotonous" way. During the tutorial, this young man explored speaking text, soft palate exercises, and breath support. Although he made minor improvements, nothing really made much of an impact. Finally, he was asked to speak the text in Chinese, his mother tongue. It was fascinating to hear his use of rhythm and language and how much richer the text was, even to the non-Chinese listener. It became apparent that many of the sounds had a rather nasal twang, and that many of the Chinese sounds used the palate in the dropped position rather than the lifted position that the majority of English sounds require. Part of the "monotonous" quality to his speaking of Shakespeare in English had to do with the fact that his soft palate took on a fixed position when he spoke, which did not allow for the normal flexibility and responsiveness. The young man then worked on loosening the soft palate, speaking the text with the yawn, and speaking the text first in Chinese-Mandarin and then again in English, singing the text in Chinese and then singing the text in English. The switching back and forth from Chinese to English was the key. This enabled him to eventually find the same freedom he had discovered in the exercises and incorporate this freedom into the speaking of the text so that that. over time, having identified the habit of what he was doing, he was able to approach the English text with the appropriate ease and flexibility necessary to allow the natural rhythm of the text. The older habit, completely appropriate for Chinese, had to be halted internally to allow him to develop a new relationship to the language.

What is important in both these examples, however, is the fact that once the coach acknowledged the actor's heritage as part of the vocal process, the actor managed to find a stronger commitment to the text; to use his full self in approaching the text, which enabled him to find his full voice. This is one of the most important issues in tackling voice tension. It is rarely a simple case of addressing the muscle in and of itself, but must be coupled with an understanding of the psychological components to achieve any level of success.

SIMPLE EXPLORATIONS TO HELP ELIMINATE VOCAL TENSION

Here are some simple exercises designed to address particular issues. With all these exercises, the approach should be one of exploration rather than going for an end result. Each individual responds slightly differently and if one exploration does not work, one should just go on to another. There is no right or wrong, just a chance to look at the vocal experience from another angle, which generally opens up new possibilities. Any sense of judgment creates further tension, so the coach must "believe the actor can do it." This will communicate unconsciously to the actor and create a more positive and productive working environment.

Tension in the Tongue Root

This results when someone is "driving the sound" by tightening the root of the tongue, attempting to find power by pushing with the back of the tongue and the tongue area below the chin. Generally, this habit is compensating for lack of appropriate support and an effort to achieve something within a performance.

Sit in a relaxed, upright position. Release the tongue out so that the outline of the tongue meets the outline of the lower lip. If the tongue won't rest comfortably in this position, gently hold the tongue. One should make sure the tongue is not being pressed down with too much force nor that the jaw is tightening to help out the situation. Then speak the text, slightly slower than usual, making sure to convey meaning clearly. After speaking a section of text in this fashion, which feels ridiculous, slide the tongue back into the mouth and speak the text again. Often the text will become clearer and the vocal tone richer because the exercise

gives the tongue root and jaw an opportunity to relax. Because one has to take the text more slowly, the breath support improves, as does the clarity of the thought.

Tension in the Jaw

Massage the jaw hinge gently. Then, with clean fingers, place forefingers gently between the upper and lower back molars, as one speaks the text. Then remove the fingers, but continue to keep the same space between the teeth as one speaks. Generally, one finds a fuller, easy sound by simply opening the jaw in a more relaxed fashion.

Another approach to alleviate jaw tension is to rub the hands together, place them on the jaw hinges, and then tilt the head over to one side, resting the head in one hand and then massaging the opposite jaw hinge. Then come back to center, with both hands on the jaw hinges and tilt over to the other side and massage the hinge of the other jaw. Come back to center and notice if the jaw muscles have relaxed.

Tight Soft Palate and Nasality

If the text sounds pitched and with an overbalance of nasal resonance, the problem is usually a dropped soft palate. There are a number of soft palate exercises but the simplest is to count from one to ten on a wide yawn then take the text on a yawn, so the actor can get the sense of the space inside the mouth. Then the actor speaks the text again, without actually yawning but allowing the sensation of yawning to inform the delivery. The actor generally discovers more sense of space in the mouth and a better balance of the nasal and mask resonators because of the lift of the soft palate.

Dealing with a Raspy Sound

If the actor tends to use too much force in speaking, resulting in a raspy, forced sound, then having the actor imagining the sound out the back of the neck is useful. In groups, partners can work together, putting a hand gently on the back of the neck and having the actor sigh a "huh" into the hand. This generally takes the pressure off the larynx by putting the attention elsewhere. One can also successfully apply the same idea to text. Moving down the body, an actor can put his or her hand at the back of the neck and sigh "huh" into the hand. The hand should pick up sound vibrations. If the actor is pushing vocally too much, the vibrations will be less. So, the more the actor releases with ease, the greater the sound vibrations. This is useful when actors are experiencing laryngeal pushing and tightening of the muscles around the larynx. Similarly, the actor can "kinesense" (sense kinesthetically) the sound moving out the skull. The hand can be placed on the skull and the actor can become aware of sound vibrations in the head. These can also be done as partner exercises.

If the actor tends to vocally push, it can be quite useful to a performer to conduct an activity while speaking the text. For example, if the actor puts away books, or wipes the blackboard, this can often take the pressure off the words and allow the actor more vocal ease.

Improving Support

In dealing with support, the most important thing is the movement of the intercostal muscles. This is the only effort required in breathing, while other efforts interfere with effective breath support. Attempting to suck in a big breath generally tightens the upper chest muscles, impedes free flow of sound and is counterproductive. It is important for actors to understand the anatomy of the diaphragm because too many people have an inaccurate picture of exactly what it is and what it does. One must remember the diaphragm extends around the full circumference of the lower ribs and expands and drops like a drum, causing a vacuum, which draws in the breath and releases up as the ribs contract on the release of breath. The main focus of the actor should always be on allowing the ribs to swing out, rather than contracting in. Putting emphasis on contracting the ribs in toward the body on the release of breath and sound creates a tendency to pull down and constrict the shoulder and neck muscles, resulting in tension around the larynx.

Lie on the floor, in fetal position, with the upper arm over the head and the lower arm under the head, so the neck is not crunched. Have a partner start at the top of the ribs closest to the ceiling, up beyond the collarbone and say, "These are your ribs." The partner moves all the way down, piece by piece saying, "These are your ribs" all the way down to the lower ribs. Then the first person sits up and compares the rib freedom of each side. In most cases, the individual will experience much more awareness of the full extent of the rib case and the movement of the ribs on the side just worked with. Then one can repeat the same thing on the other side. This exercise also helps to sense the differentiation between the ribs and the shoulder girdle. Many actors squeeze the upper arms to the upper ribs and this constricts support. The elbows and ribs are enemies and like a little space between them.

It is important to remind actors that the spine lengthens on the outtake of breath, which in a way seems counterintuitive. However, if the actor can work with that image, some wonderful things can happen. Instead of the typical pull down, tighten, and squeeze for "power" ("bluff acting"), the actor can find the length and width in the release of the thought, thereby eschewing the typical squeeze actors often resort to, which does nothing but create vocal tension and unbelievable acting "moments." The squeeze obstructs free expression because it tightens the breathing mechanism and pulls everything inside, rather than sharing it out. Actors can explore finding the ease of full expression if they really let it release and sense the length as they release the text. The bigger the stakes, the more release the actor needs.

An actor can move one arm pointing toward the ceiling and the other to the side as she or he speaks the text, so as to remind her or himself of length and width. Then repeat this, imagining one is moving the arms and notice if one has more sense of ease.

If the actor is having difficulty finding appropriate support, ask the actor to lift the arms out to the side, with each intake of breath and then, while speaking the text, take the arms back down to the sides of the body. This usually helps the actor to engage the back area of the ribs and opens up the support. Sometimes the actor, if open to something playful, can imagine angel wings and move the arms in this manner while speaking the text.

If an actor does not seem to be embodying the text, then here are a few ideas to help the actor "get into his or her back." The actor can imagine one is wearing a sound cape, and that the sound and ideas of the voice are moving through the cape. The actor can speak to someone, picturing the person behind him or her, imagining a mouth in the back, as if one is speaking from one's back. If the actor doesn't click with the mouth image, then even just speaking to someone behind can help the actor use his or her full breath support and gain a fuller kinesthetic awareness.

Tension in the Neck and Shoulder Areas

A simple Alexander idea is to practice text, pretending one has a second head on top of one's real head. One immediately finds length and width and more ease in the speaking of the text. A guided body check can prove useful as well:

Sense the width of the back,

The distance between the eyebrows and the back skull,

The occipital joint, sense the head moving up and away from the body,

The distance between the shoulder blades,

The back of the arms,

The backs of the legs,

Sense the sitting bones,

The soles of the feet on the floor,

The distance between the ankles and the toes.

This helps ground the actor, reminding him or her of the full body connection, which in turn aids the release of tension around the neck, jaw, and shoulders. Addressing the overall psychophysical use generally makes addressing any specific tension areas, such as jaw tension, neck tension, soft palate inflexibility, and so forth, much easier.

Constructive Rest

Lie on the floor or a table, with the knees up toward the ceiling, feet flat on the ground, with a book under the head. The book should allow the neck to lengthen so that the neck is not overly arched or the head so high that the chin is pressing down on the larynx. One then thinks in a number of directions—out through the top of the head away from the torso, in the direction up through the knees, feet solidly on the ground and the thought of the back lengthening and widening. If one does this for several 5-minute sessions a few times a day, one notices positive changes quite quickly: more ease in the shoulders and neck, thereby more freedom in the voice, more sense of ease in movement, and more of a sense of ease of height. Often, an added benefit is an improved sense of well-being.

Ways to Deal with Monotone Delivery

An actor speaks in monotone when he or she has not fully comprehended the "geography" of the text; that is, how one phrase and thought builds into the next. The actor needs to allow the voice to reflect the rhythm of the text and the pitch to appropriately reveal the meaning, using the sounds of the words to convey the message. Here are some ways to help the actor discover the connection of the meaning to pitch and rhythm in an intuitive manner. The actor can sing and dance the text and then go back to speaking it. This exercise achieves two things. One, the actor becomes more physically relaxed, allowing the natural breath support to take over and, two, the movement and singing help the actor find the inherent rhythm and musicality of the text, which allows the actor to connect to the language in a deeper and more released way. Often it is useful to ask the actor what kind of music he or she likes. Then one says to the actor, "Here are the lyrics (the actor's text) and you are the composer. You need to find the right music for these lyrics that fit the meaning." With verse speaking, actors have achieved great success with country and western delivery, rap, jazz, and opera singing. This gives the actor the opportunity to experience the words in a new way. In general, when the actor returns to speaking the text after this exercise, the actor speaks it with much more variety and vocal build of ideas.

Another exercise involves the coach at the piano. The coach gives the actor a lower pitch to start with and then gives the actor a new ascending pitch for each new idea, as the thoughts build. Once the thought idea is completed, the coach can then return to a lower pitch and build again. The actor chants the text on the particular pitch, rather than speaking it or fully singing the text. Then the actor goes back to speaking the text without the piano and usually approaches the text with more variety and nuance.

Precision of Language

If the actor is having difficulty finding precision in the language, then have the actor speak the line of text word by word, (ie, to . . . to be . . . to be or . . . to be or not . . . to be or not to . . . to be or not to be . . .) then repeat the whole thought. This is an exercise I learned from Patsy Rodenburg and I have nicknamed it "Lego blocks," because the actor begins to sense the shape of each idea and how each word builds on the word before. Actors tend to run words together, which obscures clarity of meaning. Awareness of each word as a string of thoughts, like a string of pearls, is particularly important in classical text, but any text benefits from this exploration.

Exploring Imagery

Often, vocal tension arises out of a lack of clarity about what the character actually is saying. A simple exercise I have developed has proven quite useful. The actor draws each new image on a blackboard as specifically as possible, even abstract ones. This often helps the actor grapple with each new part of the thought, which the actor may have overlooked. The time taken to really delve into each image specifically helps the actor relax into the language, deepen the support, and hence use less tension in the speaking.

Asking the actor to close one's eyes and visualize each image as the actor says it is a tool I have found particularly effective for dealing with tension. Often, tension stems from the physical manifestation of not giving each image and idea its full importance. Picturing the text helps find the specific image behind each thought.

One can also take a similar approach in a group by using sound. This idea came to me when I led a workshop of Buffalo storytellers in a workshop a number of years ago. One participant was sight impaired and I was quite shocked by the fact that almost my entire repertoire of metaphors involved sight. So when this gentleman performed his story, the group developed appropriate sound effects to support the images in the story. When he spoke the text again, without the group's sound effects, he was able to find many more levels in the ideas and the voice responded accordingly, expressing the ideas with changes in pitch, rhythm, dynamic, and so forth. I have often since asked students to close their eyes and have the group make sound effects and often this has quite a dramatic impact. Working individually with an actor, one might ask the actor to think through the text and just make sounds appropriate to the ideas. Then the next time the actor speaks the text, the actor should have a more kinesthetic response to the language, with more vivid images and textures to the ideas.

SUMMARY

Unless one fully takes into account the specifics of each thought, one cannot really help an actor fully realize his or her vocal potential. It is not enough to free the sound, but the thought must be carved out with commitment and precision and a full kinesthetic relationship to the *language*. Coaches need to approach the actor with a sense of openness as a guide. This works much better than taking a "corrective" attitude, which usually serves to render the actor self-conscious. Finding vocal ease requires commitment to healthy technique, daily vocal preparation, openness, and a genuine desire to communicate. The actor and coach must delve into the text as deeply as possible to allow the thought to propel the sound, the nuances, and delicate dynamics of thought. Both coach and actor must include the overall personality of the actor in addressing vocal tension.

REFERENCES

1. Linklater K. *Freeing the Natural Voice.* New York, NY: Drama Books; 1976. (Basic introduction to the Linklater approach to voice work.)
2. Wade A. *Voice and Text Professional Workshop* through VASTA (Voice and Speech Trainers Association); University of Arizona, Tempe, Ariz; January 1994.

3. Berry C. That secret voice. In: Hampton M, Acker B, eds. *The Vocal Vision.* New York, NY: Applause Books; 1997. (A collection of essays including Catherine Fitzmaurice's article "Breathing Is Meaning" and other articles related to voice pedagogy, controversial issues in teaching, and various techniques.)

4. Gelb MJ. *Body Learning.* New York, NY: Owl Books; 1996. (History and explanation of the Alexander Technique and resources for further study.)

ADDITIONAL RESOURCES

Berry C. *Voice and the Actor.* New York, NY: Applause Books; 1991.

Berry C. *The Actor and the Text.* New York, NY: Applause Books; 2000. (Deals with the visceral connection of voice and text as well as text analysis.)

Linklater K. *Freeing Shakespeare's Voice.* New York, NY: Theatre Communications Group; 1992. (Explorations of voice/text and psychophysical work.)

McCallion M. *The Voice Book.* New York, NY: Theatre Arts Books/Routledge; 1998. (Explores many aspects of voice/speech/text; particularly good in dealing with the Alexander technique and voice.)

Rodenburg P. *The Right to Speak.* New York, NY: Theatre Arts Books; 1992. (Basic vocal approach; deals with the voice as it relates to the "right to express" and self-image in our society.)

Rodenburg P. *The Need for Words.* New York, NY: Theatre Arts Books; 1993. (More voice/text explorations.)

Rodenburg P. *The Actor Speaks.* New York, NY: St. Martin's Press; 2000. (Deals with voice curriculum and vocal demands in various performance situations.)

Sataloff RT. *Professional Voice: The Science and Art of Clinical Care.* San Diego, Calif: Plural Publishing, Inc; 2005. (Basic medical overview, explanation of voice disorders, with color illustrations.)

Sataloff RT. *Vocal Health and Pedagogy.* San Diego, Calif: Plural Publishing, Inc; 2006. (Good overview of interdisciplinary voice care from both medical and artistic perspectives.)

Plural Publishing has many books on voice and voice care. CDs and tapes on voice and voice care are available from the Voice Foundation (1721 Pine Street, Philadelphia, Pa 19104.).

Chapter 13

TREATMENT OF INJURED SINGERS AND PROFESSIONAL SPEAKERS: THE SINGER/ACTOR, SINGER/DANCER, AND SINGER/MUSICIAN

Jeannette L. LoVetri

Actors, dancers, and musicians are often called upon to sing. Each of these groups of professional voice users will encounter unique challenges in singing and will have specific issues to address if they are to remain vocally healthy or to recover from vocal injury. To assist a performer to return to healthy vocal use for singing and speaking, it is necessary to understand as many factors as possible that could contribute to vocal injury.

THE SINGER/ACTOR—THE LARGER CONTEXT

In New York City and other major theatrical centers, there is a difference between someone who sings and can act (singer/actor) and someone who acts and can sing (actor/singer). This may sound odd, but it comes from the fact that actors and singers are trained very differently and think of themselves in ways that are distinct from each other. This is also true of those who are primarily dancers (dancers who sing) and musicians (someone who can play and sing). These are not inconsequential differences, as they are significant factors in how each of these performers uses his or her voice when singing. In New York professional circles, "actor" is a term that can be used to refer to both men and women. In this chapter, the use of this word will be a reference to both males and females.

The following are quotes from ads for auditions that appear in the weekly New York theatrical trade publication, *Back Stage*:

> "Thoroughly Modern Millie"—Seeking male dancers who sing . . .

> "Evita"—Seeking singers who move, dancers who sing, male and female . . .

> "Disney Cruise Line"—Seeking musical theater performers, trained vocalists and actors who move well, or trained dancers who can sing on key.

> "Floyd & Clea Under The Western Sky"— Seeking Singers: male or female, who are also instrumentalists, must be proficient on the dobro/acoustic guitar/pedal steel guitar, etc. Singers who are not proficient musicians cannot be considered.[1(p8,22)]

THE SPEAKING/SINGING INTERFACE

All singers discover through life experience that the speaking voice has a direct impact on the singing voice. (Perhaps this is why we divide them into two categories even though the voice source is from the same two vocal folds). It is also true in reverse in that singing can have an impact on how an actor speaks. To ascertain the interface between speaking and singing, it is useful to take a look at the training of performers' speaking and singing voices. Training, or lack thereof, has a direct impact on the vocal patterns habitually used by the singer/actor or actor/singer so, before attempting to return a performer to healthy singing, it is important to know what these patterns are and how they were developed. Retraining an injured voice implies bringing it back to a state of normalcy, and deviation from the functional norm can have deep and old roots that must be unearthed before they can be removed.

TRAINING HISTORY—A NECESSITY

Regardless of whether the training is for singing or speaking, as has been stated, singers and actors are trained very differently. Because the level of training available runs the gamut from poor to excellent, and because not all singers and actors have formal training, performers bring a wide range of patterns with them when they begin professional work. Training *should* be helpful, but this is, unfortunately, not always the case. Some types of training can be useless, some can be confusing, others will set up conflicts between how the voice is used for singing and how it is used in speech, and still others may actually be harmful to the voice in general. Remember, too, that some singers, dancers, and musicians have no training at all for speech or singing yet work professionally.

> A *singer/actor* is someone who is trained first to sing and then learns to act. This performer would answer the question "what do you do?" with the answer, "I am a singer."

Singing training involves learning very different skills than those used in acting. Singers focus on learning to read music and on singing with enough carrying power to be heard over an orchestra without electronic amplification. A singer needs to make a clear tone, using a wide range of pitches, with deliberate control over the use of the breath and with a constant vibrato. "A good vibrato is a pulsation of pitch, usually accompanied with synchronous pulsations of loudness and timbre, of such extent and rate as to give a pleasing flexibility, tenderness, and richness to the tone."[2] Singing training will also involve learning to sing in several foreign languages and learning to use complex musical decorations called ornaments. It may or may not include formal acting training (which is separate from that used in a musical production) or movement/dance training. The goals of training someone to sing are still almost totally classical; that is, training is aimed toward opera, oratorio, art song, chamber, or other classical music. These are primarily musical goals.

Singers who are called on to act in plays without music can be quite challenged by use of the speaking voice, as frequently it will have been largely ignored during singing training. In theatrical productions, women especially are often asked or expected to use a speaking voice that sounds deep, low, and robust but may not have the ability to do so as they have only been trained as singers to sound high, sweet, and warm. Singers who find themselves in a nonmusical play may find speaking for long periods of time fatiguing. Lighter voices, especially, can be worn out by long rehearsals with continuous repetition of scenes.

An *actor/singer* is trained first in "straight" drama (no music is involved) and is asked to investigate his or her own memories, history, and points of view in learning to develop and express a character in a dramatic work. Movement training is frequently involved, and sometimes there is training for the speaking voice. Actors also analyze historic and contemporary plays and playwrights and types of productions and directing. Generally, no musical training is given. The actor may or may not at some point have some lessons in singing and/or learn songs that may or may not be classical.

Actors can be quite confused when asked to sing something that requires very precise pitch control in a range that is far above that of conversational speech, as musical ability can be divorced entirely from speaking well. If the performer is able to use a vocal quality in singing that is very similar to the same vocal quality used in speech, it is likely that things will work out well.

A QUICK LOOK AT THE BASICS

All healthy voice use, including singing, is based upon a few of the same principles. A *professional singer* is someone who gets paid for singing and must deliver musical sound on demand. The following list of prerequisites for good voice use applies to every vocal professional, both singing and speaking:

1. Excellent posture
2. A strong open chest and rib cage
3. Strong but flexible abdominal muscles
4. Relaxed strap muscles in the neck
5. The ability to take a free, full inhalation, well down into the bottom of the lungs
6. Coordination between the ribs and abdominal muscles during exhalation (This is usually called "breath support".)
7. The ability to open the mouth by dropping the jaw freely and easily and with more than the usual amount of space between the teeth
8. The ability to articulate clearly—using the lips and tongue easily and freely
9. Comfortable vocal expression in song and speech—no strain, no forcing, and no discomfort
10. A pitch range of an octave and a half to two octaves, and enough power to be heard without electronic amplification in a moderately sized room with good acoustics.

Interference with the function of any of the above can exacerbate vocal problems for anyone but lack of these skills can be a serious issue for those singer/actors, dancer/singers, and musicians who wish to sing well.

THE BODY/VOICE CONNECTION

Anyone who is in good health and physically fit has an advantage in keeping the voice functionally strong, as these things go together well.[3] Beyond this, however, the vocal performer draws on the body and its ability to move when expressing emotion and becomes acquainted with the body's sensations and feelings in order to create a character in a play or musical.[4] Skilled performers learn to be intimately aware of the body and what it can do or handle.[5] The enhanced awareness that a performer has of his or her body is also very valuable to vocal health, as performers can often sense when something is wrong, even if they do not have the specific medical terms to describe it.

RANKING THE SINGER'S TASKS

In musical theater, the amount and type of singing varies from show to show, so it is difficult to generalize about vocal function in singer/actors and actor/singers or dancer/singers. A performer who is in the chorus of an older musical show (something written before 1968) is less likely to encounter vocal problems. The earlier music was written so differently for singers than is the music of today's composers that it is usually easier to sing.

Singer/actors who must add movement or dancing into their work are also more likely to incur vocal problems because the added activity can interfere with correct use of the voice or be fatiguing to the body, or both. Singers who are in leading roles of rock musicals such as *Tommy*, *Jesus Christ Superstar*, or *Rent* are performing music that is extremely demanding emotionally, physically, musically, and vocally and must not only be very skilled but must monitor how the voice is used outside the performance to be able to maintain a full 8-shows-a-week schedule. When there are so many factors affecting the way the voice is used, even the best actor/singer or singer/actor could encounter vocal trouble, particularly if other things such as illness or stress are also present.

Any specialist who works with a singer in this last category must understand that this performer is the vocal equivalent of an Olympic athlete who needs to be treated accordingly.

FACING THE UNKNOWN: WHEN THE ACTOR IS THROWN INTO SINGING

Actors who are inexperienced singers can face a wide range of difficulties that could have a negative impact on the voice when asked to sing in a musical. This situation is not particularly unusual, and when such a performer is expected to sing, she will have little prior experience from which to evaluate her ability or the materials she is being asked to execute. This insecurity can undermine even a very confident actor. If the music is difficult or badly written, she can unwittingly push the voice or alter her breathing pattern while struggling to sing the song, and this may cause vocal fold irritation. Music directors, too, can ask the performer to do things that are musically viable but beyond the capability of the novice singer. The music director is usually a pianist and conductor who has dealings with singers but may have no training in singing or be unable to sing him- or herself. Some music directors are intimidating to young performers and have the effect of making the performer afraid to speak up lest he or she seem unqualified to be in the show.

OTHER FACTORS THAT MATTER

Because all professional shows except opera and other forms of classical music are now electronically amplified, a lot depends on the sound system and the sound engineer of any given show. The "sound man" can make or break the performer if he is unfamiliar with singers and the sound system plays a big role in what the performer hears. Without a good monitor (stage amplifier facing the singer) or good acoustic feedback within the theater or performance space, the performer will hear his voice in a distorted or muffled way. This, too, will cause him to push the voice and can lead to vocal problems.

Typically, actors will attempt to sing using the same sound for music as for speech. This is an excellent way to begin and for most music it is the correct approach. However, some of the most popular shows that have appeared on Broadway over the last 40 years are quite demanding, particularly rock-and-roll based shows. Singing this music demands a strong vocal instrument, lots of power in the breathing mechanism, and a good deal of physical movement. The range of the songs is typically high and can involve powerful emotional expression as well. Those who do not have strong vocal technique may quickly run out of options in terms of vocal resources.

Certain roles demand very loud singing or speaking, sometimes in unusual or difficult positions (lying down, bent over, twisted alignment, etc). In productions that use heavy or restrictive costumes, the performer may have a great deal of weight in the costume itself. It may be made out of restrictive materials that can affect head/neck alignment or place stress on the neck and throat muscles or the rib cage position and interfere with the ability to freely inhale and strongly exhale. For example, the Broadway musical *The Lion King* has a number of roles in which the actors play animals, and must both sing and speak with "animal" voices and wear heavy costumes. Singing or speaking in a very high pitch range or a very rough vocal quality can cause fatigue if done repeatedly over an extended period of time.

THE DANCER'S DILEMMA

Many dancers are professionally mute for their entire careers. Those who belong to a dance company can survive well without ever uttering a sound while flying across the stage on their winged feet.

Dancers who are lucky enough to belong to a professional dance company where no vocal utterances are ever required, however, are the rare exceptions. More often, at some point in his or her career, a dancer will be called on to speak or sing as a part of a performance. The dilemma faced by these dancers is that they may not be prepared, psychologically or vocally.

Dancers who have not had speech or singing training or who have had little experience using the voice professionally are often quite frightened by the prospect of doing so. This fear only makes it more difficult to produce a free healthy sound, as it inhibits both the breath and the voice itself. Additionally, dancers who have had no vocal training may suffer from habitually restricted movement of the muscles that affect vocal production, making it difficult for the dancer to learn new vocal skills quickly even if the dancer is willing and unafraid.

Professional dancers usually begin training at an early age. No matter what style of dance is studied, little anatomy or physiology is included in dance training except at the most elite schools, so the dancer may not have a good grasp of any of the vocal muscle systems, and likely knows very little about the voice and how it works or how it relates to the body as a whole.

All of this means that dancers are ripe for vocal problems if they are also in a situation where the voice must be used similarly to those just described for singer/actors. Even though they are coordinated and strong, dancers can be very specifically focused on using the body for dancing, *and only for dancing*, and be unable to include awareness of the voice and how it is being used. The issues of using the voice well would become doubly difficult, as the dancing would be a diversion of mental and physical energy, away from the voice itself.

Dancers frequently have tension in the genioglossus, hyoglossis, mylohyoid, diagastric muscles,[6] and the muscles of the root of the tongue connecting to the hyoid bone. They can have tight, stiff jaw (masseter and medial pterygoid[6] muscles), making it difficult to get the mouth open enough to be useful in terms of volume and acoustic efficiency or resonance amplification. Because a long "swanlike" neck is considered a mark of beauty in a ballet dancer, dancers often have very stretched sternocleidomastoid (strap)[5] muscles in the neck, which make it difficult for the larynx to float loosely in the throat. The overall tensions, if not released gradually over a period of time, can cause the dancer to push the voice to make it seem louder or more professional, and this in turn actually makes things worse.

Effective treatment of a vocal disorder would warrant looking at the ability of the dancer to easily move and be aware of all the external muscles affecting the sound. Each of these areas would need to be approached individually so that they could be more relaxed, movable, flexible, and eventually stronger. This would include work on stretching the jaw, developing greater flexibility in the tongue, activating the face and mouth muscles, and loosening the neck and shoulder muscles. The stomach muscles (rectus and transversus abdominis, and the obliques)[5] in particular need to be flexible enough to allow for some forward movement during inhalation. Dancers' stomach muscles are very strong and sometimes they are so taut that little movement is possible. This inhibits the ability of the diaphragm to descend during inhalation and consequently restricts the amount of air intake. Ballet dancers are taught to breathe laterally, meaning that the ribs move out to the sides during inhalation so that the rib cage does not rise and fall during dancing. This type of inhalation

is less efficient for singing but is better than a locked rib cage which cannot move at all, making inhalation very shallow.

MUSICIANS

A musician has to fall into one of two categories: either she is capable of singing while playing the instrument or she has to stop playing it to sing. The people who play brass or woodwinds are in the second group. The rest of the musicians can sing while they play. The odd group would be the violinists and violists, who could conceivably make vocal sound but would find it difficult to move the mouth to pronounce words, as the jaw has to anchor the instrument to the shoulder in order for it to be stable.

Playing an instrument definitely helps make the performer more musically confident when he or she has to sing, but the postures used in each of the various instruments do affect the way the voice works. Some instruments are less likely to cause vocal problems for the performer than others, but a great deal rests on the way each individual actually plays.

The Alexander Technique is beneficial to instrumentalists both for their own technique in whatever instrument they play and for helping them find a good use of the body for singing as well. If the posture of the musician is relatively good while playing the instrument, learning to breathe correctly and keep good alignment while singing should be an achievable task. If, however, the performer is wrapped around his guitar or saxophone or falling into the piano or cello, things can be more challenging. Also, if the performer is singing early music while gently strumming a lute, it would be much less worrisome than if he is banging a set of drums in a heavy metal band while pumping out background vocals. The second performer would have a more difficult job getting to good vocal production habits unless he or she was quite able to adapt in several areas easily and simultaneously. Also, in the case of someone who has to play with an embouchure, the way in which a player applies the mouth to the mouthpiece of a brass or wind instrument,[7] the function of the lips, jaw, mouth, and the structures inside the mouth itself, including the soft palate, the back of the tongue, and the larynx and the vocal folds all have an impact on the production of the instrument's sound. In a professional musician, these muscles are quite strong and do a different job than they would for someone who is a singer, and only a singer. Horn players who must develop strong air pressure in the mouth and strength in the muscles surrounding the lips will also keep the jaw in a relatively raised position. All these muscle patterns are antithetical to good singing and can cause the musician to sound unpleasant or to experience pitch fluctuations or diminishment of vocal range.

As with dancers, musicians have to be cross-trained to function optimally in both playing and singing. The muscle groups involved in playing need to be massaged (externally, where possible), relaxed, stretched, and moved so that they can allow for greater flexibility and ease of movement. Postural imbalances must be addressed through stretching and strengthening and perhaps also through physical therapy and medical massage. On the positive side, though, brass and wind instrumentalists have good breath control and this facilitates breathing for singing, as it is possible to easily adapt the breathing techniques used for playing to singing.

PITCH-RELATED ISSUES

Actors and dancers and even musicians may also have pitch-matching issues that professional singers do not have. This means that these individuals may not easily "sing on key" or "on the note" or have major issues with pitch control (sharping—singing too high or flatting—singing too low to be accurate). Until these issues are addressed through training (and good singing training can train anyone to sing on pitch accurately), the added insecurity about "being able to stay on pitch" would be yet another stress factor that could inhibit correct and healthy singing.[6]

APPROACHES TO RETRAINING A DISORDERED OR INJURED VOICE

Many of the same principles that apply to working with a disordered or injured speaking voice also apply to working with the voices of those who sing. The primary difference is that the exercises are applied to pitches that are specific (musical scales and arpeggios) and often sustained for longer durations and at louder volumes than necessary for conversational speech. Also, because the work is directed toward vocal fold function rather than articulatory issues, there is an aspect of acoustic acuity necessary, on both the part of the singer and the teacher, that typically would not be called for in speech.

A singing voice specialist (SVS) is a singing teacher who is familiar with healthy vocal function and is able to discuss any vocal health issues with a speech-language pathologist and otolaryngologist. The SVS will understand the diagnosis made by the medical and clinical professionals and be able to work as part of a team in helping the singer return to good healthy singing. Working in this way, the SVS can be assured that others are also able to support and evaluate the progress of the singer and validate the health of the vocal mechanism through objective measures and tools.

BEGIN WITH WHAT CAN BE SEEN AND TOUCHED

All singing training begins on the outside of the body with posture and alignment and with specific exercises for the various parts of the body that affect the way the sound is produced. Training also begins by teaching the singer to have a more deliberate and specific approach to breathing that must be consciously coupled with sound-making for the vocal output to be freely and correctly controlled. It should also teach the singing actor, dancer, or musician how to listen objectively for correct vocal and musical function. Returning to normal singing function means returning to normal function in the following areas.

Posture

The importance of posture cannot be overstated.[6] The larynx works best when situated in the throat without any undue muscle tension from muscles that are not necessary for phonation. The relationship of the head, neck, shoulders, and rib cage to each other is a crucial ingredient in allowing the muscles of the upper torso to function properly. If a singing professional has vocal problems, and if those problems are chronic, it is important to evaluate the relationship between the head and neck, the neck and shoulders, and the upper chest with the lower back. Misalignment or tension in any of these muscles will affect the ability of the larynx to function optimally. It is helpful for the performer to work with a postural alignment system such as the aforementioned Alexander technique, one of the various approaches to yoga, or other bodywork disciplines that facilitate correct alignment. If the head juts forward, protruding out in front of the body, allowing the ribs to sag, the larynx will not be able to move freely and the vocal folds will be affected by this restriction. If the head is dropped back so that the cranium is collapsed into the cervical spine, the neck muscles will shorten and the contraction will restrict the muscles of the neck and throat, ultimately affecting the larynx in a similar fashion. These are just two of the possible problems that can aggravate vocal fold issues and make it more difficult for the singer to function optimally; potentially, there are many more.

Breathing

Singing can demand more than twice the air pressure and as much as five times more range than speech. In order for the singer to be able to generate sufficient air pressure for loud sounds and higher pitches, it is necessary to work on increasing the singer's ability to deeply inhale and to control the air as it goes out during singing. This involves using the intercostal muscles in the ribs and the abdominal muscles in a coordinated and deliberate manner while exhaling during a sung phrase. For this to work properly, the body must stand erect, but without rigidity, and the torso must be balanced so that it is possible to walk and move with grace and ease at all times. The ribs must remain open and stable during both inhalation and exhalation and the singer must inhale by drawing the air down into the bottom of the lungs, simultaneously allowing the abdominal wall to move forward, down, and/or out. When sound is being made, the singer must learn to deliberately contract and tighten the abdominal muscles to keep the air pressure constant while the lungs are emptying. This is a learned behavior that takes time to master. There is some variability from person to person

in how this is accomplished, but breathing patterns that do not generally conform to these principles may not be sufficient to keep vocal production healthy.

The Face and Head

The muscles of the singer's face and head greatly affect the sound that is being sung. The mandible (jawbone) must be able to drop significantly more in singing than it does in speech and remain in a dropped position for long periods of time. The tongue must be relaxed even when the mouth may be wide open, and this is a learned behavior for most people. The jaw can also be dropped too far down and interfere with the muscles of the throat or with the tongue, so the amount of the opening must be evaluated in relationship to other structures. The muscles of the face and the lips change the shape of the mouth, which affects the quality of the sound; and the tongue, both in front and in back, plays a crucial role in shaping the vowel sounds both for accuracy and for purposes of expressiveness. Although most novice singers can make simple movements of the face and lip muscles and the jaw, the exaggerated movements necessary for singing are sometimes beyond the ability of an inexperienced singer to initially control and can require time and patience to develop to optimum responsiveness and efficiency. Singing high notes and loud sounds requires that the jaw be dropped quite a bit. At the same time, the face and lips must also be shaped and the tongue positioned so that there is no interference with the muscles inside the mouth and throat, and there must be good solid help from the breathing mechanism. This, too, requires a high degree of coordination and also takes time to learn.

Internal Structures

The musculature in the velopharyngeal port (the back of the mouth and throat) has a profound affect on the singer's voice. The shapes made inside the mouth and throat, and the modifications of those shapes by the tongue, determine not only what vowel we hear but how that vowel sound comes across as acoustic output. Singer's call this "resonance" and it is the crucial ingredient in most singing, as it is a part of what makes the singer's voice unique. Because none of these structures are deliberately movable, except perhaps in a very skilled and experienced singer, creating change in them is often an elusive and confusing process unless the SVS understands how to stimulate vocal function through specific exercises. If internal change does not occur, the sound remains the same and the faulty habits that produced that sound also continue.

The larynx has a very important role to play, as the vocal folds determine both the pitch and the basic tonal quality of the sound.[8] They also regulate the airflow, depending on the quality of the sound the singer is producing. Much has been written and discussed regarding vocal production but it is generally conceded by the scientific and academic voice communities that the main body of the folds, the thyroarytenoid muscle, is responsible for producing the vocal quality that is called *modal* or speaking voice quality. The muscle that stretches and thins the folds, the cricothyroid, helps produce the quality that is called *loft*.[8]

There are many other terms or names for these vocal qualities. The most common term is *vocal register*.[8] A register is essentially a group of tones that have the same texture or quality. This definition, which is an aural one, says that one group of tones sounds like speech and the other does not. Typically, vocal sounds are divided into two basic qualities: chest register and head register, named by the sensations felt in the body while the sounds are being made. *Modal* would be chest register and *loft* would be head register or "falsetto." The easiest way to understand this difference is to think of a man speaking in his normal voice and in a falsetto or childlike quality. The simultaneous combination of these two qualities would give a balance of both.

The use of registers is a key ingredient in style and a primary element in singing voice training. Classical singers are taught to "blend" the registers so that there is a smooth sound from the lowest to highest pitches. Theater singers, and others who sing the various styles of commercial and pop music, do not necessarily blend the vocal registers. In fact, some styles specifically require that the singer stay in the chest or modal quality throughout the entire sung range (see "belting" below). If the performer does not understand how to sing in the correct register quality, he or she might be unable to produce the appropriate sounds for the music being performed.

Proper use and development of registers is a key ingredient in helping a singer/actor, dancer, or musician understand healthy vocal production. Development and strengthening of both chest and head registers assist the entire vocal mechanism to work freely and efficiently. Lower voiced males typically need to develop the head or falsetto register to strengthen it and help expand their range upward and lighten the amount or pressure on the larynx and vocal folds in higher pitches. They can then also integrate the head register quality into their lower pitch range, making it warmer and more appealing. Women sometimes need to do the same, as not all women's voices are head register dominant, as was the case a generation ago. Lighter higher voices (including classically trained tenors and sopranos, lyric mezzos, and baritones—particularly those who have been trained in an older more conservative approach) also usually benefit from developing the chest register on the lower pitches to give the voice more strength and richness.

Contemporary commercial music, the new term for all nonclassical styles, places a strong emphasis on the use of chest register. Learning to sing with this quality in a free and healthy way is of paramount importance to all contemporary performers.[9] It is possible to produce high tones in a speech-based chest register quality, but this is more likely to cause vocal dysfunction issues as, to be done safely, it requires greater and more efficient output of all the systems involved in producing vocal sound. Singers of any kind of commercial music who have been injured must be guided toward correct register function in order to sing well and remain healthy.

Emotional Issues

All artists are emotional. It comes with the territory. Performing often magnifies emotional response and asks for its powerful expression, repeated on demand, over and over. No one's throat was meant to do this, day in and day out. In music that is particularly demanding, adding emotional factors into the mix is often enough to overload the vocal system and cause the vocal folds to become fatigued or injured. Singers must learn to deal with these demands, as it is part of what they are expected to deliver as professionals, but it can require enormous stamina, skill, and care to do that successfully. Tension brought on by chronic or acute stress tightens the muscles, inhibits breathing, and takes a toll on the voice and body, so adding personal emotion to professional emotion can complicate things still further. Any singer who has had vocal problems is stressed, and this must be addressed as the voice is guided back to healthy function, so that the worry does not also cause vocal function issues.

CONSTRICTION—THE BIGGEST ISSUE

The biggest vocal difficulty of singers who perform in shows that have vigorous, demanding music, as is found in many of today's musicals, is constriction. The three groups of constrictor muscles (superior, middle, and inferior) often become engaged when the singer has to hit high pitches in a loud chest register or "belt" quality and does not have sufficient strength in the muscles of the body and throat to manage this task.

> The nature of the belt: it is an attempt to extend the normally "short" female chest register upward.) When secure, the belt produces an edgy, driving sound. Because of the tension involved in holding the position, vocal qualities associated with relaxation as well as all those associated with the integrated head register, are not possible. Sweetness of tone, ductility in phrasing, flexibility of movement are closed out. There is no such thing as a quiet belt, or a beautiful one. (Osbourne, as cited in Potter[10])

Men belt, too. Carrying the chest register quality above approximately E/F/G$_4$ without modifying or darkening the vowels, at a loud volume, would constitute belting.

The constriction narrows the sidewalls of the pharynx, raises the base of the tongue, pulls the larynx up, and tightly compresses the vocal folds. Sometimes, but not always, the external throat and neck muscles bulge or protrude. In all but the most unusual singers, this constriction is not deliberate, nor desired, and often becomes a chronic pattern affecting all vocal production. The performer may be unaware that anything is wrong until and unless the vocal folds themselves develop problems or until professional musical standards can no longer be met.

The side effects of this type of constriction are numerous and varied. Aside from pathology, they can include loss of high range or certain pitches, loss of pitch control, difficulty with sustained notes, breathiness in middle pitches, easy fatigue of the voice, extreme nasality, and difficulty with articulation, as words can become swallowed or garbled.

This problem is the most difficult one to address, as it cannot be handled directly. In general, the tension must be taken off layer by layer, starting on the outside of the body with the head position and with the jaw. The head must remain level and positioned directly over the shoulders and torso, and the upper chest must be lifted but only from below by the abdominal and back muscles and not by the pectoralis muscles or shoulders. The tongue must be loosened, but in the back, and this is only possible indirectly through exaggerated movements initiated in the front. Furthermore, the pressure must be taken off the larynx so that the folds can release, and this must be done through a combination of lowered volume and pitch range. All of this, hopefully, will have an effect on the inner musculature where the constrictive patterns reside and, secondarily, on breathing patterns as well. Constriction in the throat will inhibit a free and easy inhalation/exhalation cycle, and release of constriction will allow the larynx to rest in a lower, more comfortable position in the throat, facilitating easier and fuller breathing.

If the problem is long-standing, the patterns can be resistant to change and the retraining can take too long to be of practical value, in which case the SVS and the performer may have to accept less constriction overall, rather than the elimination of constriction, as the final outcome of their work together. If the vocal folds are diagnosed as being healthy, this is sufficient.

SUMMARY

Many factors that have an impact on the vocal health of singing actors, dancers, and musicians can be generalized but, in the final analysis, each individual performer must be evaluated uniquely. Each person will have a current vocal health status or diagnosis; a history of training; habits of speech, singing, breathing, and movement; and specific performance needs and demands. All these factors must be incorporated into any retraining or treatment program. The SVS must work as a member of the voice care team of otolaryngologist, speech-language pathologist, and perhaps other professionals, to serve the performer's need to return to healthy singing in a timely and efficient manner.

REFERENCES

1. *Back Stage*, September 29–October 5, 2005, New York, NY: 8, 22.
2. Seashore CE. *Psychology of Music*. New York, NY: McGraw-Hill; 1938.
3. Emmons S, Thomas A. *Power Performance for Singers*. New York, NY: Oxford University Press; 1999:67.
4. Bunch M. *Dynamics of the Singing Voice*. 4th ed. Wien: Springer-Verlag; 1997:14.
5. Perkins WH, Kent RD. *Functional Anatomy of Speech, Language, and Hearing, A Primer*. Boston, Mass: College-Hill Press; 1986:28–32,132–140.
6. Sataloff RT, Carroll L. The singing voice. In Sataloff RT, ed. *Professional Voice: The Science and Art of Clinical Care*. New York, NY: Raven Press; 1991:381.
7. *Oxford Essential Dictionary of Difficult Words*. American ed. New York, NY: Berkley Book, Oxford University Press; 2001:151.
8. Sundberg J. *The Science of the Singing Voice*, Dekalb, Ill: Northern Illinois University Press; 1987.
9. LoVetri J. Contemporary commercial music: more than one way to use the vocal tract. *J Singing*. 2002;58(3):249–252.
10. Banfield S. (1979). Stage and screen entertainers in the twentieth century. In: Potter J, ed. *The Cambridge Companion to Singing*. Cambridge, UK: Cambridge University Press; 1979:65.

Chapter 14

PERFORMANCE ANXIETY: IDENTIFICATION, ASSESSMENT, AND TREATMENT

Philip J. Lanzisera

Performance anxiety is one of the most common experiences involving negative emotions. Indeed, it is ubiquitous in human experience. Most individuals will acknowledge such anxiety, and the most commonly reported "social" fear is public speaking, a form of performance anxiety. Virtually all musicians, instrumental and vocal, experience some degree of performance anxiety.[1,2] For experienced musicians, stressful performance situations may actually enhance musical performance.[3] Performance anxiety, however, can seriously impair the musician. Powell[4] estimates that 2% of the population is susceptible to "debilitating" performance anxiety. In this chapter we describe the nature of performance anxiety including its place in human experience, its physiologic and cognitive components, its phenomenology, the differentiation between normal and clinical varieties, self-management, and formal treatment.

PERFORMANCE ANXIETY AS A HUMAN PROCESS

Anxiety is a process whereby danger is recognized, information is obtained relevant to the perceived danger, and the organism is mobilized to solve the prob-lems posed by the danger. It is an innate mechanism and can be observed in infants. The brain mechanisms that perceive danger are primitive parts of the brain residing in the brainstem and limbic system. Those brain centers communicate with "higher" cortical areas and produce the more overt cognitive components of the experience. For the most part this system is cue-based, meaning that it is responsive to discrete sensory configurations some of which are innate (eg, fear of snakes) and some of which are acquired by cue-based conditioning. This system can be responsive to linguistic processes when language serves to "transform the function of a stimulus."[5] These conditioning processes do not require conscious awareness to operate. Indeed, most of the processing that occurs in anxiety occurs outside of awareness and, actually, prior to full conscious appraisal of the situation.[6] The extent to which these "outside of awareness" processes influence the conscious appraisal of the situation varies.

As one can imagine, because anxiety serves a realistic protective function, evolution perfected the capacity to detect danger and experience and respond to anxiety. As with most functional capacities, the capacity (or propensity) to experience anxiety is not simply present or absent. Some individuals will experience anxiety much more easily or intensely, and others will experience it much less so.

Part of the evolutionary process is the ability of the brain to be "perfected" after birth. Thus, as with most propensities, early experience will shape it so that it is more responsive to some stimuli than to others, more or less easily soothed, more or less easily generalized, and attached to some symbolic representations and not to others. It is important to realize that this early shaping causes modifications in neuroanatomy both at the synapse and intraneuronally.[7] Different neurobehavioral functions have different "critical periods"[8] during which neurodevelopment is most easily modified by environmental shaping and after which such shaping occurs with great difficulty and only to a lesser extent.

Finally, as is implied by the above, one will experience anxiety only if relevant triggering stimuli are detected in the environment. Thus, the likelihood that a given individual will develop clinically significant performance anxiety is a function of many genetic influences, key early shaping experiences, and how all those things tend to bring the individual into contact with situations in which performance anxiety is relevant.

Although one might wonder whether it would be better to have very low anxiety susceptibility, we should note that without the capacity for anxiety, humans die at younger ages because they take risks that "wiser" individuals avoid, as a result of which they are not available for reproduction. Simply put, we need anxiety to survive. But, we should ask, does performance anxiety fit into this scheme, do we need it for survival?

Indeed we do. Humans, like primates and many other animals, are social creatures. Simply put, without others of our own kind, we have a difficult time surviving. First, we have a very prolonged period of helplessness during which we are fully dependent on our mother's (or mother surrogate's) care for sustenance and protection. Second, we need the group to which we belong to supply secondary protection (from outsiders and other predators) and to provide food (via hunting). We need to remain a member of our group. Virtually all social creatures form hierarchies and individuals have to fit into that hierarchy in some way to keep their places in the group.

Modern humans live in very complex social spaces so that we can rightly say that each of us is a member of several different communities and that those communities may be complementary or competitive with one another. I am, for example, a member of my family of birth together with my parents and siblings, and I have a place in that community. I am also a member of my own nuclear family together with my spouse and our children; I have a place in that community as well. In addition, I am a member of my work community, my professional community, and various other communities. There may be conflicting loyalties and demands, and my place in one community might be far more secure than my place in another community. As long as I perceive my place to be secure, I am not likely to feel much anxiety. As I perceive that place to be less secure, I am likely to feel more anxiety. What will "tell" me that I am or am not secure will vary depending on how my anxiety sensitivity was shaped by my early experience.

Performance anxiety occurs when we feel that our place in the community of musicians, for example, is threatened by the judgment of those for whom we are performing. Performance anxiety requires that we detect that our performance in a specific situation will have a bearing on our place in a community of value and that we determine that there is some chance that we might not perform well enough to keep our place in that community. We do not have to be consciously aware of either of these components. Indeed, we can feel anxious when we consciously believe that we are quite capable of performing well and will do so. Our conscious beliefs are often not our only beliefs and often not the beliefs most fully activated in a situation.

Performance anxiety tends to occur in individuals who have high expectations and demands for themselves[4] and occurs when the individual believes he or she will not live up to those expectations or those of the audience and will be negatively evaluated by self and others.[9,10] If the individual believes he or she "must" perform well but cannot and will suffer some terrible social loss because of failure, the situation will be very threatening. Anxiety is the natural response in such a situation and alerts the individual to take appropriate action. That one is likely to gain confidence in one's ability to meet expectations with experience is the most likely explanation for the fact that more experienced musicians tend to feel less anxiety than less experienced musicians.[2]

Performance anxiety has cognitive, somatic, and behavioral components. These components feed back on one another in such a way as to create a positive feedback system helping to create more and more anxiety. It may lead to "split attention," which has been demonstrated to lead to impaired performance, particularly in individuals who are just learning complex skills.[11] This may be because the novice needs to be able to direct attention to the mechanics of performance. If the more experienced performer attempts to cope with anxiety by focusing on the mechanics of musical performance, the problem could be seriously compounded. The experienced performer relies on having automated certain musical skills. "Choking" in experienced individuals appears to be related to excessive self-monitoring and self-coaching during performance.[11,12] This is particularly true for highly practiced sensorimotor skills such as musical performance.

THE PHENOMENOLOGY OF PERFORMANCE ANXIETY

Most commonly, individuals begin to experience anxiety prior to beginning a performance. For some the first recognized experience is somatic but for others it may be a thought. There is almost always some kind of thought that helps to trigger the anxiety. This is because as soon as the performer gets ready to perform, he or she begins to think about what the performance is going to be about, how prepared he or she is, and how the performance is likely to go. In addition, the performer thinks about the audience and about what the audience is likely to think of the performer. To the extent that the performer thinks the audience will be critical, anxiety is more likely to occur. If there is a formal critic in the audience, the performer is more likely to feel anxious,[13] and as the size of the audience increases the likelihood of anxiety increases. The performer may flitter back and forth between thoughts about the audience and thoughts about his or her own capacity to perform up to perceived expectations. If there is a discrepancy, and often performers have a more negative view of their capacity to perform than does the audience,[14] that discrepancy gives rise to the perception of danger and risk, which initiates the somatic responses. Some thoughts may be "hot thoughts," thoughts that have a powerful emotional significance to the person and which are not easily questioned. It is as if the danger the thought points to is so important that it has to be taken seriously.

Remember, the anxiety system is designed to overpredict danger not "miss" it.

The somatic components are those of which the performer is usually most aware. These include increased heart rate, altered breathing, nervousness, sweating, jitteriness, muscle tension or spasm, and gastrointestinal sensations including nausea. Not everyone will experience each of these symptoms, but most will experiences several of them. These experiences may be mild in some cases but may be overwhelming and incapacitating in others, and individuals tend to experience their anxiety symptoms in a sequence that is characteristic for them.

There are a number of behavioral consequences of this process. For the vocal artist of great concern are the effects on tone and on the smoothness in the respiratory and vocal apparatus. As the performer becomes aware of the sense of tightness in these areas, the sense of danger can be intensified by negative thoughts such as "I must sound terrible." In addition, increased arousal can interfere with working memory,[15] which can result in forgetting a line or losing place in the score. Such a lapse will further increase anxiety.

Wilson[16] in his discussion of performance anxiety compares the commonly held belief that performance increases as arousal increases from zero to some specific point after which performance deteriorates gradually (the well-known inverted-U function) with a competing notion that at some point the combination of physical arousal and worry becomes catastrophic after which performance precipitously decreases. Anxiety is, at its heart, an arousal mechanism. Although it can facilitate appropriate arousal, communicate importance to the performer, and energize the performance, combined with worry it can be disastrous.

As anxiety (or physical arousal) increases one becomes more aware of one's surroundings and of one's own internal physical experiences. This can help to make our behavior more accurate and in tune with the demands of the external world. Individuals prone to social anxiety tend to shift their attention toward internal cues as sources of information about threat far more than to the demands of the external environment.[17] This results in an excessive focus on internal cues. This can lead to impairment of attention and concentration leading to errors. Motor functions can become impaired by tremor or spasm. Working memory can become impaired[15] leading to difficulty unless the material is learned to the point of automatic functioning. Together these result in decreased performance. As anxiety increases further, the anxiety itself becomes traumatic. The anxiety takes over more and more of the individual's focus of attention and becomes all the individual sees. Even if the performance is "adequate," the level of anxiety might be so high that the individual cannot recognize the information value of the "adequate" performance but only experience the trauma of the anxiety.

A lapse or excessive focus on anticipated negative evaluation can lead to a catastrophic response during which the individual feels that the world is caving in and the somatic symptoms increase in intensity. The performance may quickly deteriorate at this point. The deterioration of the performance confirms all the negative thoughts that the performer had about his or her capacity and sets up expectations for what will happen in future performance situations. Such a situation can be traumatic to the performer and lead to avoidance of performing. The performer dwells on the experience of failure, and the recollections may become even more dramatic and devastating than the original experience. Furthermore, avoidance tends to intensify anxiety rather than decrease it. Thus, the problem can worsen even though the individual successfully avoids having even a second failure experience.

NORMAL VERSUS CLINICALLY SIGNIFICANT PERFORMANCE ANXIETY

The above is a description of the worst kind of outcome, terror and fright during a performance that leads to severe withdrawal from performance. This is not, of course, the most common outcome. Almost everyone experiences performance anxiety, usually much more mildly than the terror described above. It is important to review, then, the difference between "normal" and "clinically significant" performance anxiety.

As with most psychological problems, the boundary line is not always clear. The single most important point of distinction is the degree of functional impairment. "Normal" range anxiety tends to be self-correcting or mild in terms of its impact on a person's functioning. Typical social support or "self-help" is sufficient to

correct the problem. We should go just a bit further, however, and assert that some degree of "normal" performance anxiety is critical to good performance.

The mere presence of anxiety in performance situations, however, does not warrant a formal diagnosis. Performance anxiety should be considered normal and even helpful when it is at lower levels. It helps to heighten awareness and motivate behavior. It might even help the individual "feel" the audience and enliven the performance. When, however, it either impairs the actual performance or causes so much distress that performing hardly becomes enjoyable, we should consider the problem to be a diagnosable disorder. The formal diagnosis is that of social anxiety and requires that physical symptoms of anxiety occur when the individual is exposed to a feared social situation (the performance), the individual recognizes that the anxiety is unrealistic, the situation is either avoided or endured with intense anxiety, and the anxiety interferes significantly with functioning or leads to preoccupation with having the anxiety.[18] (The anxiety must not be due to drug use or other medical conditions.) So, if the individual avoids performance situations, "freezes" at times, or becomes so distressed before or after a performance that other aspects of life are interfered with, a formal diagnosis is warranted.

SELF-MANAGEMENT OF PERFORMANCE ANXIETY

There is a wealth of self-help material for anxiety problems, and the interested individual should look through them in a local bookstore to find one that is appealing. It is probably more important that the book seem to fit the individual's style of thinking and solving problems than describe any specific techniques to a psychologist's satisfaction. That having been said, we can look at some general principles and specific techniques of self-help applied to social anxiety. The professional interventions are built upon the same basic approaches. Figure 14–1 depicts the key processes and decisions involved in both self-management and professional management of performance anxiety.

Prior to discussing the more "psychological" approaches to self-management, it is critical that we

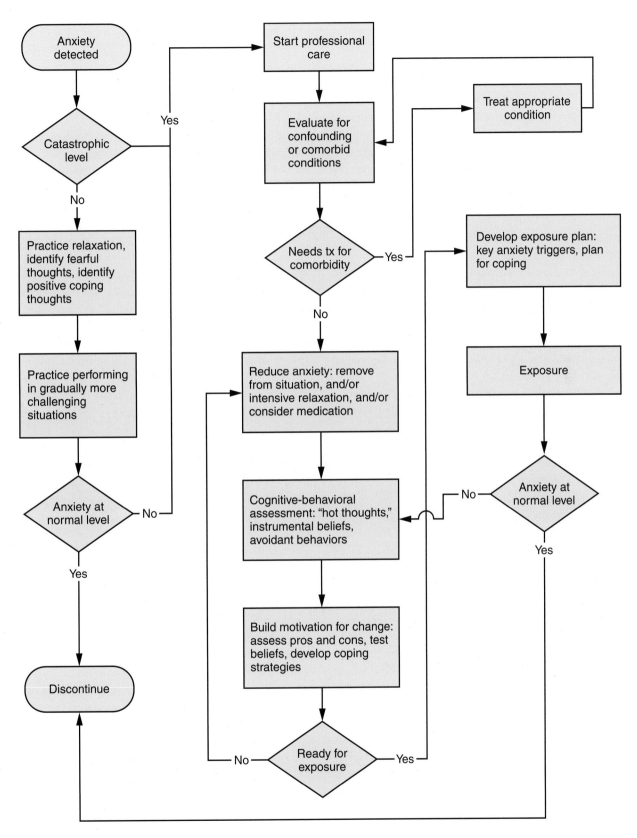

Figure 14-1. Flow chart of the processes and decisions involved in both the self-management (*left-hand side*) and professional treatment (*middle and right-hand side*) of performance anxiety.

discuss the role of preparation. It is unrealistic to think that one will perform adequately if one is not prepared. Not only is the performer's level of experience (and, hence, overall preparation) relevant to the degree of anxiety experienced, but also performers report that worry about their level of preparation is a typical anxiety thought.[2] When possible, practice a piece to the point that its performance is automatic. This reduces the likelihood that divided attention will impair the performance. If one is in a situation in which a performance is required for which one is not adequately prepared (hopefully, for reasons beyond one's control), one has to be realistic about evaluating one's own performance. At the very least the performer should set his or her sights on a level of performance that is realistic for the situation.

Most self-help and formal treatment approaches for performance anxiety are based on a cognitive behavioral approach to treatment, and the foregoing discussion was based on a cognitive-behavioral understanding of anxiety. Relaxation training, stress inoculation training, mindfulness and acceptance, and exposure and rehearsal are the primary components.

Relaxation training involves learning how to relax in the face of stress and how to control or moderate anxiety symptoms or the intensity of those symptoms. We use these methods not to end the anxiety symptoms but to help an individual manage the symptoms. They are not designed to eliminate anxiety but to make working with it easier. There are several approaches to relaxation training. The two basic components are breathing control and muscle relaxation.

Anxiety often leads to a shortening and quickening of the breath. This is, obviously, not good for a singer. The experience of such breathing changes can trigger a precipitous increase in anxiety as the singer has thoughts such as "I won't get through that passage." It is of great advantage for the signer to learn to slow the breath and deepen it. (As with everything else discussed in this section, it is very important that the individual practice this frequently when not under stress so that this practice can make this something the individual can do even under stress.) Count from one to five over a period of 5 seconds all the while breathing in. Be sure that the lungs are completely full at the end of the count. Then begin to breathe out over the same length of time, counting to five, and be sure that the lungs are empty at the end of the count. As

you are breathing out, be aware of how letting the breath out is relaxing. You can picture all the tension in your body going with that breath. Repeat that in-and-out sequence 12 times (or for 2 minutes). By the end of that sequence, most individuals report feeling far more relaxed and calm physically. Deen[19] found that a similar exercise designed to integrate relaxed breathing and awareness of relaxation during that breathing had a significant effect on performance anxiety among vocal performers.

Muscle tension may develop anywhere in the body, but tension in the vocal apparatus, neck, and shoulders may be of particular concern to the vocal performer. For many individuals, using the above breathing exercise is enough to facilitate relaxation of these muscles, particularly if some focus is placed on them and allowing them to relax passively during the breathing exercise. If, however, the muscles are very tense, progressive muscle relaxation[20] may be more effective at helping individuals reverse this tension and produce deep states of relaxation. Often we begin with a few minutes of relaxed breathing as above, and then proceed through the muscles of the body in a systematic way. Start with one arm and hand, then the other, then the legs, trunk, shoulders, neck, tongue, jaw, and face. In each case tense those muscles briefly, hold the tension long enough to be aware of it, and then release those muscles suddenly, fully and completely. Let each of those muscles relax further for a minimum of 30 seconds and for up to 2 minutes being aware of the relaxation that is deepening in the muscles. Repeat the same muscle group a second time before moving on to the next group. Note that we save those muscles of greatest concern to the musician for last. These muscles are often those that tense earliest in anxiety and that are hardest to relax. Relaxing other, easier muscles makes relaxing these less difficult. After going through all the sets of muscles, return to relaxed breathing for a while longer. Be sure to do this slowly, taking sufficient time with each muscle group to allow it to relax deeply.

Once one has learned these breathing and muscle relaxation techniques well, one can usually find ways of abbreviating them. Sometimes one or two quiet, deep breaths together with picturing all the muscles relaxing is sufficient to reduce tension and bring about a greater sense of relaxation. Incorporating some image such as picturing the muscles to be rubber bands that are unwinding may be helpful, or thinking of how a dog lies in the sun breathing quietly may be very helpful in inducing relaxed feelings. Doing this before a rehearsal, practice, or performance can help make it a regular part of one's routine, making it more likely that one will be at least physically relaxed prior to performance.

Self-administered stress inoculation involves identifying thoughts that are involved in the anxiety response, learning to test those thoughts, and developing alternative thoughts. The first step is for the individual to observe him- or herself in the performance situation to identify the thoughts that tend to occur. Write them down as quickly as possible after the performance situations. After a few occasions, one can then find which ones occur most frequently and which ones seem to be the most powerful triggers. One can use a "Thought Record" to help in this process. Once you have identified some key thoughts, ask yourself what there is about that thought or idea that is so threatening or what really could go wrong. Ask what the worst possible outcome could be.

Then ask yourself how likely it is that each of these things could really happen or how realistic the thought is. Suppose the thought is, "the audience will think I'm terrible." Maybe the worst possible outcome is that the critics will say such terrible things about you that you will be banished from the stage forever and become penniless and homeless. Then ask yourself two key questions: is there any evidence that the audience would really have such thoughts, and how likely is it that the worst-case outcome would come true. In addition, one should ask how useful that thought is to promoting a good performance. Usually this helps foster more realistic thinking. Then, develop realistic but helpful coping thoughts. For example, in response to the thought "the audience will think I'm terrible," a more appropriate thought might be, "I'm likely to do well and the audience will likely see that, but even an error or two won't make them think I'm terrible." You might have the idea that you will "choke" and make a fool of yourself. It would be more realistic to think, "I might make an error or two but am not likely to "choke," and I have had many good performances." You might add that a good enough performance is much more likely than a horrible one. Review all the times you have coped well with the pressures of performance.

Finally, if possible reframe the situation from one of danger and threat to one of possible opportunity and challenge. Skinner and Brewer[9] found that individuals who focus on a situation as a challenge rather than a threat experience much less anxiety in a performance situation. For example, work on thinking of the performance situation as an opportunity to feel more and more comfortable with an audience and one's own capacities. Again, be realistic.

Write down a very brief summary of what you have learned. Include the thoughts you developed to reframe the situation or counter the "hot" thoughts that you tend to have. That summary should fit on a small index card you can keep with you or put in your musical score. Just before a performance, go through your relaxation routine and, while relaxed, review your "coping card" to set your mind on helpful and adaptive thoughts.

Note that the thoughts developed to counter the anxiety thoughts are not "pie in the sky" hopefulness. You are not counting on winning the lottery. You are being realistic. You are anticipating some errors (as that is very common in musical performance). You are also recognizing that the consequences will not be dire and that they are of such a sort that you can live with them. It does no good to tell yourself things you cannot really believe.

You can help the process of cognitive restructuring along if you remember that identical situations can be viewed differently by different people or by the same person at different times. Individuals who see performance situations as challenges or opportunities rather than threats feel more comfortable in the situation.[2,9] One can reframe a threat into a challenge or opportunity by the way one phrases the situation to oneself.

Mindfulness or acceptance[21] is a key component in anxiety management. We often develop true fears of our emotions and attempt to avoid experiencing them,[22] and we sometimes think of the anxiety as the danger rather than merely serving to suggest there could be a danger present. As much as one might want to order anxiety away, one cannot do that; we have to accept the fact that it will be there. Mindfulness involves letting oneself experience a feeling in detail while not getting "caught up" in that emotion. It is a skill that has to be developed over time by practice. Start by observing mild emotions and "seeing yourself" having them. Notice how they affect you and how you can still act and function despite them. As you build this ability, you will develop a greater ability to accept the anxiety. This is important because were you to insist that you not feel anxiety before or during a performance, you would almost never perform, and you would likely feel even more distress when the anxiety refused to submit fully to your efforts at control. One has to be willing to feel anxiety. The more willing you are to feel the anxiety, the less distressing the anxiety becomes. The less willing you are to feel the anxiety, the more distressing it becomes (you become anxious about being anxious). Remember you can feel anxiety and still perform. Recall how many great musicians have had very intense performance anxiety. They have had to be willing to experience the anxiety and perform anyway.

The above strategies are all preparatory for the "real" component of self-management, exposure. The functioning of the brain structures that produce anxiety can only be changed by experience. That experience occurs during exposure when you discover that you can be successful and that disaster does not occur. It is very important that the level of anxiety that one feels not be so great that it becomes traumatic. Except when under professional care, it is best to engage in exposure gradually. Fortunately, music teachers often help students do this naturally. Children first perform in front of their loving parents, then in front of peers, and then perform small recitals before performing larger ones. In this way they move from a supportive and encouraging environment in which performing is an opportunity to receive praise to situations in which performing could be met with higher expectations and some degree of critical appraisal. Thus, when the individual has little experience and could justifiably worry about being adequate, the situation will evoke, instead, thoughts of reassurance and support from the audience. As training goes along and the individual has reason to anticipate more and more "adequate" performances, that individual will find it easier to deal with an audience that is more critical.

One can engage in a partial form of exposure without any risk at all. One can imagine the scene of the performance in great detail and even imaging making an error. One can picture oneself recovering from the error. One can picture the audience's response and even a less than ideal response. One can practice quieting oneself during the performance. It is very important to make what one imagines as real as possible. Rather than making it "just a daydream" in which one is performing wonderfully to the audience's intense rapture with your music-making, imagine being anxious. Over time intensify the image. Feel the butterflies in the stomach; feel the tightness in the chest; think of the heart rate going up; think of the audience having paid for a great performance Then, use all the techniques discussed above to deal with those images and experiences. This becomes practice in managing anxiety in a real situation.

All this work in imagination is a preparation for "real" exposure. Perform first in situations that are relatively low in threat or challenge and build to those that are more threatening or challenging. You should feel "comfortable enough" and able to perform adequately at a lower level of threat before going on to a higher level of threat. Performance anxiety has been found to increase as size of the audience increases and when the audience contains critics.[23] One should build the "threat or challenge" into one's exposure with this in mind.

PROFESSIONAL TREATMENT OF PERFORMANCE ANXIETY

One should seek professional treatment if the above self-management approaches are not successful in reducing performance anxiety or if the level of anxiety is "catastrophic" and one's ability to perform is seriously threatened. Even though most common professional treatment approaches will be quite similar to the above, the professional will be able to catch some parts in the anxiety response that the one experiencing the anxiety will not catch and will have tools available to help identify hidden thoughts and fears. Most clinicians will use a cognitive-behavioral approach such as that outlined by Rodebaugh and Chambless.[24]

Evaluation

First, the clinician will perform a thorough evaluation of the individual with performance anxiety with a view toward the presence of confounding and comorbid conditions. Powell,[4] summarizing the literature in the area, concludes that about one-third of individuals with performance anxiety will have some other psychiatric disorder. It is not uncommon for someone with performance anxiety to have generalized anxiety disorder (GAD),[19] which is a debilitating, chronic, and intrusive worry about all sorts of common problems. Social anxiety disorder is also frequent. Depression may be less frequent, but it must be recalled that persistent difficulty doing one's job (making music) can generate a strong feeling of failure and serve to precipitate a depressive episode. Still, Powell reminds us that two-thirds of those with performance anxiety do not have other psychological conditions.

The clinician must also look for substance use problems. Not only are substance use problems fairly common among the general population, but also it is fairly common for individuals to treat their own anxiety with a variety of substances both pharmacological and recreational. Unfortunately such self-medication seldom works and can often lead to other problems because individuals, erroneously thinking that it is merely that they are not using enough medication, tend to increase their use of self-medications when they don't work.

The clinician should also recall that there is a significant difference between performance anxiety and many other forms of social anxiety disorder. In performance anxiety, there is often a much greater emphasis on negative self-appraisal. In most forms of social anxiety, the emphasis is almost totally on a negative appraisal coming from others. The clinician should carefully explore the performer's self-expectations and the presence of perfectionistic demands. Finally the role of the demands placed on the performer by family and teachers must be considered. How the performer views these demands and what the performer sees as the consequences of failing to live up to those expectations may be of great importance in the creation or maintenance of the anxiety. It is even possible, although not common, that the anxiety serves to solve some interpersonal conflict for the individual. The anxiety, then, would be reinforced by the reduction in anxiety the individual feels by virtue of avoiding the conflict. This form of reinforcement is called "negative reinforcement" and is the strongest type of reinforcement, and the resultant learning is hardest to extinguish.

Cognitive-Behavioral Therapy

Very commonly, the clinician will use some form of "stress inoculation" training as a part of the treatment. Stress inoculation training consists of identifying likely stressful situations, what the individual sees as "the problem" in the situation, and then developing specific ways of coping with those problems. The clinician will help the individual to identify specific actions or self-statements that can be used at various points in the situation that the person finds stressful. For example, the clinician will help the individual develop a strategy for self-soothing or refocusing on one's abilities and past successes. Through this, the individual gains confidence that he or she will be able to manage the stressful situation. Of course, it is the real-life management of the stressful situation that "stamps in" the newfound confidence. In a meta-analysis of 37 studies, Saunders[25] found stress inoculation training to be quite effective at reducing anxiety and enhancing performance under stress. Even though just one session of stress inoculation training can be helpful, one should expect treatment to last a minimum of six to seven sessions. It is probably realistic to think that individuals who have tried the self-management techniques above and have not been able to manage their own anxiety will require even more sessions as there are likely to be many hidden obstacles or cognitions that will take time to find and confront.

Confronting one's anxiety is difficult. Often the clinician has to work with the performer to help the latter develop the will and desire to confront the anxiety. The clinician will assess the performer's readiness to start each stage of the treatment and will reassess that readiness and the individual's response to the interventions attempted. It may be necessary to "cycle back" to an earlier stage in the treatment when an obstacle is met or a new "hot thought" discovered during the process of exposure.

The individual will be asked to engage in "homework" between sessions. Because in all psychological treatments it is the "patient" not the "therapist" who does the changing,[26] this homework becomes critical to the change process. Much of what constitutes professional treatment is helping the individual identify the internal obstacles to change and organizing him or herself toward changing those obstacles. The individual has to work on those changes between sessions for the treatment to be efficient and effective.

Because the individuals who present to a professional, as distinguished from those who manage their own anxiety successfully, will present a number of challenges to the clinician, it is important that the approach be flexible and incorporate strategies most likely to affect that individual's particular combination of difficulties.[27] The clinician should draw from cognitive, behavioral, interpersonal, and psychodynamic approaches.

Exposure is the basic tool in treating almost any anxiety disorder. Most commonly one starts with identifying situations that tend to be anxiety provoking and then ordering them in ascending order of intensity of anxiety. Then the key features of those situations are determined and the list refined further taking those key features into consideration. Once the list is complete, the clinician leads the individual up the list starting with situations that provoke very little anxiety. Once such "easy" situations no longer trigger any appreciable anxiety, the clinician invites the individual to move up the list. This is done progressively so that the individual never has to experience more anxiety than can be managed. Very commonly this is combined with careful relaxation training so that the experience of relaxation can be "paired" with the cues that have triggered anxiety in the past. This sets up a new conditioned (learned) experience that is incompatible with the previous anxiety.

This process has to be highly flexible and the clinician will most commonly go back and forth between exposure and a cognitive-behavioral analysis of the problem. At each point in exposure, the clinician will test the effectiveness of the exposure and, implicitly at least, the prior cognitive-behavioral analysis. The clinician will not assume that a reduction in anxiety is due to having challenged the cognition previously identified as relevant but will be open to the possibility that a different cognition was operative in this instance. Failure of a particular intervention is as much data for the assessment as is the earlier assessment, and such failures are a routine part of the treatment of even moderately complex cases.

At times psychodynamic approaches might be useful in managing performance anxiety, particularly when the individual has strong tendencies toward feeling shame and inadequacy or when the anxiety "solves" an interpersonal conflict. Psychodynamic approaches examine how various thoughts and behaviors serve to protect one from anxiety or other emotions about which one has felt conflicted. There is always a personal story behind these types of fears and conflicts. For example, if one has been shamed in the past for proud or boastful behaviors, one can develop a fear of performance because it is (sometimes literally) blowing one's own horn. The clinician helps the individual to recognize those fears and confront them mentally before encouraging behavioral exposure. McCullough[28] describes the use of a behaviorally enlightened psychodynamic therapy for performance anxiety. This will involve careful identification of the nature of the guilt or shame together with an exploration of the "narrative" behind that experience. This facilitates a more appropriate appraisal of the situation and greater tolerance of the affect.

Pharmacotherapy

A number of medications have been used to manage anxiety disorders. In general, and with some exceptions, the research data do not demonstrate any superiority for medications over psychological treatments in the management of anxiety and no real advantage to combining them except in the most severe cases. Furthermore, individuals who are treated with medications are very likely to need to use them for a very long time and may not be able to discontinue them without difficulty. There is an old saw in medicine, "what gets you well keeps you well." Long-term maintenance on medications for anxiety is more and more common. Because they have no major advantage over behavioral therapy as monotherapy, their use should likely be limited to more severe situations in which the individual is on the verge of making damaging choices to quit performing or needs some initial help in starting the process of behavioral treatment.

Most commonly today, SSRIs (selective serotonin reuptake inhibitors) are used to manage anxiety disorders in general clinical practice. These drugs, which include such household words as Prozac (fluoxetine) and Zoloft (sertraline), are used to treat anxiety and depression and can be quite effective in doing so.

They must be used consistently and are useless on an "as-needed" basis. Because they can not be used on an as-needed basis and have some significant side effects, they should probably be reserved for use when the individual with performance anxiety has other comorbid conditions for which they would be appropriate.

There is one class of drugs that should clearly be avoided for performance anxiety, the benzodiazepines. These include Xanax (alprazolam), Valium (diazepam), Klonopin (clonazepam), and a number of other compounds. These drugs are central nervous system depressants and can impair cognitive and motor functioning.[29] In addition, these drugs interfere with exposure.[30] This may result from one or more of several processes including the tendency of these drugs to interfere with short-term memory and their function as cues which signal safety in the exposure situation preventing the individual from learning that the situation is not dangerous. Finally, benzodiazepines may lead to a bias toward perceiving internal cues of anxiety.[31] This, as noted above, can lead to an increase in anxiety experience and interfere with performance.

Many performers rely on beta-blockers on an as-needed basis. These drugs are commonly used for hypertension and cardiac arrhythmias. One of their effects is to slow cardiac acceleration. The individual does not feel as much of a rise in heart rate and is, supposedly, less likely to respond to that experience as a signal of impending anxiety. Turner and colleagues[32] found that there was no difference between atenolol (a beta-blocker) and placebo in reducing social anxiety in a performance situation. There is little doubt that knowing they are "in the system" might give the performer some confidence, but it is most likely more a placebo effect than a pharmacologic effect. If the individual comes to believe that having such a drug on board is critical to controlling anxiety, the lack of it, for whatever reason, may actually intensify anxiety.

In all, then, unless there are significant comorbid conditions that would justify the use of one of these medications or the anxiety has gotten so highly disruptive and traumatic that some immediate, short-term pharmacological reduction in anxiety is needed to enable the individual to start the process of behavioral treatment, behavioral treatments should be the sole treatment modality for performance anxiety.

SUMMARY

Performance anxiety is a near-universal problem for vocal musicians. For most it does not cause disability but it can interfere with one's functioning and make music-making far less enjoyable than it should be. One's own demands for excellence and an intolerance for imperfection can predispose an individual to develop more problematic performance anxiety. Performance anxiety can most often be managed on one's own with the use of cognitive and behavioral techniques. If one cannot manage it on one's own, clinicians will most commonly use similar cognitive-behavioral techniques and will add strategies for identifying covert thoughts and beliefs that block change and will build motivation and tolerance for exposure. While medication is not usually indicated and often contraindicated, it is occasionally useful for the most acutely impaired. Above all, it is important to know that the pressure a performer experiences that can lead to performance anxiety is also a motivator to move toward excellence and can energize the performer and the performance. In this way, what might otherwise be experienced as anxiety could be experienced as the thrill of performance.

REFERENCES

1. Kaspersen M, Gotestam K. A survey of music performance anxiety among Norwegian music students. *Eur J Psychiatry.* 2002;16:69–98.
2. Tamborrino R. *An examination of performance anxiety associated with solo performance of college-level music majors* [dissertation]. Bloomington, Ind: Indiana University; 2001.
3. Hamman DL. An assessment of anxiety in instrumental and vocal performances. *J Res Music Ed.* 1982;30:77–91.
4. Powell DH. Treating individuals with debilitating performance anxiety: an introduction. *J Consult Clin Psychol.* 2004;60: 801–808.
5. Hayes SC, Barnes-Holmes D, Roche B. *Relational Frame Theory: A Post-Skinnerian Account of Human Language and Cognition.* New York, NY: Kluwer Academic/Plenum Publishers; 2001.
6. Yiend J, ed. *Cognition, Emotion, and Psychopathology: Theoretical, Empirical, and Clinical*

Directions. Cambridge: Cambridge University Press; 2004.

7. LeDoux J. *The Emotional Brain: The Mysterious Underpinnings of Emotional Life.* New York, NY: Touchstone; 1996.

8. LeDoux J. *Synaptic Self: How Our Brains Become Who We Are.* Harmondsworth, UK: Penguin Books; 2003.

9. Skinner N, Brewer N. The dynamics of threat and challenge appraisals prior to stressful achievement events. *J Pers Soc Psychol.* 2002;83:678-692.

10. Tobacyk JJ, Downs A. personal construct threat and irrational beliefs as cognitive predictors of increases in musical performance anxiety. *J Pers Soc Psychol.* 1998;51:779-782.

11. Beilock SL, Carr TH. On the fragility of skilled performance: what governs choking under pressure? *J Exp Psychol:Gen.* 2001l;130:701-725.

12. Beilock SL, Kulp CA, Holt LE, Carr TH. More on the fragility of performance: choking under pressure in mathematical problem solving. *J Exp Psychol: Gen.* 2004;133:584-600.

13. Maroon MT. *Potential Contributors to Performance Anxiety Among Middle School Students Performing at Solo and Ensemble Contest* [dissertation].

14. Rapee RM, Lim L. Discrepancy between self- and observer ratings of performance in social phobics. *J Abn Psychol.* 1992;101:728-731.

15. Ashcraft MH, Kirk EP. The relationships among working memory, math anxiety, and performance. *J Exp Psychol:Gen.* 2001;130:224-237.

16. Wilson GD. *Psychology for Performing Artists.* London: Whurr Publishers; 2002.

17. Pineles SL, Mineka S. Attentional biases to internal and external sources of potential threat in social anxiety. *J Abn Psychol.* 2005;114:314-318.

18. American Psychiatric Association. *Diagnostic and Statistical Manual.* 4th ed. Washington, DC: Author; 1994.

19. Deen DR. *Awareness and Breathing: Keys to the Moderation of Musical Performance Anxiety* [dissertation]. Lexington, Ky: University of Kentucky; 1999.

20. Bourne EJ. *The Anxiety and Phobia Workbook.* 3rd ed. Oakland, Calif: New Harbinger Publications; 2000.

21. Hayes SC, Strosahl KD, Wilson KG. *Acceptance and Commitment Therapy: An Experiential Approach to Behavior Change.* New York, NY: Guilford; 1999.

22. McCullough L. *Changing Character: Short-Term Anxiety Regulating Psychotherapy for Restructuring Defenses.* New York, NY: Basic Books; 1997.

23. LeBlanc A, Jin YC, Obert M, Siivola C. Effect of audience on music performance anxiety. *J Res Music Ed.* 1997;45:480-496.

24. Rodebaugh TL, Chambless DL. Cognitive therapy for performance anxiety. *J Consult Clin Psychol.* 2004;60:809-820.

25. Saunders T, Driskell JE, Johnston JH, Salas E. The effect of stress inoculation training on anxiety and performance. *J Occup Health Psychol.* 1996;1: 170-186.

26. Tallman K, Bohart AC. The client as a common factor: clients as self-healers. In Hubble MA, Duncan BL, Miller SD, eds. *The Heart and Sole of Change: What Works in Therapy.* Washington, DC: American Psychological Association; 1999.

27. Lazarus AA, Abramovitz A. A multimodal behavioral approach to performance anxiety. *J Consult Clin Psychol.* 2004;60:831-840.

28. McCullough L, Osborn KAR. Short term dynamic psychotherapy goes to Hollywood: the treatment of performance anxiety in cinema. *J Consult Clin Psychol.* 2004;60:841-852.

29. Streufert S, Satish U, Pogash R, et al.. Effects of alprazolam on complex human functioning. *J Applied Soc Psychol.* 1996;26:1912-1920.

30. Birk L. Pharmacotherapy for performance anxiety disorders: occasionally useful but typically contraindicated. *J Consult Clin Psychol.* 2004;60:867-879.

31. Steward SH, Westra HA, Thompson CE, Conrad BE. Effects of naturalistic benzodiazepine use on selective attention to threat cues among anxiety disorder patients. *Cog Therapy Res.* 2000;24:67-85.

32. Turner SM, Beidel DC, Jacob RG. Social phobia: a comparison of behavioral therapy and atenolol. *J Consult Clin Psychol.* 1994;62:350-358.

Chapter 15

SURGICAL ANATOMY, PLANNING, AND CONSENT

Michael S. Benninger

SURGERY IN THE SINGER

It is not by chance that the chapter on surgical therapy in the singer is the last chapter in this book. Fortunately, surgery is only rarely needed to manage a voice problem in a singer. Most voice disorders in singers can be improved or completely resolved through appropriate assessment, diagnosis, and nonsurgical treatments. These may include lifestyle changes, modification of voice use, speech therapy from a voice pathologist, or ongoing voice instruction from a singing voice teacher.[1]

There are times, however, when surgery is the preferred treatment option. This chapter discusses decision-making processes to identify those singers who should consider surgery, the preoperative evaluation, surgical planning, the critical surgical anatomy, and the informed-consent process and documentation.

IDENTIFYING THE PATIENT WHO IS A SURGICAL CANDIDATE

There are numerous singers who present with findings that theoretically could be amenable to surgery. In principle, most mass lesions can be removed with surgery, yet few truly require it. So, how do you determine which patient should be considered for surgical treatment? This question is not easily answered. There are as many variables that need to be considered as there are voice-disordered patients. Those variables include the singer, the environment, the time needed for recovery, and the comfort levels of the singer and the surgeon. Needless to say, the determination of surgical candidacy requires a caring, thoughtful, and empathetic approach. Singers must understand that surgical treatment is only one step in the rehabilitation of a vocal injury. Once determined, candidacy does not mean that surgery will result, as candidacy is only the initial step in the ultimate decision to perform surgery.

The evaluation techniques that have been discussed in the preceding chapters are particularly important in an individual who is being considered for surgery. A thorough history and physical examination should be bolstered by appropriate objective tests and subjective observations to make the diagnosis and to confirm the degree of voice dysfunction. Videostroboscopy is particularly useful in assessing the impact on vocal fold vibratory characteristics, as well as giving an impression of firmness and chronicity.[2] The VHI, as described in chapter 5, is very useful in helping to determine the impact of the lesion on overall life quality. A person who has notable dysphonia but is still able to perform within defined expectations and scores well on the VHI may not be a good surgical candidate even if he or she has a chronic lesion that is poorly responsive to conservative treatments.

All pertinent evaluations should be performed at the initial visit and then again following behavior modifications, voice therapy, and singing instruction. It is imperative to assess whether or not further nonsurgical therapy may be of value. It is also important to understand the degree of the singer's compliance with these treatments, as poor compliance prior to surgery will usually mean poor compliance after, with the potential for less than optimal results. It is my opinion that it is better to err on too long a period of time for conservative treatment before surgery than too short. I have been surprised more than once that a patient who had gone through a long period of conservative treatment with suboptimal results eventually had positive results later.

A failure of conservative treatment does not alone determine which singers are surgical candidates. A singer with nodules and chronic dysphonia secondary to vocal nodules who is still able to perform (even if suboptimally), and who is not able to change performance schedules, may not have significant improvement until the schedule can be changed. A singer with reflux and persistent hoarseness will not benefit from laryngeal surgery for Reinke's edema, but after failing aggressive reflux treatment might benefit from surgical fundoplication. By maintaining open communication among voice team members and the patient, a clear and conservative treatment plan is shared by all and open to change when appropriate.

The primary indications for laryngeal surgery in singers are mass lesions on the vocal folds. Although there has been considerable debate and a lack of consensus regarding nomenclature for vocal fold mass lesions, some constant descriptive terms are helpful in describing the lesions and allowing for a general understanding of what the pathology is among health care providers. These descriptive terms may vary somewhat between centers so it is important for the members of each vocal care team to have consistency within their group. It should also be noted that the tentative diagnosis used to describe the preoperative lesion may be altered at the time of surgery when the surgeon has been able to carefully palpate, assess, and examine the lesion directly. I try not to give my definitive impression to the patients preoperatively, as there

have been a number of times where my diagnosis changed in the operating room.

That all being said, I prefer to classify lesions based on the location on the vocal fold, the likely histopathology, the effect on vibration seen during videostroboscopy, whether or not the lesion is unilateral or bilateral, and a general impression of firmness or chronicity. Although this is a clear simplification, bilateral and nearly symmetric lesions in the mid to anterior one-third of the vocal folds are often vocal nodules in women.[3] Similar appearing lesions in men are typically not nodules. Most otolaryngologists and voice pathologists have seen lesions that have been defined as "nodules" but did not respond appropriately to voice therapy; and the results after surgery revealed a cyst with a contact nodule on the opposite vocal fold (Figures 15-1A and 1B). "Vocal nodules" that have responded little or not at all to voice therapy and vocal hygiene are of particular concern. Not only is it possible that one or both masses is a cyst but there also may be a sulcus vocalis. Videostroboscopy has been found to be useful in clarifying the nature of some of these lesions.[2]

On occasion, it is difficult to identify whether or not a unilateral lesion should be classified as a cyst or a polyp. In some cases this distinction may be relatively simple (Figure 15-2), while in others it may be quite difficult. It is also often difficult to determine the difference between chronic nodules and more insidious lesions such as sulcus vocalis (Figure 15-3). It is critically important to inform patients that a suspected diagnosis made preoperatively may be changed once the lesion is better evaluated in the operating room. It is also important to inform patients that the magnitude of the procedure may need to be changed in the operating room, or, on rare occasions, may need to be aborted based on the intraoperative assessment and diagnosis.

Granulomas are typically found on the posterior aspect of the vocal fold, usually on the vocal process of the arytenoids, and although usually unilateral, they may also be bilateral (Figure 15-4A). Granulation tissue can also form on other areas of the vocal folds, and some refer to them as granulomatous polyps (Figure 15-4B). Typical granulomas rarely require treatment, as aggressive reflux treatment and appropriate behavior modification and voice therapy will usually allow them to resolve spontaneously, whereas granulomatous polyps more often require surgery.

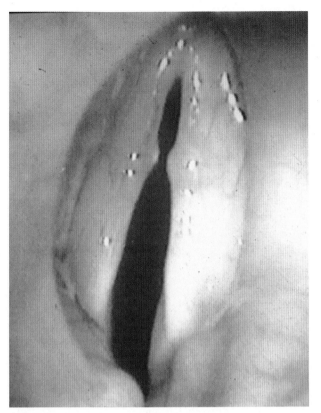
A.

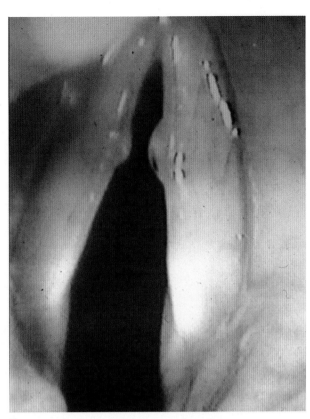
B.

Figure 15-1. Poorly responsive "vocal nodules." **A.** Low magnification suggesting asymmetric nodules. **B.** Higher magnification revealing cyst on the right vocal fold with contact nodule on the opposite vocal fold.

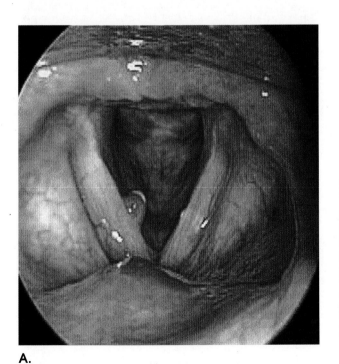
A.

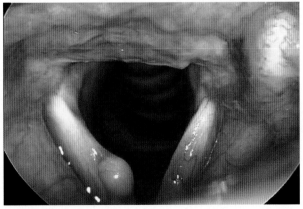
B.

Figure 15-2. A. Unilateral laryngeal polyp. **B.** Unilateral laryngeal cyst.

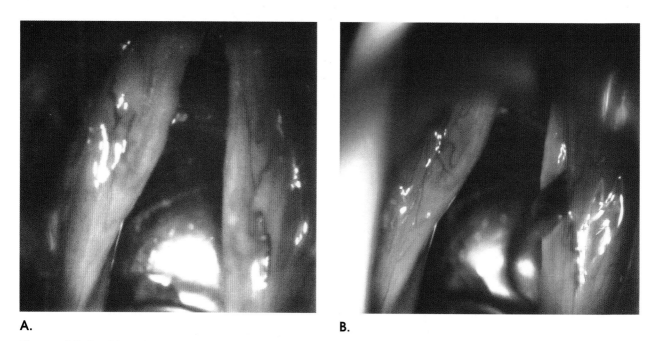

A. **B.**

Figure 15–3. Chronic, recalcitrant "nodules" failing conservative treatment. **A.** Chronic appearing bilateral swelling. **B.** Intraoperative palpation reveals deep bilateral sulci.

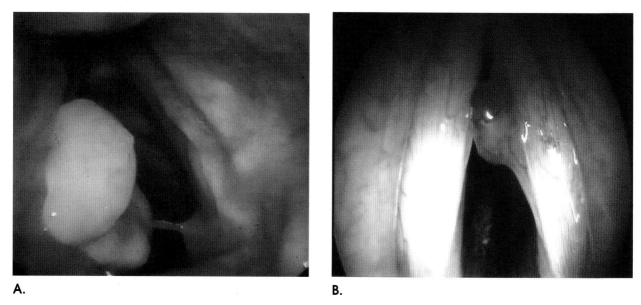

A. **B.**

Figure 15–4. **A.** Classic vocal fold granuloma on the vocal process of the arytenoids. **B.** Granulomatous polyp on the free margin of the vocal fold.

Even if obvious mass lesions are noted on the vocal folds, it does not necessarily imply that surgery is necessary. When a singer is evaluated in the clinic, it is sometimes difficult to determine if the lesion is new or has been there for some time. I have been impressed with the number of singers who have had an acute change in voice where a mass is noted, and where there were older photographs or videos of the larynx that show that the mass had been there for some time, even when there was an intervening period of normal voice quality. Making decisions regarding surgery in these situations may be difficult. If possible, and if the singer has been seen in the past, it is always helpful in obtaining any older medical records or images. In some cases, a chronic mass lesion may have been present for a long time and some other factor resulted in the recent voice change. In such cases, surgery may not be of great value.

Another critical and important issue is the singer's expectations from the evaluation and recommendations. Some singers are not concerned about the impact of the mass (which could potentially be surgically removed). In some cases they just want reassurance that the problem will not progress or permanently affect their voice. In other cases, they are concerned about the possibility of a cancer, particularly in those singers who smoke. There are singers where the raspy or breathy voice afforded by the mass lesion is actually part of their voice signature and is, therefore, desirable. This is true for some cabaret singers where removing the lesion could be catastrophic. The bottom line is that every singer is different, with different voice demands, and different expectations. It is important for the voice surgeon to establish a strong relationship with the singer, know his or her singing style and demands, then be honest about the problem and explain the treatment options and their ramifications. Then, the surgeon should take the time to hear the singer's concerns and allow him or her to participate in the discussion and ultimately make the decision. When the surgeon is specifically asked what he or she feels is the best option for the singer, taking a balanced approach and being honest about the expectations is the best approach.

During the preoperative evaluation it is very important to identify any other significant medical problems that need to be considered. In some cases other physicians may need to be brought into the care team. A thorough history of medications is mandatory to be certain that they will not adversely affect the surgical outcome (see chapter 9). With the number of alternative and homeopathic medications available, it is also important to identify these as some of them may be contraindicated in the surgical patient. For a full description of the potential side effects of these products please refer to chapter 10.

INFORMED CONSENT

This is the basis of the informed-consent process. The singer should be aware of each available and reasonable option, their advantages and disadvantages, and a consistent plan for each. If the singer has not already achieved appropriate resolution of the voice problem from nonsurgical therapy, and if a significant impact on the singing voice remains that is potentially amenable to surgery, then surgery should be discussed with the singer. The first question that a surgeon should ask is, "Am I comfortable with my own skills in surgically managing this problem?" If the answer is "No," then there should be follow-up questions: "Are there others that are more competent to surgically manage this patient?" or "Is the problem complex enough that others would also be uncomfortable in managing this?" These questions allow the surgeon to re-evaluate his or her role in the rehabilitation of the singer. The surgeon may then perform the surgery, refer the singer to another surgical laryngologist, or consider that the risks could potentially outweigh the benefits at this time and pursue other avenues.

Once the surgeon has determined that surgery is the best option, and that he or she is competent to perform the surgery, then the benefits and risks of the surgery should be discussed with the patient in detail. These should not only include the risks related to the effect on the larynx and voice, but also other potential issues such as anesthetic complications, injury to the teeth, postintubation laryngospasm with pulmonary edema, or other risks specific to the patient's health. These discussions should be thoroughly documented in the medical record and a consent form should be signed and witnessed with a copy for the patient. The patient should never be coaxed into surgery. In addition, it is important to discuss with the singer that it is impossible to determine how one will heal and that there is a risk that the voice may not improve or could theoretically worsen due to the aforementioned risks, and that the results could be permanent. These discussions will vary based on the severity of the surgical problem. In most cases they should be part of an open discussion, emphasizing the positive aspects, suggesting that improvement is expected, and allaying the singer's fears while increasing the singer's confidence in the surgeon. Reviewing photographs and videos and drawing templates on paper are very helpful in describing the surgery and in gaining the patients understanding of the surgery. It is also helpful to describe the entire process from preoperative steps to leaving the recovery room. The more informed the patient, the greater their psychological comfort and the stronger the relationship with the surgeon. This will also help to buffer any potential litigation issues if there is a suboptimal outcome.

Other objective tests may also be helpful to clarify the need for surgery and may be useful in assessing the effectiveness of surgery when comparing preoperative to postoperative results. These tests may be more relevant based on the specific test and the nature of the problem. For example, airflow analysis may be useful in vocal fold paresis or paralysis or very large masses, but may be less valuable in Reinke's edema. Objective tests are useful for monitoring nonsurgical treatments but do not take the place of laryngeal videostroboscopy (LVS). In addition to LVS, outcomes instruments like the Voice Handicap Index (VHI) are important. They help not only to assess the severity of disease and the response from the patient's perspective to treatment but may also help clarify whether or not the patient is a surgical candidate.

SURGICAL PLANNING

Once the determination has been made to proceed with surgery, and the informed-consent process has been completed, a number of important issues need to be considered as part of the surgical planning. The first is the timing of the surgery. How does it fit into audition, recital, or performance schedules? How does it fit into family, social, or other occupational schedules? When does the patient want to proceed? It is important to be flexible, understanding, and supportive of the singer's schedule and timing needs. As there will be some recovery time before singers can resume their voice use after surgery, this also needs to be built into the schedule. In general, for superficial vocal fold masses such as nodules or superficial polyps, it is not unreasonable that the singer may begin some gentle singing within 4 to 6 weeks following surgery. They can gradually advance their voice use so that they can perform by 2 to 3 months after surgery. If the problem

appears more significant, then it may take longer. It is reasonable and preferable to overestimate the time to recovery. It is often easier for the performer to add in an engagement than to cancel one because recovery was underestimated. It also helps to emphasize that the healing process may be slow and that postoperative voice use should be tempered.

I typically tell patients that they should have little voice use for at least 2 weeks following surgery. I see them around that time and obtain LVS assessment. If there is a return of vocal fold vibration, and if the mucosa is healing well, I will begin advancing their voice use. I see them again 2 weeks later, and if they continue to do well, I will ask them to begin some gentle singing vocalizations. I generally do not allow them to begin dramatically advancing their volume or range until 6 weeks and only then if everything is going perfectly. The value of a singing voice specialist at this time is important as the singer will often discuss details of singing with that person rather than anyone else. The typical patient can begin performing between 8 to 12 weeks. It is important to note that this time frame may vary significantly. Close observation and examination of patients is critical to optimize their return while still avoiding any potential setbacks. It is generally best to err on being conservative. If recovery is planned prior to surgery and then adjusted, if necessary, once the magnitude of the surgery is known, all involved will be comfortable with the recovery time.

Another consideration that should be made preoperatively about the perioperative treatment is the importance of integrating the voice pathologist and singing teacher into the treatment plans. It is important to coordinate these visits, determine the appropriate roles for each practitioner, and elucidate to the patient the specific roles. Treating a singer is a multidisciplinary endeavor and this is particularly true for the surgical patient. It may be important to begin singing instruction before the surgery to maximize the effectiveness of these treatments postoperatively.

SURGICAL PLANNING: MICROANATOMIC CONSIDERATIONS

The other part of surgical planning is conceptualizing the surgery and what may be expected to be encountered based on the evaluation of the lesion and the relevant surgical anatomy. Although the anatomy of the larynx is well described in chapter 2, a review of the microanatomic principles of the larynx and how they relate to surgery is valuable. The layered structure has been well defined by Hirano[4,5] (Figure 15–5). There is mucosa, three layers of the lamina propria, with the most superficial being Reinke's space and the deepest layer being the vocal ligament. Deep to the ligament is the thyroarytenoid (vocalis) muscle.[4] These layers tend to vibrate independently at lower frequencies and more as a unit at higher frequencies. These layers are relatively independent and with differing composition of collagen and cellular matrix with the predominant collagen fibers of the vocalis ligament running parallel to those of the mucosa. Injury to both the mucosa and the ligament will cause disruption of this orientation so that there are adhesions between these deep layers and mucosa.[5] This can lead to stiffness and limitations in the vibratory characteristics of the vocal fold.

Fortunately, most lesions of the vocal folds such as nodules, polyps, and superficial cysts such as mucus-retention cysts, are limited to the mucosa and superficial layer. Surgery, therefore, confined to the mucosa and Reinke's space as is usually possible in such lesions, will lead to maintenance of the orientation of the layers with normal or near-normal vibratory characteristics.[5] Deeper lesions, such as epidermoid cysts and sulci, may not result in completely normal vibration.

The surgeon needs to plan the type of anesthesia, perhaps even having a discussion with the anesthesiologist prior to surgery. Although venture-jet ventilation is an appropriate consideration, with this technique the surgeon and anesthesiologist need to work closely together to make sure that the ventilation does not move the vocal folds while the laryngeal surgeon is manipulating the vocal folds.

Specialized equipment for laryngeal surgery should be available. There have been great advances in laryngeal microsurgical instruments that recognize the microanatomic principles of vocal fold surgery. Smaller instruments that allow for atraumatic manipulation of the vocal folds have been developed. Although most surgeons have moved away from laser surgery for many benign lesions, in skilled hands the outcomes would be expected to be similar to those obtained with microinstruments.[6] Another significant innovation in surgical instruments has been the orientation of the handle of the instruments. In these instruments, thumb activation does not result in any perceptual movement of the distal, active part of the instrument (Figure 15–6). This results in better stability and may potentially reduce the risk of movement error.[7]

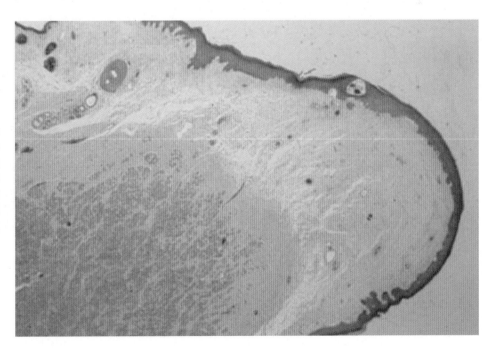

Figure 15–5. The microanatomy of the vocal fold showing the mucosa, three layers of the lamina propria, and vocalis muscle.

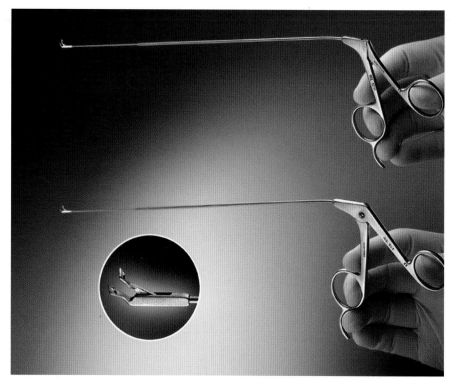

A.

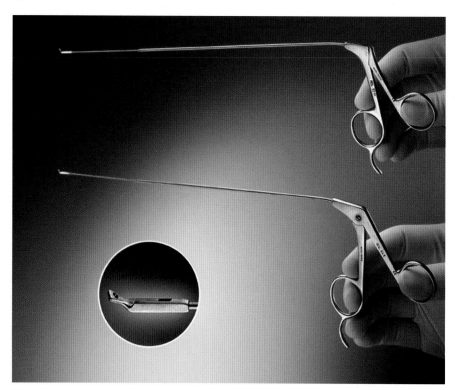

B.

Figure 15–6. Laryngeal microinstrument with thumb-activated handle that allows for minimal distal movement with closure. Notice the difference between the lower (traditional handle) and upper (thumb-activated handle) instruments in relationship to distal tip motion. **A.** Instrument open. **B.** Instrument closed.

SUMMARY

Planning for surgery in a singer requires the establishment of a strong relationship between the surgeon and the singer. In essence, they need to develop a partnership of care. In most cases, the diagnosis should be confirmed with appropriate objective tests, LVS, and a trial of voice therapy prior to determining the need for surgery. The decision to proceed with surgery should lead to a thorough discussion of the risks, benefits, and alternatives (informed consent) and this should be properly documented. The surgery should be planned where possible around the schedule of the performer and a contract should be developed regarding the approximate timing of the postoperative voice use and performance schedule. The surgeon should plan the surgical technique but be flexible to modify the technique based on the intraoperative findings. He or she should make sure that suitable instruments are available to treat the problem. The surgeon also is responsible for coordinating the surgery with other health care providers including the anesthesiologist. Finally, the surgeon should be involved in the postoperative care along with the speech pathologist, the voice teacher, and the singer's agents or managers.

REFERENCES

1. Benninger MS, Johnson A, Jacobson B, eds. *Vocal Arts Medicine. The Care and Prevention of Professional Voice Disorders.* New York, NY: Thieme Medical Publishers; 1993.
2. Sataloff RT, Spiegel JR, Hawkshaw MJ. Strobovideolaryngoscopy: results and clinical value. *Ann Otol Rhinol Laryngol.* 1991;100:725-727.
3. Benninger MS, Jacobson B. Vocal nodules, microwebs and surgery. *J Voice.* 1995;9:326-331.
4. Hirano M. Phonosurgery. Basic and clinical investigations. *Otologia (Fukuoka).* 1975;21:239-262.
5. Benninger MS, Alessi D, Archer S. et al. Vocal fold scarring: current concepts and management. *Otolaryngol Head Neck Surg.* 1996;115:474-482.
6. Benninger MS. Microdissection or microspot CO_2 laser for limited vocal fold benign pathology: a prospective randomized trial. *Laryngoscope.* 2001;110 (Suppl 92):1-17.
7. Benninger MS. Laryngeal microinstrumentation: a novel design to reduce movement. *Otolaryngol Head Neck Surg.* 2003;129:280-283.

Appendix

VOCAL HYGIENE

Vocal hygiene is a daily regimen to achieve and maintain a healthy voice. Vocal hygiene includes maintaining adequate rest and hydration (6 to 8 glasses of water per day), minimizing exposure to noxious chemicals, no smoking of cigarettes or other tobacco substances, and avoiding excessive shouting, screaming, or other nonessential loud voice use.

Proper nutrition is also part of a good vocal hygiene program. Excessive weight may lead to faulty use of the respiratory muscles that are important for generating the power of the voice. In addition, excessive weight adds to overall body fatigue and may restrict a singer or actor from certain roles that require a high level of physical activity.

The following tips apply to keeping and maintaining a healthy voice:

- Good general health.

- Regular exercise to maintain adequate muscle tone.

- Rest when fatigued or injured.

- Use a reduced voice usage schedule when tired.

- Rehearse only after warming up.

- Use ear protection when the sound level is high.

- Have your hearing checked regularly.

- Review past recordings of your voice; note the changes if any.

- Avoid long telephone conversations prior to rehearsals or performances.

- Warm up your voice prior to singing.

- For school children—adequate hydration prior to after school rehearsals. A few minutes of stretching also helps.

Do's and don'ts of vocal hygiene

- Drink 6 to 8 glasses of water per day (there is no substitute for plain water).

- Reduce or eliminate caffeine and caffeinated drinks—coffee, tea, colas, and so forth.

- Rest before performances. Allow plenty of time between long airplane flights and rehearsals or performances.

- Eat a balanced diet. Avoid crash diets. They may contain substances that change the way you feel and produce voice.

- Examine the details of food supplements. Excessive vitamin E may cause blood vessels in the vocal folds and other parts of the body to rupture.

continues

- Do not clear your throat. Excessive throat clearing is an indicator of a problem and should be addressed by an otolaryngologist.

- Laugh. The muscles of the body relax during laughter.

- Do not shout.

- Do not whisper with strain.

- Eliminate and avoid all tobacco products.

- Avoid areas of noxious chemicals/fumes.

- Do not smoke cigarettes, cigars, or pipes.

- Avoid second-hand smoke.

- Do not use recreational drugs.

- Do not share the prescription medications of other performers (such as antibiotics).

- Avoid over-the-counter medications. Your voice is too important. Consult an otolaryngologist who specializes in the care of performers.

- Review all prescription medications with your doctor in relationship to potential impact on your voice.

- Minimize alcohol. Like caffeine, it dries out the mucous membranes that cover the vocal muscles, inside the mouth and throat.

- Be cautious about weight lifting that requires grunting or straining. Use lighter weights and more repetitions if possible.

- Eat light meals with plenty of water before rehearsals and performances.

- Take steps to reduce stress. Exercise, rest, and counseling are proven ways to reduce stress.

- Humidify your studio and bedroom during winter months. If you have mold allergies, try not to let the humidity get too high.

- Be cautious about voice use in environments with loud background noise, such as clubs or airplanes.

- After an injury or sickness, consult your vocal coach or singing teacher to see if you have modified or changed your vocal techniques.

- Women—select birth control medications with the help of a physician who understands the effects of hormones on the voice.

- ***Do not sing when sick***—A cold or upper respiratory infection changes the way you use your breathing muscles, may cause the vocal folds to swell, and may affect the way you hear your voice.

- ***A hoarse voice, change in the sound of the voice, or noticeable voice fatique for 2 weeks requires attention by a qualified voice care team—otolaryngologist, voice pathologist, and voice teacher.***

Glossary

abduction: the action of bringing the vocal folds apart. Vocal folds abduct during the act of inhalation.

acoustic analysis: evaluation of the sound properties of voice. Measures considered important to acoustic analysis are fundamental frequency (F_0), jitter, shimmer, signal-to-noise ratio, and maximum frequency range.

adduction: the action of bringing the vocal folds together to produce voice. Vocal fold adduction may occur at voice onset, during the production of voiced consonants such as /b/, /d/, and /z/, and during coughing or throat clearing. The vocal folds also adduct during swallowing.

aerodynamic analysis: evaluation of the amount of air and rate of airflow available to set the vocal folds into vibration. Measures include flow or phonation volume, phonation time, and airflow rate. Subglottic pressure, glottic resistance, and glottic efficiency are also measures that can be extracted using equipment designed for aerodynamic analysis. Pulmonary function tests, which measure an individual's amount of lung capacity and use of air for breathing, could also be considered parts of aerodynamic analysis.

airflow rate: a measure of speed of airflow between the vocal folds during voice production. This generally is measured in millimeters per second (ml/sec) or cubic centimeters per second (cc/sec). The value is obtained by dividing the total amount of air expelled, for example, while saying "ah" (/ɑ/) by the amount of time it took to produce that sound. Higher airflow rates (>200 ml/sec) are associated with "breathy" or "weak" voice, and low airflow rates (<80 ml/sec) may indicate tight, strained voice. Trained singers are able to maintain steady airflow rates across various fundamental frequencies.

apron: the part of the stage that extends from the curtain to orchestra pit.

aria: a song usually from an opera for solo voice with instrumental accompaniment. Arias also are found in oratorios and cantatas. Arias provide lyric interludes that draw the listener away from the primary action of the opera.

arpeggio: the notes of a chord sung (or played) in succession. Arpeggio exercises have many uses, but among the more common ones are range extension, flexibility, and legato singing (the negotiation of intervals in a smooth and connected manner).

articulation: in speech-language pathology, the shaping of resonated tones into vowels and consonants by the tongue, lips, and jaw. It is considered to be the "endpoint" of a model of the process of speech production. Musically, articulation refers to the way a phrase is executed. In vocal pedagogy, it is the production of consonant sounds. Proper articulation in singing is achieved when the production of consonants is accomplished without tension and the process does not interfere with the production of tone. The result is good tone quality with clear diction.

attack: in speech-language pathology, the onset of sound or the act of bringing the vocal folds together to produce sound. A *hard glottal attack* is a voice onset in which the vocal folds are brought together and pressure is built up beneath them so that on release there is a popping sound. This usually occurs at the beginning of a sentence or breath group and is most noticeable on initial vowels. When used habitually, this is an abusive method of producing voice. An *easy attack* or *easy onset* is a method of voice production in which the vocal folds come together more gently.

The coordinated attack (simultaneous release of air and onset of voice) is considered ideal for singing.

baritone: a male voice with a range higher than a low bass voice and lower than a high tenor voice.

baroque: the period of music that begins in the early 1600s and extends to about 1750. This period saw the birth of opera.

bass: the lowest range of the male voice. There are bass profundos who sing serious roles, bass fuffos who sing comic roles, and bass bel cantos who sing art songs.

bel canto: an Italian term meaning "beautiful singing," which became associated with a vocal style in the 18th century. Bel canto style emphasizes phrasing, tone, and technique, valuing beauty and purity of voice and considering beautiful tone to be more important than any other aspect of interpretation.

belting: a style of singing used in several types of popular music, generally by female voices, where the chest voice or chest register is pushed upward, often beyond its limits. The effect is a dramatic sound, is relatively loud, and sounds pushed. A similar manner of production in classical music is referred to as *chesting*.

blocking: when the director moves people around the stage by the stage prior to singing during the preliminary phases of rehearsal.

break: a sudden, audible shift in register, also referred to as a *crack*.

breathy: In speech-language pathology, this is a vocal quality associated with the release of excessive air during phonation. Breathiness occurs as a result of inefficient vocal fold closure. Breathiness can be "functional," meaning produced as a result of inappropriate voice production, or "organic," meaning produced as a result of vocal fold weakness or paralysis or due to a mass interfering with vocal fold closure. In vocal pedagogy, a breathy tone is the opposite of a *focused* tone. It is like a picture out of focus—unclear, lacking definition. It may be used consciously as an interpretive effect, but with that exception it has a negative connotation in the vocal studio. Pathologic causes include edema, nodules, and polyps. Where no pathology is present, the cause is likely to be inefficient *breath support*, inefficient laryngeal control, poor vocal *placement*, or a combination of the above. Although breathiness is not harmful to the singing voice, it indicates inefficient use of air and is generally considered to be esthetically unpleasant. It is the lack of breath support that may cause more serious vocal problems.

bridge: the transitional area between vocal registers.

Camarata: a group of 16th century Florentine philosophers who argued against the polyphony of the times for a more classical presentation that emphasized the words and emotional content of a composition.

cantabile: a musical expression that results in singing or playing in a tuneful manner.

cantata: a musical form, generally for chorus and soloists, based on a primarily narrative text; the most famous cantatas are those written by Bach, all of which take scriptural texts as their starting points—some are even for solo voice and instrument.

cantilena: a lyrical melody line, obviously meant to be sung or played "cantabile."

canzone: a short, lyrical operatic song; the term itself may have originated in Provence and could have referred to arias, which have no narrative quality at all, but simply reflect the singer's state of mind. Cherubino's "Voi che sapete" in Mozart's *The Marriage of Figaro* is called a canzone.

canzonetta: literally, a little "canzone;" Mozart used the words "canzone" and "canzonetta" frequently to differentiate between the more serious (and longer) arias and the shorter (and more conversational) solo works in his operas.

cavatina: a short, simple solo song, occasionally instrumental rather than vocal, that was popular in 18th century Italian operas.

chest voice: used to describe the lower notes of a vocal range, thus named because of the sympathetic vibrations produced in the chest while singing with the thicker vocal configuration required to produce those tones.

classical: the period in music that comes after the baroque period and before the romantic; the dates are roughly 1756 (which is the birth of Mozart) to 1830 (3 years after the death of Beethoven). Although the period is not as long as the baroque period, it represents the greatest standardization in orchestral form and sonority; even composers who lived beyond 1830 continued to use the standard "classical" orchestra of pairs of flutes, oboes, clarinets, and bassoons, four horns, two trumpets, three trombones, strings, and timpani.

coda: the last musical thoughts in a composition; in strict formal terms, a piece might contain exposition (which sets forth the principal themes of the work), development (which uses that material in new and varied fashions), recapitulation (where the principal material is restated almost verbatim), cadenza (for a last-minute vocal improvisation, sometimes based on the early materials in the work), and coda (where one last little idea is put forward by the composer).

coloratura: a type of soprano, generally, but also the description of singing that pertains to great feats of agility—fast singing, high singing, trills, embellishments, and so forth. Some coloratura sopranos during this century have been Lily Pons, Roberta Peters, Joan Sutherland, and Beverly Sills. An example of coloratura is Marguerite's "Jewel Song" from Gounod's *Faust*.

commedia dell'arte: a style of dramatic presentation popular in Italy from the 16th century on; the commedia characters were highly stylized and the plots frequently revolved around disguises, mistaken identities, and misunderstandings. The principal commedia characters are Pierrot, Harlequin, and Colombine. Operatic spoofs of the commedia characters can be found in Leoncavallo's *Pagliacci* and Strauss' *Ariadne auf Naxos*.

compass: refers to the total range of a piece of music or to a singer's tone range.

comprimario: a singer who takes the secondary character roles in an opera; from the Italian which means "next to the first"; confidantes, maids, servants, messengers, and medical personnel generally fit under the heading of comprimario roles.

continuo: the small group of instruments that accompanies the recitatives in baroque music; as a general rule, the continuo group comprises cello and harpsichord or organ, although in some of the larger works of Monteverdi (*Orfeo, The Coronation of Poppea*), the continuo group can comprise a dozen or more instruments.

contralto: the lowest female voice; the term comes from two Italian words, which signify against ("contra") the high ("alto") voice. In baroque operas, the contralto generally represented a certain character type on stage: either comic (a sort of female basso buffo), or spooky and other worldly, or just plain matronly. Marian Anderson and Maureen Forrester have been legendary contraltos in the concert and operatic world.

counterpoint: the putting together of two or more independent musical lines; when the same musical tune is repeated several times, in different vocal ranges, the result can be a fugue or a round.

countertenor: a high male voice, generally singing within the female contralto or mezzo soprano range; popular in the baroque period, the countertenor frequently portrayed young, virile men or innocent, blushing adolescents—the voices were generally quite powerful, and not considered effeminate. This vocal range is sometimes referred to as "male alto."

covering: a technique of making the transition through vocal registers that aids in maintaining an evenness of vocal quality and color. Used primarily by men, this technique involves vowel modification, generally rounding and darkening the vowel (/ɑ/ to /o/ or /ɔ/, for example) to prevent the sound from becoming "spread" or "white."

crack: see **break.**

crescendo/decrescendo: increasing/decreasing. Primarily relating to increases and decreases in loudness.

cul-de-sac resonance: a voice quality in which the tone appears to be "caught" in the back of the mouth. This can occur when there is nasal blockage. Often, tongue retraction can give the voice this muffled quality.

deus ex machina: literally, "god out of a machine," a literary or staging device that refers to some last-minute salvation of a tricky situation by a god or goddess who has been watching the entire plot unfold from afar. In the baroque period, elaborate scenery was devised whereby a particular god (more often than not Amor, the god of love) would descend from above the stage in a little cloud or carriage.

director/producer: depending on the locale of the producing company, the person who creates the staging for a play or an opera; in America, this person is called the director, or the stage director, as opposed to the conductor who leads the orchestra. Throughout Europe, this person is known as the producer and the orchestra conductor is frequently called the director!

diva: a female opera star of great rank or pretension; the original Italian word means "goddess."

dramma giocoso: an opera that combines serious elements, enacted by aristocratic personnages, with comic relief, played out and commented on by earthier peasant stock. The most famous example of dramma giocoso is Mozart's *Don Giovanni*, although the composer himself never actually called it such—only Lorenzo da Ponte, the librettist, did.

"drinking in the tone": imagery that conveys the feeling that the tone reverses its direction and comes back to its source. This concept is used by some to aid in sustaining the tone.

duet: a musical composition for two performers.

dynamics: varying degrees of loudness and softness, and intensity of a sound.

dysphonia: a disorder of voice production resulting in poor voice quality. Occasionally, adjectives are added to this term such as *functional, musculoskeletal tension,* or *spasmodic,* which refer to qualities of the dysphonia or to its suspected cause.

edema: a medical term for *swelling.* When referring to the vocal folds, this usually occurs as a result of infection or as a reaction to irritation or vocal abuse.

embellishment: the addition of extra notes to an already established melody line; in the days of Handel, and again in the flourishing of 19th century Italian bel canto, the process of embellishing a vocal line whenever it is repeated was the standard practice. Some composers, like Bach and Mozart, wrote out their own embellishments—others trusted the instrumentalists and singers to add their own.

entr'acte: a musical composition played between acts or between scenes within an act of an opera.

entrée: a musical composition, used mainly in the French baroque period by its greatest practitioners, Rameau and Lully, which has a martial, aggressive quality; the entrée generally was played to introduce an important character or group of characters. In some French baroque works, such as Rameau's *Les Indes galantes,* each act was called an entrée.

erythema: a medical term for *redness* occurring as a result of infection and in cases of contact irritation, especially at the vocal processes of the arytenoids or in the posterior commissure of the larynx.

falsetto: the diminutive of the Italian *falso,* "false." This is the lightest and highest vocal register, produced with extremely thin vocal folds. It also enables a bass or a baritone to imitate a female voice. Some voice teachers use the term interchangeably with *head voice.*

fioritura: understandably confused with coloratura but meaning almost the same thing; taken from *fior,* which means "flower" in Italian, fioratura refers to the actual flowery, embellished vocal line within an aria. All coloratura sopranos have to sing fioritura at some point or another, but there is no such thing as a fioratura soprano.

flow volume (or phonation volume): The amount of air (in liters or milliliters) expelled during one phonation after a maximum inhalation.

formant: the resonant frequency of a speech sound. It appears as a prominent band of energy on sound spectrography. There are four or five formants in most speech sounds (including fundamental frequency). Researchers have identified a "singer's formant" that is present in Western-style classical singing. This appears as a clustering of energy in the high frequencies. In the male voice, this can vary between 2.3 and 3.8 kHz.

full voice: to sing with complete breath support and resonance at a relatively loud volume, as opposed to *half voice,* which implies a lighter, less supported and often unfocused tone. *Full voice* can indicate either volume level or the technical effort made to produce the tone.

fundamental frequency: the number of times per second that the vocal folds vibrate (in hertz). Although there are several frequencies or harmonics in a sound recorded at the lips, the fundamental frequency (F_0) reflects the tone generated at the vocal folds. For women, average conversational fundamental frequency is approximately 220 Hz. For men, average conversational fundamental frequency is 125 Hz.

glissando: sliding rapidly up or down a musical scale.

glottal fry: a type of voice production in which the vocal folds are vibrating in a rhythmic, but abnormal fashion. The sound to the ear is one of a popping, bubbling sound. Glottal fry occurs due to a reduction in airflow and subsequent decrease in *subglottic pressure.* It is often heard at the end of a sentence when a speaker runs out of air and drops pitch; however, it can be produced over a range of frequencies.

glottis: the area of opening between the vocal folds. Occasionally, this term is used to refer to the general area of the vocal folds.

grand opera: opera that is sung from start to finish, as opposed to opera that may have spoken dialogue; grand opera frequently treats serious, dramatic subjects and, in French operas, of the 19th century, was generally epic in scale with a full scale ballet inserted in the middle of the work.

harshness: a quality of voice that is heard as a grating or "hard" sound. There is an aperiodic sound to harshness. Sometimes used interchangeably with *hoarseness.*

hauptstimme: this refers to the principal musical material of a work. In the operas of Schoenberg or Berg, early 20th century German composers, the main melodies are marked with an "H" to indicate that the composers considered those the principal tunes.

head voice: most voice teachers use this term interchangeably with *falsetto*. Others use it to denote the upper part of the range when produced with relatively light registration, but still fully supported, as differentiated from pure *falsetto*.

heldentenor: a type of tenor voice that harkens back to the golden age of Wagnerian singing; the typical heldentenor has an unusually brilliant top register (high notes) combined with a muscular lower voice, almost like a baritone, and is capable of long passages that require great vocal stamina. Tristan and Siegfried are great heldentenor roles. One of the great heldentenors of the century was Lauritz Melchior.

hoarseness: a quality of voice that is heard as harshness with breathiness. Hoarseness is often differentiated between *dry*, that generally heard in cases in which the vocal folds are not closing adequately, and *secretions* (eg, saliva) are pooling in the region of the vocal folds.

hooking: a technique that combines vowel modification (usually a more open vowel moving to a more closed one) with pushing lower registration to higher notes. This is generally thought to be esthetically unpleasant and bears a negative connotation in the voice studio.

hypernasal, hyponasal: to the speech-language pathologist, *hypernasality* refers to a disorder of resonance in which too much sound is escaping through the nasal cavity during speech. This is due to velopharyngeal incompetence (the soft palate is too short or too weak to seal off the oral from the nasal cavities). *Hyponasality* refers to a vocal quality in which sounds that should be nasalized (/m/, /n/, and /ŋ/) are not; these sounds become (/b/, /d/, and /g/). There is a great deal of variation in the degree of nasality across the dialects of English. *Excessive nasality* (beyond considerations of dialect) usually denotes a structural, neurologic, or functional abnormality. These terms are not common in the vocal studio, but their meaning is. Hypernasality is often referred to as *nasal twang* or simply *too nasal*, whereas hyponasality or insufficient nasal resonance is often referred to as *too far back* (placement), *too dull, too dark, too covered*. Although what is "right" is as much an esthetic and expressive choice as it is anything else, the singer is generally trying to balance nasal resonance with oral and laryngeal resonance.

When control of nasal resonance is primarily a problem with function of the velum, hyper- and hyponasality are regarded as relatively minor vocal problems.

imbroglio: operatic scene in which diversity of rhythm and melody create chaos and confusion; the original meaning of the Italian word was "intrigue."

intensity: a measurement of the amplitude of a sound, expressed in decibels (dB). Intensity is the acoustic correlate of loudness. *Dynamic range* refers to the range of intensity an individual can produce, from softest to loudest sound.

intermezzo: a short musical entertainment, which in its earliest manifestation might be played between the acts of a longer, more serious operatic work; the intermezzo was almost always of light-hearted character, and never involved more than three or four singers. One well-known operatic intermezzo is *La serva padrona* (The Servant as Mistress) of Giovanni Pergolesi (1733), which was sung between the first and second acts of a much larger, and quite forgotten, work *Il prigioner superb* (The Model Prisoner).

jitter: frequency perturbation or the cycle-to-cycle variations in the frequency of vibration of the vocal folds. There are several ways to measure jitter and various types of equipment use different methods to extract this value. In general, high jitter values are correlated with a decrease in the quality of the voice.

legato: from the Italian meaning "to tie" or "bind together." As a musical direction, it is one way of performing a musical phrase, meaning to connect the notes smoothly and evenly in a musical line. It is also used conceptually in vocal technique, based on the fact that the voice is an instrument intended to change pitch smoothly, without articulating or punctuating the change with movement of the larynx. It also implies the unbroken connection of breath, vibration, and resonance. The opposite of legato is marcato (in a marked punchy style) or even staccato (in an even shorter, more aggressive style).

leitmotiv: a short musical passage, sometimes no more than three or four notes, that instantly calls to mind a character or situation in a musical drama; although Wagner may not have invented the device, he is certainly the best-known user of it. This example is the glance motive from Wagner's *Tristan und Isolde*.

libretto: the text of an opera; the literal translation is "little book," which reminds us that, in a Broadway show, the texts of the songs are called the "lyrics" whereas the spoken text of the rest of the play is called the "book."

lied: a German song; the pronunciation is "leed" and the plural is lieder (pronounced "leader"). In some pre-Wagnerian German operas, the songs that the characters sing are called "lieder" as opposed to "aria," which would be the Italian determination.

lift: the note at which transition from one register to another register occurs.

maestro: a title of courtesy given, especially in Italy, to conductors, composers, and directors; translation (from the Italian), "Master."

manufactured sound: tone that lacks ease and "naturalness" of production, sounds labored or overly technical.

marking: a rehearsal technique intended to save the voice, marking can be done in a variety of ways, including singing very softly, singing up or down an octave to make the range more accessible, and speaking words in rhythm.

mask: the area of the face around the nose and eyes where one might wear a mask. This is often used in teaching the concept of *placement* as a student may be directed to "sing in the mask" or "feel the vibration in the mask."

masque: a staged performance in which music, poetry, song, and dance are blended; although the word is French, and pronounced "mask," the form is more frequently associated with English works that appeared in the time of Queen Elizabeth I.

mean phonation time: the average time to produce a sustained vowel. Often used in assessment as a measure of the "health" of the respiratory and phonatory systems, the average value ranges from 18 to 20 seconds, although this can vary greatly with age.

messa di voce: as a musical direction, the meaning is to *crescendo* and *decrescendo* on a single note. Also used as a vocal exercise. Historically, a singer who could execute *messa di voce* successfully on every note in the range was considered to have complete mastery of vocal technique.

mezza voce: the Italian term for half voice, or literally "medium voice," as contrasted with full voice. When singing mezza voce, the singer reduces the volume to intensify the emotion. This may be a musical directive intended to achieve a certain dramatic effect in performance. It is also a method of singing used in marking.

mezzo-soprano: the female voice range that lies between the soprano, which is the highest, and the contralto; the tone of a mezzo-soprano can either be voluptuous (in the case of Delilah or Carmen) or it can be thinner and more agile (which might describe Rosina in *The Barber of Seville*).

mixed voice (voice mixte): a tone sung with mixed registration, but with a preponderance of head voice.

opera buffa: a style of opera that revolves almost entirely around comedy; perhaps an outgrowth of the Italian intermezzo, the opera buffa as a form was popular in the baroque days as well as in Italy of the early 19th century. Its counterpart is *opera seria,* which implies opera almost entirely about lofty ideals or with tragic consequences.

opéra comique: a misleading term, French in origin, which would seem to describe opera that was funny; in fact, opéra comique describes opera in which there is some spoken dialogue as opposed to grand opera in which there is none. As a matter of fact, both Gounod's *Faust* and Bizet's *Carmen* were originally conceived with spoken dialogue and are, thus, opéras comiques even though their subject matter would seem to make them "grand" operas.

operetta: light, frothy musical entertainments that generally do not pertain to terrifically important subject material; spoken dialogue, dancing, practical jokes, and mistaken identities seem to be the trademark of the operetta form, most popular in late 19th century Vienna or France, under the hands of the Strauss family or Offenbach. *Die Fledermaus*, *The Merry Widow*, *La Périchole,* and Noel Coward's *Bitter Sweet* are all operettas.

optimal pitch: the ideal habitual speaking pitch for a certain individual. Optimal pitch was thought to be located approximately one-fourth from the bottom of one's total range. This concept now is considered to be outdated, and speech-language pathologists tend to help people find their "comfortable" range of habitual pitch.

opus: a single work or composition; from the Latin; the plural form of "opus" is "opera" and it was that term that the Camarata (see above) adopted as their new stage presentations combined the musical work, the dramatic work, and the staging work—thus making "works."

oratorio: a musical composition (generally not staged) for chorus, orchestra, and soloists, whose text is generally religious, serious, or philosophical in nature; a long version of a cantata. It was to orato-rio that Handel turned when the English public turned sour on his staged operas, although the story line and characterization of the oratorios are often totally operatic. *Messiah* and *Israel in Egypt* are oratorios; *Julius Caesar* and *Rinaldo* are not.

orchestra: the group of musicians which accompa-nies a staged presentation; in early operas (from 1600 to about 1750); the orchestra might consist of a few strings, pairs of oboes, bassoons, flutes, trumpets, and continuo (see above). The orchestra grew from the time of Mozart through Beethoven, Berlioz, Wagner, Verdi, Puccini, and Richard Strauss so that nowadays an opera orchestra can easily consist of 90 to 100 players. In America, the first floor of a theater is called the orchestra, whereas in England that area is called the stalls.

ornamentation: the extra notes, like appogiaturas, scales, trills, or cadenzas that can enhance a melodic line when it has to be repeated. Ornamen-tation and embellishment are probably inter-changeable terms.

overture: the instrumental introduction to a musical drama or oratorio; frequently the overture will incorporate musical themes that will later be heard in the course of the opera. In *Don Giovanni*, the ominous theme of the Stone Guest (from Act II) is heard as a premonition at the beginning of the overture, thus setting an emotional tone as well as providing musical structure to the entire work.

parlando: literally, "speaking"; this Italian term directs the singer to imitate speech in singing. The "patter songs" of Gilbert and Sullivan operettas frequently employ a great deal of parlando singing.

partial: a component of sound sensation that is usu-ally distinguished as a single tone and cannot be further distinguished audibly, but contributes to the timbre of a complex sound. This may be higher or lower than the audible frequency and may be either harmonic or inharmonic.

passaggio: the Italian word for *passage*, which describes the area of the voice between registers where preparation for a change in registration should take place.

phonation: the process of the production of voice. To the speech-language pathologist, it may be described as "breathy," "strained," or "normal." The singer's main concern is to initiate sound so that the vibration of the vocal folds is coordinated exactly with the release of supported air and per-ceives that the tone is initiated by the air.

pitch: the location of a sound on a scale ranging from high to low.

placement: a process of the imagination by which the voice is directed to a certain area of the body (usually the head) and the subsequent awareness of resonance in that area.

polyphony: literally, "many voices"; the mixing together of several melodic lines in a pleasant fash-ion. Counterpoint is certainly an element that cre-ates polyphony.

portamento: the smooth movement in singing or playing a stringed instrument from one note to the next, effectively sliding over all of the notes in between; a portamento can only be achieved in legato singing or playing and is frequently com-pared to "glissando," which literally means sliding from one note to the next.

prelude: the instrumental introduction to an individ-ual act within a musical drama, whether opera or operetta; some composers use the words over-ture, prelude, and entr'acte interchangeably.

prima donna: the female star of an opera cast; in Verdi's time it was considered a matter of course to differentiate the roles in terms of their dramatic and vocal importance, such as "Prima Donna," "Seconda Donna," "Terza Donna," and the like. It did not until recently come to describe the per-sonality of the singer, rather than the importance of her role in the opera.

projection: the quality of vocal production that refers to the ability of the voice to travel through space and be heard over the musical accompaniment.

prompter: a member of the musical staff of many large opera houses; the prompter sits in a small box practically invisible to the audience, under the apron of the stage, and gives singers and choristers the vocal cues seconds before they are required to sing them. In many international houses, where singers perform without benefit of long musical rehearsal periods, a prompter can be invaluable as a memory aide for a jet-lagged singer.

proscenium: a misunderstood term; most perform-ers, even designers, refer to the proscenium when they actually mean the proscenium arch. The proscenium, to be technically exact, is the part of the stage between the curtain and the orchestra pit—and the architectural arch that encloses the curtain is called the proscenium arch. Even so, proscenium is used in a larger, more general sense, in the meaning of a stage constructed with a cur-tain, as opposed to a thrust stage where the stage has no formal enclosure.

prosody: the pattern of stress or inflection of a sentence or utterance. Prosody is the contribution of voice to language through the use of pitch, loudness, and duration.

prova: rehearsal; from the Italian word for "test"; often in Italy, one hears of a "prova generale," which means the final dress rehearsal. In Germany, a rehearsal is called "probe" (PROE beh); in German houses, one frequently hears of a *sitzprobe* (a rehearsal with orchestra where the singers sing seated on chairs at the front of the stage instead of moving about) or *wandelprobe* (where the singers actually go through the motions of their acting while the orchestra plays the music) or *generalprobe* (which is, in essence, the last dress rehearsal).

raked stage: a stage that slants upward away from the view of the audience; in the earliest opera houses, the stage was so slanted so that the audience member sitting in the back of the theatre could have an easy view of someone standing at the back of the stage. Many opera houses in Europe today have stages that are permanently sloped like this.

range: the division of the human voice according to six basic types: soprano, mezzo soprano, contralto, tenor, baritone, and bass.

rasp: a tone quality that sounds harsh and gravelly, somewhat like a protracted throat clearing, while maintaining a semblance of pitch. Thought of by some rock singers as a vocal style.

recitativo: a musical form within an opera that, by imitating rapid speech, advances the plot; this is not the same as parlando, which is a style of singing, but rather a formal device that links together the arias and choruses. Those forms generally express states of mind, whereas the recitative describes a course of action.

recitativo accompagnato: is accompanied by the full orchestra. The introduction to Donna Anna's "Or sai chi l'onore" in *Don Giovanni* is an example of the "accompagnato" style, where the orchestral sonorities are capable of varying the mood of the narration more than the simple harpsichord accompaniment could.

recitativo secco: is accompanied by the continuo instruments. Numerous passages abound in the operas of Mozart and Rossini of the "secco" style.

register: a group of notes produced with similar laryngeal function, yielding like quality of sound. Opinions among singers and teachers vary as to how many registers there are (from one to three)

and whether to call the lowest *chest* or *pulse*, the middle *middle* or *modal*, and the highest *head* or *loft*.

resonance: the amplification of certain components of the tone produced at the vocal folds along the vocal tract (above the vocal folds and including the oral and nasal cavities). An individual's vocal resonance is determined by the shape of his or her anatomy and by the way this configuration is changed during speaking or singing. Often used mistakenly in the voice studio as interchangeable with such terms as *timbre, tone, color,* or *quality of voice,* the singer is concerned with esthetic result of achieving a good balance of resonation among the naso-, oro-, and laryngopharynx.

respiration: the process of breathing. For speaking, we use a relatively small proportion of our available lung capacity to produce voice. People with quite impaired respiration (reduced lung capacity and ability to move air in and out of the lungs) can produce voice without severe difficulty. However, breathing for singing is much more dynamic, more athletic, and more exaggerated than it is for speaking. Breath control is achieved through the development and coordinated interaction of the abdominal and intercostal muscles in an opposite manner from the way they are used in everyday speech. That is, instead of inhalation being active and exhalation passive, the process is conceptually reversed. On inhalation, the abdominal muscles "relax" outward and downward, aiding the contraction of the diaphragm while the rib cage expands. *Breath support* occurs when, as opposed to a passive release of air, exhalation becomes an active and dynamic force by engaging the lower abdominal muscles and moving the air through the expanded rib cage. The rib cage should remain expanded as the process is repeated.

ring: vibrant tone quality with a predominance of high partials in the frequency range of approximately 2800 Hz.

ritornello: the instrumental prelude to an individual song within a cantata, concerto, or aria; in baroque Italian operas, the ritornello (which comes from Italian meaning "a little return trip") could be heard not only at the beginning and the end of the aria, but as a dividing mark between stanzas.

romantic: the period of music between 1830 and the turn of the 20th century; composers of romantic music frequently found inspiration in other than musical ideas, such as nature, painting, birdcalls, or rainstorms. Beethoven was probably the first romantic opera composer, although the most famous are Wagner and Verdi.

scooping: an upward slur, most often defining an attack that begins below the pitch. Scooping may also occur within a vocal line, and is differentiated from the *portamento* by the fact that it is usually not a conscious act. Generally considered by voice teachers to be unmusical and technically detrimental.

shimmer: for the speech-language pathologist, it is intensity perturbation or the cycle-to-cycle variation in the amplitude of the sound signal. As with jitter, the methods for measuring shimmer vary, and shimmer may be expressed as a percentage, in decibels, or in some other value. Increased shimmer values generally correlate with hoarseness. To the voice teacher, shimmer is a tone quality that is highly desirable. The voice is used properly, has a good vibrato rate and projects well.

signal-to-noise ratio: the ratio of the periodic signal produced at the vocal folds to the "noise" or aperiodic signal. Someone with a great deal of hoarseness would have a low signal-to-noise ratio; that is, the "signal" and the "noise" might be very similar in loudness.

singspiel: early German musical drama, which employed spoken dialogue along with musical numbers; Mozart's *The Abduction from the Seraglio* and *The Magic Flute* are both examples of this genre, as are Weber's *Der Freischutz* and Beethoven's *Fidelio*. The singspiel is very similar to English ballad opera or French opéra comique.

"sitting on the breath": a sensation of the voice resting on the supported breath, achieved by maintaining constant breath pressure, a relaxed throat, and an expanded thorax.

soprano: the highest range of the female voice; the soprano voice ranges from lyric (a light, graceful quality) to dramatic (obviously fuller and heavier in tone).

sotto voce: a musical direction that asks the performer to sing, or play "under the voice," or in a subdued manner. Singing sotto voce can be compared to declaiming in a stage whisper and can be very effective in a large theatre.

soubrette: a lightweight soprano voice or type of soprano role, frequently found in comic operas or operettas; the soubrette usually possesses a flirtatious demeanor and street-wise manner, as in the case of Adele in *Die Fledermaus*, or is a particularly fetching country innocent, like Adina in *The Elixir of Love*.

spin: describes tone quality that is free and apparently effortless in production and projects or carries well. Implicit is the presence of true vibrato.

spinto: a kind of voice that is "pushed" toward another; from the Italian "spingere" (to push); thus a "lirico spinto" soprano is a lyric voice that has some qualities of the heavier dramatic range. Frequently, sopranos who have essentially light voices will take on the role of, say, Mimi in *La Bohème* (to portray her youthfulness and frailty) and push their voices to ride over the orchestra, thus developing a "spinto" sound. Licia Albanese, the great Italian soprano, would be a prime example of this type of soprano.

sprechstimme: literally, "speak voice"; a kind of vocal instruction often found in the operas of Schoenberg and Berg, where the singer half speaks and half sings a note. The declamation sounds like speaking, but there is a duration of pitch that makes it seem almost like singing.

staccato: Italian for "detached," "separate," "short." A type of singing or playing that is characterized by short, clipped, rapid articulation; the opposite of staccato is legato.

stage right/stage left: the division of the stage from the performer's point of view; thus, when a singer goes stage right, he or she moves to his or her right but to the audience's left.

straight tone: a tone produced without *vibrato*. Because vibrato is normally present in a mature, well-produced voice, a straight tone is considered symptomatic of some constriction in the throat, of a problem with breath support, or both. Straight tone singing can be executed at will and is used by some singers for stylistic effect, and in that case is an esthetic choice.

subglottic pressure: the amount of pressure just below the vocal folds. An adequate amount of subglottic pressure is crucial for the regular vibration of the vocal folds. Subglottic pressure is created by a steady stream of air originating from the lungs and regulated by the amount of tension and mass of the vocal folds. Subglottic pressure is raised to produce increased loudness.

supernumerary: a performer who appears in a non-singing role; a "super" might have a solo walk-on to deliver a message or might be included as part of a large processional, for example. In the old days, supers were often referred to as "spear carriers."

swallowed tone: tone that is constricted in the throat and therefore lacing high partials and forward placement.

s/z ratio: a value obtained by dividing the amount of time an individual produces the sound /s/ on a maximum inhalation by the amount of time to produce the /z/ on a maximum inhalation. If the vocal folds are healthy, then the times should be roughly equivalent, or equal to 1.0. The upper limit for "normal" is considered to be below 1.4.

tempo: the speed of a musical passage or composition; the tempo may range from very slow ("largo" in Italian, "langsam" in German) to extremely fast ("presto" in Italian, "schnell" in German).

tenor: the highest natural male voice.

tessitura: Italian for "texture." When referring to a song or role, *tessitura* means that range wherein the majority of pitches lie; for example, the tessitura of Lucia di Lammermoor is quite high, that of Santuzza in *Cavalleria rusticana*, although it is still a soprano role, is low enough that the role could be sung by a mezzo soprano. When referring to a singer, *comfortable tessitura* describes that portion of the singer's range produced with the greatest ease and beauty.

timbre: the distinctive quality or "color" of a voice produced by the combined effect on the ear of the listener of the fundamental tone and its harmonic overtones.

tremolo: describes undesirable vibrato, whether too fast, too slow, or too wide.

trill: two adjacent notes rapidly and repeatedly alternated.

twelve tone: a system of composition put forth in the early part of the 20th century by Arnold Schoenberg whereby (in very simple terms), each note of the chromatic scale should be used as part of a melody before any other note gets repeated. Many composers have used this system, which is also called "serialism," but the best known operas in this style are Berg's *Wozzeck* and *Lulu*, Schoenberg's *Erwartung*, and Roger Sessions's *Montezuma*.

upstage/downstage: the position on stage farthest or nearest the audience; because of the raked stage that was so prevalent in early opera houses, the farther "back" a singer went on the stage, the "higher" he seemed to become in stature—thus the distinction of being "up"-stage. When a singer is directed to move downstage left, he goes toward the audience and toward his left side; to the audience, he seems to be coming forward and moving to the audience's right.

verismo: literally, "truth"; a style of theatre made popular in the latter part of the 19th century in which ordinary events and characters participate in melodramatic situations. Bizet's *Carmen* was considered an early and powerful example of verismo and so are most of the operas of Puccini and Mascagni.

vibrato: a regular and relatively even pattern of oscillation above and below a pitch, which occurs naturally at a frequency of approximately six to seven times per second in a mature, well-produced voice; the slightly wavering quality that a singer has in his or her voice while sustaining a tone; if the vibrato becomes terribly pronounced, it is pejoratively called a wobble. Though beauty is subjective, most voice teachers agree that vibrato adds warmth and beauty to tone. It is also one of the measures of the health and function of the voice. Some singers will drain their voice of any vibrato for a particularly haunting effect.

videostroboscopy: a technique to visualize the vocal folds under full light and under "strobed" or flashing light. In stroboscopy, a light flashes onto the vocal folds at a rate slightly slower than the rate of vibration of the vocal folds. When seen by the human eye, this gives the illusion of slow motion. The images are recorded on videotape and can be reviewed as often as necessary. An otolaryngologist or speech-language pathologist may use a rigid endoscope or a flexible fiberoptic scope for this procedure.

vital capacity: the maximum amount of air that can be exhaled after a maximum inhalation.

vocal abuse: encompasses a range of behaviors, from poor vocal hygiene (smoking, inadequate hydration) to misuse and overuse of the voice. For the speaker, this is the etiology of most "benign" voice disorders. For the singer, overuse will become apparent sooner in an untrained or poorly trained voice, but also occurs in well-trained voices that are doing too much: too long, too loud, too high, and so forth. Misuse may be the result of poor vocal technique or the conscious imitation of unhealthy vocalism. It may also result from an improper or insufficient warm-up/cool-down period, singing in an inappropriate tessitura (that part of the vocal range within which lies the majority of pitches as opposed to the total range), or singing beyond one's natural range. Unfortunately, some forms of vocal abuse have come to be considered stylistically acceptable, even desirable among certain vocal styles.

vocal focus: *focus* describes a tone that, through correct production, effectively turns all of the air used to produce it into clear, vibrating singing or speaking sound. Although often used interchangeably in the vocal studio with the term *vocal placement*, focus is better described as the result of good vocal placement and its unencumbered connection to breath support.

vocalise: a vocal exercise.

voce di capra: Italian for "voice of the goat." Characterized by a quick, bleating pulsation of the tone.

whistle register: the female equivalent of male falsetto. The highest notes in a female voice.

wobble: uneven and unusually slow fluctuation of pitch.

zarzuela: a Spanish popular musical presentation that blends dialogue and music in skits and dramas ranging from one to three acts that deal satirically with aspects of daily life. The derivation of the name is intriguing: early zarzuelas were performed in the Palacio de la Zarzuela in Madrid, so named because it was surrounded by a field of brambles ("zarza" being Spanish for bramble).

Index